THE ISLAND SERIES

THE ISLE OF MULL

D1434301

THE ISLANDS SERIES

‡Achill
†The Aran Islands
 The Isle of Arran
 The Island of Bute
*Canary Islands: Fuerteventura
*Corsica
*‡Cyprus
*Dominica
*The Falkland Islands
*Grand Bahama
†Harris and Lewis
†The Isle of Mull
 Lundy
 The Maltese Islands
†Orkney
*Puerto Rico
 St Kilda and other Hebridean Islands
*‡The Seychelles
†Shetland
*‡Sicily
*‡Singapore
‡Skye
*‡The Solomon Islands
*Vancouver Island

in preparation
 Alderney
*Bermuda
 Cape Breton Island
†Gotland
 Mauritius
 Rhodes
†St Helena
 Tasmania
*Tobago

* Published in the United States by Stackpole
† Published in the United States by David & Charles
‡ The series is distributed in Australia by Wren

THE ISLE OF
MULL

by P. A. MACNAB

DAVID & CHARLES

NEWTON ABBOT : NORTH POMFRET (VT)

o 7153 4354 8

First published 1970

Reprinted 1973

Printed in Great Britain by
W J Holman Limited Dawlish
for David & Charles (Holdings) Limited
South Devon House Newton Abbot Devon

To my family
and the people of Mull

CONTENTS

ILLUSTRATIONS

Photographs other than those acknowledged are by the author

IN TEXT

The Isle of Mull
Land over 500ft is shown stippled

INTRODUCTION

THE anthem of Mull, *An t'eilean Muileach*, a popular gaelic song composed by the Mull bard Dugald MacPhail, is a fittingly descriptive introduction to this island of contrasts. In English it runs

'The Isle of Mull is of isles the fairest,
Of ocean's gems 'tis the first and rarest;
Green grassy island of sparkling fountains,
Of waving woods and high tow'ring mountains.'

For the island is a place of high hills and bare moorlands, yet with lush growth and tall trees in sheltered glens, or with stunted shrubs grasping a precarious living along the wind-swept and spray-battered cliffs which face the western ocean. Although its coasts are rocky and heavily indented with bays and sea-lochs, in the south-west there are fine sandy beaches backed by green *machair* lands and little crofting communities. In the north-west one comes unexpectedly upon a few beaches of dazzling white shell sand, separated by low cliffs.

In fact, Mull is a typical Hebridean island, beset by the economic and social problems common to the highlands and islands of Scotland. At the same time it has certain individual characteristics, of which its geology and its archaeology are perhaps the most outstanding; these aspects are treated more extensively later in this book. Properly speaking Mull is an island group, consisting of one large island and a number of smaller ones to the west.

The isle of Mull itself has a character and charm entirely its own—an island still comparatively unspoilt. Unlike other mountainous islands of the north-west, all but the highest and most rugged of its hills have a green pastoral beauty, with rich grazings extending far up to the summit ridges. The attractions of the island were certainly missed by Dr Johnson, during his visit with Boswell on a drab, wet October day in 1773. Dr Johnson described it as 'Mull, a dreary country, much worse than Sky [Skye] . . . a most dolorous country . . .' Boswell, slightly more discerning, disagreed : 'A hilly country . . . diversified with heath and grass, and many rivulets.'

Mull is also distinguished by the fact that it is commemorated on the maps of Britain's former colonies and dominions more generously than any other part of the British Isles—in Glengorm, Glenmore, Glenforsa, Inch Kenneth, Knock, Ulva, Kilmore, MacLaine Plains, and many others, especially in Australia, where Major-General Lachlan Macquarie during his governorship thirled the new continent firmly to his beloved native island by a selection of nostalgic place names. Calgary, Alberta, so named when it was founded in 1876, commemorates the happy memories that Colonel J. F. Macleod, commander of the Royal North-West Mounted Police and a native of Skye, took away from a visit to Calgary House, in Mull; it was not, as is popularly supposed, bestowed by emigrants from the village of Calgary.

Mentioned by Ptolemy, Mull is the classical Malaeius. When the Roman armies invaded Scotland they stopped short of the island's then inhospitable shores; but before them peoples of the Stone, Bronze and Iron Ages had entered Mull, and like the Celts from Ireland, the later Christians and the Norsemen, warring clansmen and latter-day crofters, all left their records behind them, in standing stones, forts, chapels, carvings, castles or habitations.

According to the census of 1821 Mull supported a population of over 10,000. Reduced in number now to some 2,000, the people live scattered among isolated sheep farms, agricultural units, forestry centres and private houses where many retired people seek peace and privacy. The ruins of old houses and even whole villages may be found in all the fertile glens and around the coast. Apart from Tobermory, there are only a few centres, and they house populations as small as 150 people.

In the south-west lies the hamlet of Fionnphort and, across the water from it, the village of Iona. A few miles inland, along the main road, lies Bunessan, a more pretentious little village, but beyond that there is no settlement of note until one reaches the east coast. There one comes to Lochdonhead, a single row of houses curving round a small bay and overlooked by high mountains. Further west along the north-east coast lies Craignure, the terminus for the car ferry from Oban and a settlement that is likely to grow. Beyond this, half way along the north-east coast, Salen is a scattered village that has expanded only slightly since its establishment at the beginning of the nineteenth century. This is the northern focal point for the road system of the island. Dervaig in the north-west was established about the same time and is one of the most attractive and least spoilt centres in the island. Everywhere in these settlements the older houses are uniformly austere in design and construction; they are steadily being brought up to modern standards.

The one real centre of population—and the capital of the island—is Tobermory, a proud little burgh, although in 1967 its population was only 617. Established as a fishery centre in the eighteenth century it rose to be an important settlement, with almost 2,000 inhabitants in the later nineteenth century. Its days of peak prosperity seem now to be past, however. Once the main shipping centre of the island, it has been displaced in this sense by Craignure, with its modern pier, which lies 22 miles nearer Oban along the Sound of Mull. Hopes for a new and brighter future for the town are growing, based on the gradual introduction of shore-based light industries.

The gaelic name of Tobermory, where a small Christian settlement dedicated to St Mary was founded in early times, is *Tobar Mhoire*—the Well of Mary. The well itself lies beside the upper village and the foundations of a very old chapel can be seen in the nearby cemetery.

Tobermory has a magnificent setting, its south-facing main street curving round the loveliest bay and anchorage in the Hebrides. This sheltered, east-facing harbour is a popular yachting centre and a haven for shipping during stormy weather. The houses rise in terraces along the steeply rising, tree-lined slopes above the bay, to the edge of the moors and uplands. More is said in a later chapter about Tobermory's place in the local administration and social services. The town has an official information centre which makes known the wide variety of attractions that are offered there and in the island generally.

THE ISLE OF MULL

LANDSCAPES

Mull itself is the third largest island in the Hebrides, exceeded in area only by Lewis and Skye. It covers about 225,000 acres and is roughly 24 miles from north to south and 26 miles from east to west. These figures, however, give no indication of the length of its coastline, which is so broken by long sea-lochs and bays and inlets that it is over 300 miles long. A glance at Mull's position on a small-scale map of Scotland reveals its relationship to the north-western highlands, north of Glen More along the great Caledonian fault. Mull appears to be the south-western portion of the mainland whose western coast is so deeply penetrated by long narrow sea-lochs. Closer examination shows, however, that the island has been separated from the mainland by the breaching of the peninsula, of which it must once have been a part, by what is now the Sound of Mull, a sheltered waterway some 35 miles long and varying in width from 5 to less than 2 miles. North of the island beyond these waters lie the mainland peninsulas of Ardnamurchan and Morvern. On the east the island is washed by the waters of Loch Linnhe and its south-westerly extension, the Firth of Lorne; east of these channels lies the mainland of Argyll. Facing the eastern end of Mull, and less than 10 miles distant, is the busy town of Oban, the main point of communications between the island and the mainland.

Mull is famed in song and story as 'Mull of the Mountains'. Its peaks are landmarks in the whole of the southern Hebrides, and from the distant hills of the mainland. Despite their height, however, the hills of Mull are more rounded, gentler, as it were, than the rugged hills of Skye or the mainland highlands, and, provided common sense is used, their exploration is comparatively easy and safe. The highest peak, Ben More, at 3,169ft above sea level, is the only 'Munro' in the Hebrides outside the Cuillin Hills in Skye (a 'Munro' is a hill of 3,000ft or more isolated by a dip of at least 500ft of relief, called after the Scottish mountaineer who first listed such peaks). The ascent of this symmetrical and commanding peak, either from Loch na Keal on the north, or from Loch Scridain on the south, need be no more than a few hours' hard hill walking.

The most arresting views in Mull lie around Loch na Keal

and Loch Tuath and the most advantageous viewpoints are from Torloisk, on the north side. The panorama of the Ben More peaks run westwards into the high headlands of Gribun and Ardmeanach, where the horizontal lava flows—one of the island's most typical and spectacular aspects of geology—end abruptly in high cliffs, for all the world resembling the silhouettes of the ram bows of old-time dreadnoughts. The cliffs are cleft by ravines and chimneys, through which many hill burns pour, reminding the onlooker vividly of Tennyson's lines :

> 'And like a downward smoke, the slender stream
> Along the cliff to fall and pause and fall did seem.
> A land of streams . . .'

Mull is indeed a land of streams—wherever you stand the sound of running water is seldom absent. When the gales blow in from the Atlantic, some waterfalls, such as Eas Forss at the east end of Loch Tuath, or Allt Airidh nan Chaisteal in Ardmeanach, are checked in their descent and blown back in spray over the cliff tops by the wind, funnelling up the rocky chimneys, until the whole headland appears to be smoking as if on fire. Diverted by the headlands, the gusts of wind also play mad tricks along the sea-lochs, creating violent eddies which raise a series of miniature waterspouts extending far out from the shore.

Beyond the western promontories of the main island, the Treshnish Islands fill the horizon with their strange outlines, like high-bowed ships sailing eternally into the south-west. Still further out lies the long low rocky island of Coll, and to the south-west of it the flat sandy line of Tiree—'the island that is lower than the waves' as the old folks used to call it—where the weather station has recorded some of the highest wind velocities around the British coasts. Dimly, on the far horizon, the higher peaks of the Long Island, from Barra Head to Harris, are spaced out at the edge of the world, as it were, for the lower parts of the islands are hidden because of the curvature of the intervening ocean. Viewed from high ground in the west of Mull on a summer evening, against the incredible colourations of a Hebridean sunset, this is a panorama which will never fade in the memory.

Hemmed in and fretted by reefs and headlands, the tides run strongly along the coasts. A choppy sea with dangerous tide-rips

15

can develop off Caliach Point in the north-west and between Duart and Lismore at the island's eastern end; elsewhere around the coast the reefs can be a danger to vessels—as Robert Louis Stevenson so vividly depicted in *Kidnapped*. Along the rocky western seaboard great stores of driftwood lie in the inaccessible coves, sometimes bored and barnacled after long journeys across the Atlantic.

Mull's scenery and landscapes are closely related to the geological structure and the history of the island. The bones of the earth are here plain for all to see, fashioned to their present-day beauty by the agencies of the weather and by ice. The surface details of the landscapes, however, have been modified by man and grazing animals in a process which can be glimpsed through the keyholes of history in ensuing chapters.

Page 17: Loch Frisa from Achnadrish Hill on the Dervaig road

Page 18: Sea-worn columnar basalt on the Ardtun shore of Loch Scridain, looking across to the trap country of Ardmeanach

1 THE STRUCTURE OF MULL

A VISITOR exploring Mull must be impressed by the number and variety of rock formations and the strange patterns in which they are arranged. A little knowledge of the island's geology and physical structure is both revealing and rewarding. The unravelling of the geological story of the island started some 200 years ago. A memoir issued by the Geological Survey of Scotland in 1924 begins: 'It may safely be maintained that Mull includes the most complicated igneous centre as yet accorded detailed examination anywhere in the world.' It is very worthwhile for the layman to see for himself some of the evidence that the intensive detective work has revealed.

The very distinctive shape of Mull, with its mountainous eastern portion and its hilly western promontories, depicts in miniature many of the physical aspects of the northwestern highlands of Scotland, even though its surface geology is entirely different from most of that of the region. The physical relationship of Mull to the highlands, which has already been noted briefly, is such that the very ancient crystalline rocks of which much of the northwest is composed run out west and form the 'basement' of the island. They are glimpsed at the surface only in limited areas, where they have been uplifted through faulting. Their ancient, worn-down surface is in Mull concealed under great thicknesses of the much younger volcanic rocks for which the island is famous.

The general directions of many of the features of Mull—coastlines, glens, lochs, valleys—frequently conform to those of similar features on the west coast, the most common running roughly northwesterly or northeasterly, with some running west-east. These directions usually delineate fundamental lines of weakness or actual faults in the rocks, established long ago when the highland area was first crumpled up into a mountainous region and long before its western parts had been broken up into islands. The north-east line of the Great Glen fault that crosses Scotland continues southwestwards through Loch Linnhe and across the southeastern corner of Mull, roughly through Lochs Spelve and Buie. Another early fault line, the surface features of which are known as the Moine Thrust Plane, that affects the western highlands and runs more north-northeasterly, is believed to be continued through the western extremities of Mull. Iona is presumed to lie to the west of this line, and indeed that island is composed of ancient rocks, largely Lewisian Gneiss. Similarly, the western part of the Ross of Mull is uplifted to the west of a more local fault running northwest-southeast through Loch Assapol, and here a belt of ancient metamorphic rock is preserved at the surface, abutting against a mass of old volcanic rock, the renowned red or pink Mull granite of the western tip of the Ross.

GEOLOGICAL HISTORY

The Lewisian Gneiss of Iona (and of the Outer Hebrides too) is probably 1,500 million years old. At a much more recent geological period than the Caledonian earth movements of some 300 million years ago, after the ancient rocks had been further deformed and repeatedly worn down by erosion, there occurred a period of intense volcanic activity that entirely altered the surface aspects of Mull in a widespread phenomenon that stretched from Greenland to what is now northern Ireland. These volcanic outpourings of 40-50 million years ago lasted at intervals through millions of years, during the Tertiary era, largely contemporary with the earth movements that formed the Alps and mountains of similar age. Disturbances of such magnitude are inevitably accompanied by local movements; foundering and subsidence occur, and indeed Mull is a centre of such subsidence. It now resembles a block of the ancient platform depressed under great thicknesses of Tertiary basalts and granites, its foundered borders in the Sound of Mull and the Firth of Lorne coinciding with lines of weakness. Glaciation and weathering have removed a great deal of the Tertiary deposits; the development of the glens and valleys has transformed the scene of volcanic fury, but much evidence remains of the vagaries of vulcanism, of fluid lava pouring forth and transporting within it semi-consolidated portions of older volcanics; ash, slag, clinker; pillow lavas and basalt columns.

Mull has two very distinctive geological regions—the hills and plateaux lying west of a sinuous line south from Salen, and the mountainous eastern core, glens and lowlands. These divisions roughly reflect the course of events during the Tertiary age. In the early stages a series of great thicknesses of liquid lava—they are estimated to have totalled some 6,000ft—were poured out of fissures and spread over the whole of Mull and beyond, each layer gradually solidifying to form the basalt spreads visible today. That these outpourings occurred at intervals over many thousands of years is revealed by, amongst other evidence, the layers of weathered material that occurs between the spreads; these are seen in exposures of sections of the basalt as reddened layers,

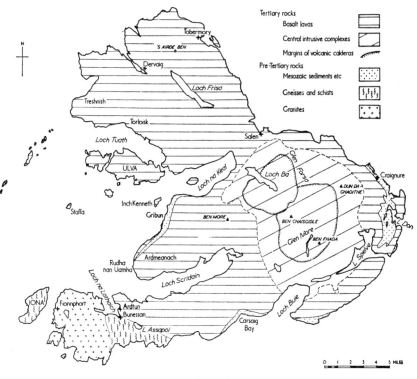

Geological sketch map

known to the geologist as red bole. Most of the western half of Mull displays the lava beds in level or inclined surfaces with the edges of the flows forming terraces on the hill sides. Ben More itself is a conical mountain eroded from a great thickness of the basalt. The basalt plateaux are known as 'trap' country—the word is derived from Swedish *trappa*, a step. The basalt itself is mostly a dark, fine-grained rock, particularly familiar in columnar structures.

At a later stage of the vulcanism, Mull became the focus of intense volcanic activity of a different kind, with two enormous and overlapping explosive centres, from which issued igneous material of a more acid composition that subsequently hardened into coarser-textured rocks, such as granite and gabbro. The two caldera or reservoirs of molten rock from which these later volcanics issued were centred more to the east, respectively on Beinn Chaisgidle and the head of Loch Ba, each of which is surrounded by a roughly circular area, outlined by a granitic dyke, that represents the collapsed core of the vent.

From this volcanic focus there also developed an enormous system of volcanic dykes and sills, respectively vertical and horizontal intrusions within the country rock, where molten rock explored the weaknesses of the earth's surface layers to relieve the stresses of the crust. The majority of the dykes run in a swarm over ten miles wide of vertical walls cutting indifferently across earlier basalts and other volcanic rocks, basement and sedimentary beds, largely in northwest-southeast direction. Sills reach far out beyond the island, some as far to the southeast as the Whin Sill that outcrops from the Northumbrian coast southwards through Yorkshire. Paroxysmal explosions occurred at places along the dykes, and also from subsidiary vents around the main centres, and this second vigorous and fiery stage of volcanic activity contrasts with the relative quiet of the all-engulfing, successive spreads of the earlier basaltic lavas. The heat and vapours of the later volcanics also deformed and even altered the character of the existing basalt through which they burst—hence, to some extent, the geological and structural contrasts between western and eastern Mull.

THE PRESENT-DAY LANDSCAPE

THE PRESENT-DAY LANDSCAPE

Landscapes are eternally in a state of change; landforms are simultaneously being born and destroyed by erosion processes. The Tertiary volcanics of Mull would be attacked by agents of erosion as soon as they had been deposited; at times this would be under tropical conditions, since the climate has not always been as it is now. Once volcanic activity had quietened down, the shaping of the island to its present-day form began in earnest. It can only be a matter of conjecture, based on the detailed studies of the geomorphologists, what courses the rivers then took, which direction they ran in, where the sea level stood. Relics of wave-cut notches and of plateau levels have been discerned. It is very probable, however, that the major features of the island were outlined and its coastline determined during post-Tertiary times, before the onset of the glacial period. The established lines of weakness would be worn down into valleys and lowlands while the more resistant rocks formed the hills, mountains and ridges. The successive lava flows were cut back into a landscape of table-lands, with trap features exposed on their flanks.

In the glacial period Mull developed its own ice-cap on its central mountains, its glaciers merging with those flowing west from the higher mainland. Glaciation emphasised some of the features of the existing landscape, deeply cutting the glens into characteristic U-shapes, scoring the valley sides with transported boulders and rocks, shifting and re-sorting the superficial deposits —soil, gravel and alluvium—and depositing these in new positions. Erratics—rocks originating in another area—are to be found deposited around the northern, eastern and southern fringes of the island, having been transported from the mainland by ice. The ice movements in general rounded the hills and scooped out the basins of the lochs, and probably, as the ice melted and the glaciers retreated up-valley, caused changes in the original drainage pattern. In the 10,000 years since then, the more recent processes of erosion have altered the landscape only in minor ways. The most marked changes have probably been due to changes in sea level, from the evidence of post-glacial beaches, at levels as high as 100ft above present-day sea level. The melting of the ice and the uplift of the land, relieved

23

of its burden of ice, account for both submergence and emergence.

In the limited area of the island most of the rivers are short and unimpressive except during times of heavy rain, when they come down in sudden floods, carrying a large volume of water to the sea. Most of the freshwater lochs are long and narrow and their situation is commonly related to a structural weakness in the rock combined with the direction and force of glacial erosion.

THE NORTH-WEST PROMONTORY

The north-western region is almost cut off from the central core of the island by Loch na Keal, which penetrates so far inland that it leaves an isthmus only about 3 miles across, southwest of Salen. Loch Tuath has similarly bitten into the west coast and now entirely separates the island of Ulva from the mainland. This region is composed largely of flat boggy moorlands which rise to the terraced uplands and isolated flat-topped hills of the trap country. A broad depression between Dervaig and Salen follows the northwesterly trend of the island structure. The hills rise nowhere above 1,456ft, which altitude is achieved in Speinne Mor on the northern uplands. Towards the west and north there are bold headlands and cliffs. The name 'Mull' means a high, wide tableland, and the suffix '-nish', which occurs frequently in local place names, implies a flat headland on a more local scale.

The volcanic dykes that cross the country between Dervaig and Tobermory have been etched into hills and valleys, the more resistant rock of the dykes standing out as ridges. Loch Frisa, narrow, 5 miles in length and the largest loch on the island, lies in Glen Aros; it is renowned for its small, red fighting trout. A string of small lochs, the Mishnish Lochs, lie in a narrow depression between Dervaig and Tobermory, a glen known as Bealach Naithir—Snake Pass—on account of the adders found there. Just north of this is a little loch, 'S Airde Ben, perched near a hill top. The hill of 'S Airde Ben is composed of a plug of volcanic material, hardened within its vent, which burst through the surrounding (and older) lava sheets. The small depression on its

24

crown that the lochan occupies and the course of the stream that drains it are probably related to erosion along a fracture line that can be traced in the neighbourhood.

A raised beach, some 25ft above present sea level, is discernible around Loch na Keal, and remnants of what is presumed to be a pre-glacial raised beach, at about 125ft, can be traced through some 4 miles along the coast of Loch Tuath, between Treshnish and Torloisk. It is backed by old sea cliffs moulded by ice, and its outer edge drops straight into the sea in a lower, younger line of cliffs. This terrace or raised beach is 70–100 yards wide, which suggests a long period of erosion. It forms a fertile shelf on which valuable crops were formerly grown in rich, volcanic soil.

Many of the western islands can be considered as part of the north-west region, with which they have affinities. They are treated in greater detail in a later chapter.

THE ROSS OF MULL

The long, flattish Ross of Mull is separated from the central core by Loch Scridain. This south-west region may be regarded as running inland as far as the isthmus between the heads of Loch Scridain and Loch Buie. Its easterly portion—east of the fault line in the Loch Assapol area—is underlain by piled-up lavas, nowhere higher than 1,500ft above sea level, and presenting some fine trap-plateau features. The surface slopes up from north to south to the high, cliffed southern coastline. West beyond Bunessan lie the crystalline gneisses, worn down to a lowland and then west of Loch na Lathaich the red and pink granite mentioned earlier. This flat, bare countryside has fine, sandy beaches on its south coast.

The cliffed southern coast to the east of this region is broken by the picturesque bays of Carsaig, with its beach of dark volcanic sand, and Loch Buie, which is backed by a small fertile plain, with the old castle of the MacLaines of Lochbuie standing at the edge of the sea.

Around Carsaig Bay, below a covering of Tertiary lavas some 150ft thick, fossiliferous sedimentary deposits outcrop extensively. They are particularly well exposed on the west side of the bay.

25

Of greater interest perhaps is the outcrop of lignite, a soft, inferior coal, in a three-foot seam at Beinn an Aoinidh, southwest of Carsaig. Although this has been worked in the past for local domestic use, it is of no modern economic value. Other seams, of varying thickness have also been found in the locality, but their formation is often lenticular and sparse. They indicate the sub-tropical conditions that must have prevailed in this part of the world during the early volcanic period, since they are witness to the growth of vegetation and its decay in intervals between the formation of lava beds.

More evidence of the climatic conditions of the time is to be found in the 'leaf beds' discovered at Ardtun, near Bunessan, an accumulation of fossil leaves and petals in a layer of mudstone lying between two early lava flows. In the long interval between the flows, the surface of the earlier flow weathered, soil was formed and trees and vegetation grew. The process of the accumulation of the leaves is vividly reconstructed in a paper presented in 1851 to the Geological Society of London by the eighth Duke of Argyll, who was at that time researching into west highland geology. The leaves of one of the layers, he said, must have been shed 'autumn after autumn into the smooth still waters of some shallow lake, on whose muddy bottom they were accumulated, one above the other, fully expanded and at perfect rest'. Botanical examination of the leaf-beds, in the thin plates into which the mudstone can be split, showed that the leaves were from trees which are now found in sub-tropical conditions —gingko, sequoia and various conifers.

Also on the Carsaig coast are found caves formed considerably above the present shoreline, presumably associated with a higher sea level. Some of these are the Nuns' Cave at Carsaig, Lord Lovat's Cave (originally Odin's Cave) near Loch Buie, and the fantastic Carsaig Arches, four miles west of Carsaig.

THE MOUNTAIN CORE

This is a spectacular region, composed of majestic piled-up lava flows, chiefly in the west, and high jutting mountains in the centre where the volcanic remnants lie.

Ben More and the West

The western part, most of which is over 500ft in altitude, centres on Ben More, at 3,169ft the highest peak of Tertiary basalt in Britain. The lavas are here believed to be 3,000ft in thickness, a great depth having already been planed off by erosion by water and ice. Westwards the lava plateau, though dissected by rivers, stretches right to the coast and forms in the peninsula of Ardmeanach sea cliffs 1,000ft high. Ardmeanach, which reaches 1,700ft in places, is separated from the bold plateaux above Gribun (which top 1,800ft) by Iris Glen—Glen Seoilisdair. This pass carries the coast road from the north across to Loch Scridain and thence to the south-western region of the island.

The whole of the Ardmeanach peninsula is characteristically terraced and trap-featuring is particularly well displayed in Burg (also called The Wilderness), its mountainous termination. Gribun has another claim to geological interest in that, on its steep western coast, there are, overlying the basement of Moine Gneiss, outcrops of sedimentary rocks which date from the pre-Tertiary era, the Mesozoic. Mesozoic rocks have had no mention earlier in this chapter, because of the paucity of their occurrence in Mull. Here in western Gribun they have been preserved beneath the lava and exposed in the sea cliffs, presumably owing to some differential factor in the thickness of the lava or in the uplift of the coastal zone during the warping that accompanied the general subsidence of the island centre. The series may be seen, in ascending order: Triassic sandstones lie unconformably upon the Moine Gneiss (that is to say, they have been laid down, after a great gap in time, upon a surface that had been much worn down); above them come in turn Rhaetic and Liassic sandstones, all apparently, to judge by their constitution, laid down under marine conditions. Beds occur too of sandstones that may be of Cretaceous age. Lava flows cap the whole series. An exposure of Rhaetic beds may be seen near Balmeanach Farm, where the Allt na Teangaidh has cut a way into the rocks. The landslips around the precipitous seaward slopes of Gribun are also spectacular—they are referred to again when the island's road system is discussed later—and careful examination shows that they vary greatly in age; one is as early as pre-glacial times. Slipping occurs over the sedimentary beds.

By far the most striking features of this district are the land-forms and structure of the basaltic lavas. Columnar structure is particularly interesting where it occurs.

Columnar basalt

Columnar form does not occur throughout the lava succession but appears to be limited to a low horizon (that is, to early lava flows) and also, to judge by the distribution of observed occurrences, to a limited western area. The phenomenon is found on the island of Staffa, at the base of the Ulva lavas, in the Wilderness area of Ardmeanach, near Tavool, in the lavas immediately above and below the Ardtun leaf-beds near Bunessan and in the Carsaig cliffs; two small islands west of Iona are also formed of very fine columnar basalt. Isolated examples occur in Bloody Bay near Tobermory.

The processes by which the structure is achieved are those of cooling and contraction after the lava sheet had spread. The differences in the character of the structure—massive regularity as seen in the lower zones, closer-spaced wavy columns as in higher zones, curving columns, horizontal jointing—can usually be related to the situation of the lava and its physical constitution. After spreading out, the lava sheets began to cool usually from base and top, though at different rates, according to the surroundings. The upper parts probably lost heat most rapidly, by convection, but irregularly because of overlying slag of varying thicknesses. The lower portions would cool slowly and more regularly from the base upwards. Contraction on cooling, and loss of contained water, led to the development of a regular polygonal jointing, in planes at right angles to the cooling surfaces; the resultant columns are, ideally, hexagonal though three- to eight-sided columns are found. The curves of the columns have developed where the cooling surface was not itself in a horizontal plane (for example, in dykes, a similar phenomenon has occurred, with columns forming *across* the dyke between the two bounding, probably vertical walls). Spectacularly curved columns have been formed in Staffa at the Clamshell Cave and at the Buchaille Rock. The immense pressure of contraction sometimes squeezed out certain constituents of the basalt, such as calcite, into the fine vertical joints, making the columns look as if they had been

28

cemented together—the flat surface of worn-down pillars in front of Fingal's Cave, on Staffa, illustrate this.

The fine examples at Fingal's Cave on Staffa are, like those of Giants' Causeway on the north Antrim coast, probably the most renowned of the columnar basalts of the Tertiary volcanics of Britain—travellers have been writing about and depicting them for two centuries at least—but many admirable examples can be seen on Mull itself or on Ulva or Gometra. On the south coasts of these islands they are most extensive and impressive, giving long stretches of the shoreline a strangely artificial appearance, as of the walls and foundations of old buildings and castles looking across Loch na Keal to Ben More and Gribun. One site in Ulva is in fact called 'The Castles'.

Describing the basaltic columns of Ulva in 1819, Dr MacCulloch wrote : 'They are often as regular as those of Staffa, although on a much less scale, and pass gradually from that regularity into the most shapeless masses. In many places they afford elegant and picturesque compositions, which although passed every day by the crowds who visit Staffa, appear to have been unnoticed. If either their number, extent, or picturesque appearance be considered they are more deserving of admiration than even those of the Giants' Causeway; and had they been the only basaltic columns on this coast they might have acquired the fame they merit. But Ulva is eclipsed by the superior lustre of Staffa; and while the mass of mankind is content to follow the individual who first led the way, its beauties will still be consigned to neglect.'

MacCulloch's Tree

This same Dr MacCulloch was the first to describe in 1819 the 'fossil tree of Burgh', regarded by the geologists of the Scottish Geological Survey in their memoir on Mull (1924) as 'the most arresting single geological phenomenon in the island'. This mute witness of the cataclysm of the beginning of the volcanic activity stands at the shore line on the exposed Ardmeanach peninsula. It is the cast of an ancient coniferous tree trunk, forty feet high, embedded in the lowest lava flow of the basalt cliffs at Rudha nan Uamha (Point of the Caves), 100 yards north of the double waterfall of Allt Airidh nan Chaisteal, the most westerly

29

point of the peninsula. There are at least two similar but less obvious trees nearby, a small one lying across the lintel of a shallow cave, the other flat in the rocks just below high-water mark. At Tavool, on the south side of the headland, there is an exposure in the bed of the stream, between the waterfall and the road, of a mass of fragments of fossilised wood.

When the first flow of lava spread across what was then a sandy land surface covered with forests, MacCulloch's Tree was engulfed and destroyed. Yet it exerted just enough cooling influence and resistance—it is nearly five feet broad—to preserve its outline in the solidified flow; the lowest three feet of the trunk became fossilised by siliceous water. Attacked by curio-hunters since its discovery, the lower part is now preserved at least from erosion by a prosaic capping of cement through the interest of the National Trust for Scotland, which owns this corner of Mull that is aptly named The Wilderness.

The local cooling influence of the tree was sufficient to modify the vertical jointing pattern of the surrounding columnar basalt, which is everywhere curved from the vertical; within the last three feet from the trunk, the columns actually lie horizontal. The cliff has been cut back by erosion until the cross-section of the tree stands exposed, with the sea washing almost to its base.

Perhaps the most wonderful fact of all is the presence of a cavity at the foot of the fossilised trunk where a quantity of the original charcoal has been preserved, apparently as fresh as when the wood was charred by the great heat millions of years ago. The original grain of the wood stands out in the exposed face of the fossilised stump.

In this remote corner of Mull the basalt formations are particularly beautiful. The sea has breached the cliffs into shallow caves, whose entrances through the columnar formations have been carved into the likeness of Norman arches. Sea pools, vivid with brilliant seaweeds, are backed by low colonnades of dark basalt, and above it all the crumbling cliffs rise in grassy terraces where only the wild goats can graze. There is an echoing loneliness along the wide, boulder-strewn beaches, broken only by the cry of a very occasional sea bird, and the constant wash of the Atlantic rollers. Those who face the long difficult walk to the tree, however, are warned to arrive there at half-tide on a *falling* tide—or risk being cut off for hours, if no worse.

The central volcanics

The eroded roots of the volcanic area centred on the calderas of Ben Chaisgidle and Loch Ba are best seen in panorama from Pennyghael on the south side of Loch Scridain, where the contrast with the basalt cone of Ben More and its surrounding plateaux is evident. Ben Chaisgidle, entirely different in its structure, only reaches a height of 1,632ft. Its surrounding volcanic ring is overlapped on the north-west by the later ring centred on the head of Loch Ba. This loch lies only 41ft above sea level, which indicates the degree of erosion and down-warping that has occurred at the core of the second volcano, down to the level where Glen Cannel merges into the loch. The half-circle of peaks around the top of Glen Cannel is the most rewarding area for lovers of hills. This is one of the two main deer forests of the island, with rich grazings and plenty of high corries where the deer find sanctuary.

Some of the mountains that surround the collapsed and eroded centres of the calderas in fact reach great heights, where the later volcanics, the cone-sheets and the dykes have thrust through and metamorphosed the existing basalt lavas, causing them to be pushed up in concentric arcuate folds and faults around the calderas. The highest peaks reach 2,300ft and over; to the northeast beyond Glen Forsa, Dun da Ghaoithe reaches 2,512ft.

Around the perimeters of the calderas, especially on the southeast side, a succession of concentric ring dykes can be traced, encircling the collapsed cores of these adjacent focal points of late volcanic activity. In this central area one may find a variety of volcanic forms: outcrops of sills and cone sheets; dykes, either upstanding like walls across the countryside where they are the tougher rock, or as long trenches where the surrounding rock is the more resistant; pillow lavas, probably cooled under water during a stage when the caldera contained a temporary loch. These last are to be seen south-east of Loch Sguabain and around the summit of Ben Fhada. If one wishes to see individual physical phenomena of these kinds it is well worthwhile becoming familiar with their typical features and their locations by reference to the relevant Memoirs of the Geological Survey.

The central glens

The glens that dissect the central part of the island are particularly striking scenically. Glen More is the longest valley in Mull, curving for twelve miles from Loch Scridain to Loch Don in the east. Its curves are in part perhaps controlled by the arcuate folding and faulting of the rocks associated with the intrusion of the ring dyke around Ben Chaisgidle. The curve is to some extent echoed by that of the upper Glen Forsa on the north-east. Indeed the two glens swing round to meet above the sharp elbow bend of the river Lussa, but only after they have each passed over a watershed in a low col.

The trough of Glen More displays some fine evidence of glacial erosion where the ice has exploited weaknesses in the rock structure, and also of glacial deposition, as the valley glacier withdrew and melted. There are rounded and smoothed valley sides; bare, striated rocks in the lower valley and beside Loch Scridain. A few miles up the glen there are the hummocks and grassy mounds of the moraines deposited by the receding glacier. A fine terminal moraine crosses the floor of the glen above Craig Cottage.

In Glen Forsa too may be seen evidence of former glaciers in striae on the rocks of the lower slopes and in the hummocky moraines and gravel fans.

The beauty of Glen Cannel in the heart of the mountains above Loch Ba has already been referred to. The outlet of Loch Ba is dammed by moraine deposits. At the mouth of the Scarisdale river, at the head of Loch na Keal, gravel spit formation may be seen.

Eastern coasts

From a point mid-way between Tobermory and Salen, along the Sound of Mull, and round to Loch Spelve, the coastline differs from that of the two western regions. It is less exposed to the prevalent Atlantic gales and waves, and is sheltered by the high central land mass. Comparatively low, with shallow bays and sea-lochs and shores of mud-flats, shingle or dark sand, it is backed for the most part by sharply rising hills. As evidence of old higher sea levels, raised beaches, with sea caves in the low cliff behind them, can be traced along the Sound of Mull between Salen and Craignure.

In the eastern part of the island, behind Loch Don, across the Lussa valley, and around the eastern end of Loch Spelve, there are broader stretches of lowland following the north-east to south-west depression of the Great Glen fault continued from the mainland. In parts of this peripheral district Tertiary volcanic rocks have been eroded, to reveal the older deposits beneath them. From Craignure Bay nearly to the sea outlet of Loch Spelve there is a 'window' in the basalts, where an anticlinal structure—an upfold in the strata like an upturned boat—with a N–S axis brings sedimentary rocks of Mesozoic age to the surface in an elliptical outcrop that surrounds an inner core of Old Red Sandstone and much older metamorphic grey slates and limestones. Erosion during the Ice Age planed across this upward bulge in the rock structure and there is little beyond small local relief and differences in soils and drainage to indicate this window that reveals the underlying rocks of an era that preceded the volcanic flooding of Mull and even more distant ages.

ECONOMIC GEOLOGY

Granite

The Ross of Mull granite of the Assapol-Fionnphort area is a decorative and useful rock, pink or red in colour, which can take a high polish. It was quarried commercially for forty years up to the beginning of the twentieth century when, because of changing methods of building construction and competition from mainland granites such as those of Peterhead and Aberdeen, the industry declined. During its exploitation thousands of tons of Mull granite were shipped around the world, particularly to North America.

The Mull granite could be split readily into large blocks, horizontally oriented. They were free from flaws and were ideal for massive building work such as docks, bridges and harbour walls. The main quarry, now abandoned, is at Tormore, half a mile north of Fionnphort slipway. It lies a few hundred yards inland from a lovely beach of white sand. Here are the ruins of the pier from which, up to the beginning of the century, the blocks were

33

shipped. They were conveyed there from the quarry by a steep tramway. At the quarry large stockpiles of hundreds of blocks are still to be seen, some of the blocks as much as 10ft long by 3ft square. All the work of cutting and finishing the blocks was done by hand.

The original method of splitting the granite was the time-consuming one of driving dry wooden wedges into cracks and

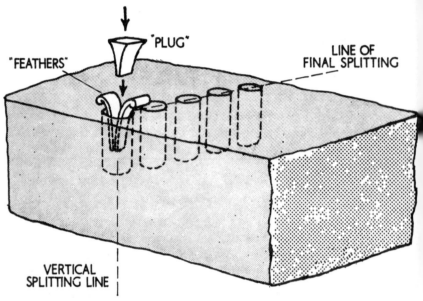

In the 'plug and feathers' method of splitting granite a series of iron wedges (feathers) were driven with the aid of iron plugs into a row of holes bored in the rock until it split under the pressure along the line of holes

holes and expanding them by constant soakings with water. This was superseded by the 'plug and feathers' method, introduced from the Mourne quarries of Ireland where it was first adopted about 1860. For this a line of holes, an inch and a half in diameter and six inches apart, was bored in the granite. Two thin iron wedges, the feathers, were inserted into each hole, forming smooth walls between which the plug, a long iron wedge, could be driven. The plugs in the row were then hammered down in turn until the rock was forced to split along the line of holes.

One giant monolith, called locally the Prince's Monument, is

Page 35: (*above*) Extensive columnar basalt on the south coast of Ulva, looking across Loch na Keal to Ben More and the 1,000ft cliffs of the Gribun coast, at the foot of which runs the road (*below*) threatened by landslips

Page 36: (above) Curving basalt
columns on the shore below a
150ft cliff on the western headland of Ardmeanach; near this
point lies the track down to shore
level which leads to MacCulloch's
Tree (below) about a mile north.
This 40ft high cast of a tree is
fossilised in a lava flow

still lying on its bed in the face of the rock opposite the main quarry. This was to have been erected in London last century as an obelisk in honour of the Prince Consort. However, a flaw was discovered at the last minute, and the project was abandoned in favour of a different style of memorial which stands in Hyde Park, and which is partly built of this granite. It is questionable whether such a large and unwieldy block could ever have been conveyed to its destination. Many of the public buildings and works of our large towns were built of Mull granite; Blackfriars Bridge, Holborn Viaduct, and the Albert Memorial in London; Liverpool Docks; Jamaica Bridge in Glasgow; Skerryvore and Dhuheartach lighthouses off Mull; and it provided the fine polished facings of many imposing buildings. Curling stones, most attractive in appearance, were also made, and for a time were in great demand.

Sandstone

There is a bed of hard grey sandstone exposed on the shore below the Nuns' Cave west of Carsaig. This was an excellent medium for cutting and shaping into ornamental stonework, such as is seen in the original carvings in Iona Cathedral, in the facings of old chapels throughout the island, and in recumbent tombstones. This quarry was first worked by the monks of Iona, and payments received for skilled work done to order went to augment the funds of the monastery. The stone at Carsaig was last worked in 1873 and used in partial restoration of the abbey of Iona in 1874.

There are other sandstones at Carsaig well suited for building work, and another outcrop at Bloody Bay, just north of Tobermory, but in every case their commercial exploitation is inhibited by distance, labour and transport problems.

Silica sand

At Gribun there is an outcrop of silica sand suitable for high-grade optical purposes; it is similar to the sand that has been worked extensively for such uses at Lochaline (Morvern) since the second world war. Unlike the Morvern one, the Gribun outcrop is badly situated for economic working, and has never been exploited.

Road metal

There is no limitation, in Mull, on sources for road metal, since the volcanic rocks provide suitable hard, fine-grained material that can be quarried almost everywhere. Small roadside pits and quarries are also used for the digging out of morainic gravels, pebbles and rotted basalts and dykes, for local use.

Coal

A few seams of coal (lignitic) exist immediately under or at the base of the Tertiary rocks in the Ross of Mull. Their quality is comparatively poor and their occurrence is impersistent and irregular. The thickest is one of three feet exposed in the burn on Beinn an Aoinidh, west of Carsaig. This seam was first worked in the sixteenth century, and for a time tenants had to supply the landlord with a certain quantity of coal as part of the rent of their holdings. Efforts to commercialise the workings in later years were unsuccessful. The last prospecting for coal was carried out in 1910, but little of interest was found. Another seam of eighteen inches appears on the east coast of the Ross, and traces are found at Brolas, Ardtun, Gribun and Carsaig Bay.

Peat

Peat has been used as fuel throughout the highlands and islands from the earliest times. Geologically speaking it is a recent, postglacial formation, of organic material, that has developed *in situ* in cool, wet conditions in ill-drained bogs and marshy areas. It must be dug out of its thick surface deposits and dried in order to form the hard, black or dark brown fuel blocks that burn with considerable heat and characteristic scent. Beds of peat are widely scattered in the glens and valleys and on the plateau tops, wherever drainage has been impeded. In the undercut bank of a burn in Glen Aros the whole succession can be seen, from the flat base of polished and ice-scored rock, covered by two feet of boulder clay, and above that, eight feet of peat ranging from black and consolidated material at the base to loose and fibrous upper layers.

Semi-precious stones

On the hills and shores both north and south of Loch Scridain there are outcrops of sills—intrusions of volcanic rock that thrust their way when molten through seams and cracks in a roughly horizontal fashion—which, because of their particular constitution, have in the process of cooling and hardening formed within themselves crystals of corundum or sapphire. The sapphires are usually small, up to half an inch or so; but in a sill just beyond the Nuns' Cave, Carsaig, and immediately above the shore, they are found up to an inch or two across. However, they are thin, plate-like and impure, and are of no commercial value.

Iona pebbles and marble

Fine white marble exists in a 40ft wide stratum running NNW and SSE in the south-east of the island of Iona. It cuts freely, polishes well, and is durable, although it tends to yellow with age. It has been used for ornamental work throughout the ages: in early times an altar in Iona Cathedral was formed from a 6ft by 4ft block of marble, and was referred to by Sacheverell in 1688. It disappeared piecemeal as a result of the superstition that a fragment of the altar carried in a boat averted shipwreck.

Early in the nineteenth century the marble was quarried extensively and supplies were sent to Leith and London; but demand tapered off and little work, if any, has been done since the beginning of the twentieth century.

On the south and west shores of Iona beautifully coloured pebbles are sometimes cast up by the action of the waves. The most famous of them is known as the Iona pebble. Seldom exceeding an inch or two in length, it is found on the shore at Port na Churaich, especially after stormy weather. It is an attractive green variety of serpentine, varying in colour from dark green to light greenish-yellow; probably derived from serpentine nodules in an undersea extension of the Iona marble.

The softness of the texture allows Iona pebbles to be readily worked into curios and tiny ornaments which find a ready sale. Their attractive qualities have been known for centuries, for in 1688, during a visit to the island, John Fraser, Dean of the Isles, compiled a quaintly comprehensive description which he presented to Sacheverell, Governor of Man:

> 'Here the sea casteth up in ane place a number of small stones of divers collours and transparents, verij fair to look upon. They realy are peculiar to the place, for the longer they lay on the

shoar they reapen, and turn more lively in their coulors. They yield to the file and admits of good polishing and engraving. Marble also of divers collours and with beautyfull vains is found on the island. It has been counted renouned, pairtly for the gouid discipline of Columbus [sic] who is buried in it, and pairtly for the monuments of the place.[1]

2   CLIMATE, PLANTS AND ANIMALS

MULL shares the climate of the western seaboard of Scotland, with cool summers and mild winters. Snow rarely
falls, and when it does come it soon disappears except
on the northern slopes of the higher hills. The incidence of frost,
too, is negligible in comparison with mainland conditions. These
circumstances reflect a combination of factors. The prevailing
winds are westerly or southwesterly and in the 'weather' that they
bring to the island, the air has been warmed during its passage
over the comparatively warm waters of the North Atlantic Drift
that flows north out of the Gulf Stream; hence the amelioration
particularly of winter conditions. The configuration of the island,
with its sea-lochs open westwards, allows the penetration of warm,
moist air. In summer, as the earth warms up, the surrounding
waters exert a cooling effect on the land temperatures and Mull
thus benefits by its very insularity.

It is noteworthy that, despite its northerly situation—about
56° 30'N—the arrival of spring, as signified by the first flowering
of certain plants, comes as early in Mull as it does, say, in the
Cheshire Plain or the East Riding of Yorkshire. Similarly, Mull
enjoys a very long growing season for vegetation, some 7–8
months, during which temperatures do not fall below a critical
level.

However, Mull is not an eternal paradise of beautiful weather!
Exposed as it is to the Atlantic gales, without any higher islands
or land mass to protect it, the island receives both a large amount
of rain and strong winds. Fierce storms strike the island with an
undiminished fury, and the narrow glens tend to funnel the wind
into the central areas. In Glen More, for instance, in addition to
the customary stout stays used to anchor them, the telegraph
poles must also be set, in certain places, into foundations of logs

41

sunk deep into the soft bogland; otherwise they would be flattened to the ground or torn right out by some of the gale winds.

In terms of the amount of rain received in a year, Mull is wetter than any of the other Hebridean islands. Records of rainfall have been kept for a long period at three points in Mull and at one in Iona. These records show that average rainfall per year varies from 81·3in (2,065mm) at Auchnacraig (near Grass Point, in the extreme east), which is in the lee of the mountain core of the island, to 48·4in (1,229mm) in Iona. Although the latter is in the most exposed westerly position, because it is so low-lying the moist air does not give up its rain until it is cooled by rising against the central mountains. On Ben More and other high places the annual rainfall reaches 125in (3,175mm), an amount equalled in the Hebrides only by a small central area in the higher and more massive Cuillins of Skye.

From the average of the four sets of rainfall records over a period of 35 years, May is shown to be the driest month, with only 3·66in (92·9mm). Thereafter the monthly average rises to a maximum of 8·40in (213·4mm) in October. This is merely an arithmetical average for the whole island, however; rain must be expected right through the year, with the smallest amounts in late spring and early summer. Moreover, most of the stations are situated at only limited heights above sea level. Gruline, at the foot of Ben More, with an annual average of 79·8in (2,027mm), more closely reflects the heavy precipitation of the adjacent mountain mass. There are local variations in the incidence of rainfall, depending on the nature of the relief and exposure, the height above sea level, the character of the soil and even of the vegetation. Peat-covered areas are commonly water-logged, and produce locally humid conditions; sandy areas are quickly drained and drier; the transpiration from lush vegetation in damp areas returns more moisture to the atmosphere and renews the cycle of rainfall, drainage and the taking up of water by plants. These natural phenomena are intensified in the conditions of high rainfall, moderate temperatures and very varied relief that exist in Mull.

The moderating influence of the surrounding waters and of the warm North Atlantic Drift is perhaps best illustrated by the relatively small range of temperatures that Mull experiences. The annual range of temperature, that is to say, the difference between the means of the warmest and the coldest months, is about 9°C (16°F). This contrasts with annual ranges in the Grampians, at about the same latitude, of over 11°C (20°F) and in the Home Counties around London of over 14°C (25°F). Sea-surface temperatures in these waters average 8°C (46°F) in winter and over 12°C (54°F) in summer; maximum and minimum temperatures are reached later in the sea than on the land.

No official records of temperature are available on Mull itself. Conditions are fairly similar, especially in the west central area, to those on the island of Tiree, 24 miles to the west, where meteorological observations have been recorded since 1931. According to Tiree's records, July and August are the warmest months, with the latter slightly the warmer. The highest absolute temperature recorded in Tiree, 26·1°C (79°F) was in July, however. January and February are the coldest months with temperatures down to about 5°C (41°F)—comparatively mild in relation to east coast temperatures, around the Firth of Tay, of less than 3°C (around 37°F). Average temperatures in the hills are, of course, lower than those of the lowlands.

The duration of sunshine to be expected is naturally related to cloudiness and therefore to rainfall. Mid-July, a notoriously wet summer month, may be expected to be rather cloudy. This generalisation is confirmed by recourse again to the meteorological data for Tiree; a sunshine index can be calculated by expressing the monthly mean of hours of recorded sunshine as a percentage of the possible number of hours of sunshine (i.e. hours of daylight). The July index is 30 per cent; that for May is 47 per cent and for June 39 per cent, for August 34 per cent and for September 33 per cent. Certainly May and June and late-August to September are periods to be recommended for visits to the island.

Up to early June the irritating attentions of midges, clegs and the common house fly are absent, and the bracken has not yet reached its tough and obscuring maturity—in places it can reach over 5ft in height, and it both conceals objects of interest and makes the going hard off the beaten track. In August to September, on the other hand, the heather is in full bloom and the early autumn colourings are superb. For the angler, salmon and sea trout should be established in the lochs and rivers they frequent,

43

METEOROLOGICAL DATA FOR TIREE

Temperatures in °C (°F)

	Jan	Feb	Mar	April	May	June	July	Aug	Sept	Oct	Nov	Dec
Monthly mean	5·3 (41·5)	5·2 (41·4)	6·3 (43·3)	7·8 (46·0)	10·1 (50·2)	12·2 (54·0)	13·7 (56·7)	13·8 (56·8)	12·6 (54·7)	10·4 (50·7)	7·9 (46·2)	6·4 (43·5)
Monthly mean maximum	7·0 (44·6)	7·2 (45·0)	8·5 (47·3)	10·3 (50·5)	12·9 (55·2)	14·9 (58·8)	16·1 (61·0)	16·3 (61·3)	14·9 (58·8)	12·3 (54·1)	9·7 (49·5)	8·1 (46·6)
Monthly mean minimum	3·5 (38·3)	3·2 (37·8)	4·0 (39·2)	5·2 (41·4)	7·2 (45·0)	9·6 (49·3)	11·2 (52·2)	11·4 (52·5)	10·3 (50·5)	8·4 (47·1)	6·1 (43·0)	4·7 (40·5)
Absolute maximum	12·2 (54)	11·7 (53)	15·0 (59)	17·8 (64)	22·2 (72)	25·6 (78)	26·1 (79)	24·4 (76)	21·1 (70)	18·3 (65)	14·4 (58)	13·9 (57)
Absolute minimum	−6·7 (20)	−6·7 (20)	−6·1 (21)	−4·4 (24)	−0·6 (31)	2·2 (36)	6·1 (43)	5·0 (41)	1·7 (35)	0·6 (33)	−3·9 (25)	−5·0 (23)
Sea temperature	7·8 (46)	7·2 (45)	6·7 (44)	7·2 (45)	8·9 (48)	10·6 (51)	12·8 (55)	13·3 (56)	13·3 (56)	11·7 (53)	10·6 (51)	8·9 (48)
Sunshine index[1]	16	26	32	40	47	39	30	34	33	26	21	14

[1] Percentage hours of sunshine/hours of daylight.

and brown trout are back on the take after their mid-season off-period.

To have the leisure to observe the passage of an Atlantic depression from a good viewpoint is an opportunity often eagerly sought by those who enjoy the changing elements, scenery and colour. To have that leisure and opportunity on Mull is to experience much beauty indeed. The procession of changing events —the passage of a warm front, in meteorological jargon—is especially striking when seen against the unpolluted atmosphere and the wide western horizons. Long wisps of high cirrus cloud spread slowly from the west, then gradually consolidate into a sheet of cirro-stratus; the cloud base becomes lower and lower over the sea as it forms a huge wedge of darkening stratus; then the low, heavy, rain-bearing clouds approach, filling the sky and driven before a strong, backing southwesterly wind; a lull, a quick veer of the wind into the west or north-west, the rain lessens, the clouds lift and a transformation takes place. Behind the 'warm front' the sky becomes crystal clear and blue, with bright fleecy cumulus clouds, the sea is bright, the whole countryside seems to rejoice in brilliant sunshine and incredible colours—and the mundane words of the weather forecast, 'Rain in the morning', have been fulfilled.

In this age of sophistication it is refreshing to return to Mull and fall again under its spell. There is still something simple in the way of living, something of older days and older ways. Indeed the island seems to have an ecclesiastic atmosphere of its own, a kind of intangible radiance that comes from near-by Iona— perhaps St Columba's shade still walks the glens and hill tracks of Mull. There is much to see there and much to explore, both on and off the beaten track, with arresting colours and a great deal of the picturesque and beautiful for the artist or the photographer.

WOODLANDS

The Natural vegetation of Mull that the first inhabitants would find was largely woodland. Trees spread northwards over Scotland after the withdrawal of glaciers during the Ice Age, and their luxuriance and type on the island would vary according to the changes in the climate that occurred after that time. It is impossible now to estimate how dense would be the forest cover, but it is certain that much of it, on seaward and exposed slopes particularly, would be stunted and wind-blasted, just as it is today. Oak, holly and hazel, with pine and birch at higher altitudes were the dominant species. The massive roots of pine trees have been found embedded in the peat bogs that have gradually accumulated, and remnants of the oak woodlands are still to be seen today.

Several factors have contributed to the considerable reduction of the woodlands since man first set foot on the island: felling for fuel or to clear the land of wild animals, such as wolves; accidental burning in the course of the periodic firing of the moors in order to improve the grazing, or wanton burning by Norse invaders; felling for wartime supplies of timber or for the manufacture of charcoal for use in iron smelting or explosive works in Argyll. By the late eighteenth century Mull was practically treeless. Dr Johnson, when visiting the island, missed his favourite stick of oak which had accompanied him all the way from London and assumed it had been stolen. 'It is not to be expected,' he said, 'that any man in Mull, who has got it, will part with it. Consider, Sir, the value of such a *piece of timber* here!' During his memorable visit to Inch Kenneth, when Sir Alan Maclean referred to the woods of Mull, the doctor replied: 'Sir, I saw at Tobermorie what they called a wood, which I mistook for *heath*. If you show me what I shall take for *furze* it will be something.'

Deforestation was continued into the nineteenth century through the burnings of the clearances and the depredations of sheep and deer grazing, since both animals nibble the tender growing shoots. Later in the century the new owners of large estates began some tree planting, and in the twentieth century the Forestry Commission has manifestly changed the scene, with plantations of spruce and larch. The work of the Commission is considered at greater length in a later chapter.

The only remaining natural woodlands are in relatively small patches of degenerate forest and scrub, mainly oak, birch and hazel, with some rowans. Wherever they are exposed to the prevailing winds or to wind-blown sea spray, the trees are stunted. Along such west-facing slopes as the south side of Loch na Keal hazel trees on the windward edge of the little woods are no taller than gooseberry bushes and are twisted and streamlined by the prevailing southwesterly wind. One can see, on the sheltered sunny side of a cleft in the western cliffs, a fine wild cherry tree; and only a few yards away, on the exposed side of the same cleft, a few skeletal shrubs grasping a precarious living, blasted by the wind deflected off the rock face.

The most extensive woods are on the north side of Loch Tuath and Loch na Keal and in sheltered Strath Coil on the lower Lussa river, where there are also many holly trees. The south-east of Mull, especially in the depression occupied by Lochs Spelve and Uisg, between Ardura and Lochbuie, and on the Laggan peninsula, has more extensive natural woodlands.

Tree planting in the nineteenth century by estate owners, for the improvement of the surroundings of their large houses, brought in exotic species. These can be seen in many favoured corners—Carsaig, Tiroran, Gruline, Ulva House, Torosay, Aros House (Tobermory) and Pennyghael. At Carsaig there are limes, plane trees, sycamores and chestnuts, beech, elm and alder, as well as tall larch and spruce. Although the Scots pine is a native tree, it is probable that the oceanic climatic and soil conditions in Mull in recent centuries contribute to its failure to regenerate successfully, especially where peat and bogland now dominate. Larch and spruce have been the more favoured species in recent Forestry Commission plantations.

MOOR AND GRASSLAND

Long exposure to grazing by cattle, sheep and deer has led to considerable modification of the grass and moorland vegetation; and, since the later nineteenth century, through neglect of areas which were formerly grazed by sheep, even greater changes have come about through the spread of bracken which grows luxuriantly in the mild, damp climate, especially on the base-rich soils that develop over the underlying basalt. In general the purple moor grass (*Molinia caerulea*) gives its typical colouring to the grasslands of the lower altitudes (below about 500ft), noticeably on the trap landscapes of the west and south. On the higher moorlands and on the more acid soils of the central area the

47

vegetation is typically that associated with fescue and bent (*Festuca-agrostis*) sheep grazing moors. However, the variety of relief and drainage conditions gives rise to a wide range of vegetation complexes and Mull has a profusion of the plants and the marine vegetation that are typical of the Hebridean region. A comprehensive botanical survey of Mull by the Department of Botany, British Museum, is in progress; it is planned to cover the five years 1967 to 1972.

While dry grass and heather moors are found on the steeper slopes, the ill-drained flats of the basalt plateau tops and in broader valley areas carry accumulations of peat. The wet bogs and moors carry a prolific growth of coarse heather, low-growing bog myrtle, coarse grasses and deep banks of sphagnum moss—the last often deceptively solid-looking over knee-deep peaty mud. Other mosses and lichens grow freely in the damp shade of birch scrub. Mull is famous for its orchis plants, found in profusion in most of the boglands, including the spotted, butterfly and scented orchis as well as some varieties peculiar to the island.

Moorland pools are commonly covered with the flat leaves of the bogbean, which, if collected and boiled, yield a concentrated juice said by the older folk to alleviate rheumatic pains. The tall white tufts of cotton grass sway in the wind above the yellow brilliance of marsh marigolds, globe flowers and buttercups and other typical inhabitants of the damp moors, such as bog asphodel, grass of Parnassus, sundew and marsh violet. Most striking in some of the lochs and the deep still pools in the burns are the flowers of yellow and white water lilies. In the shallows of some lochs beds of giant rushes ten feet or more in height grow from the bottom. Indeed water weeds grow so freely that the shallows become choked with them, to the disadvantage of anglers.

Widespread though it is, the ling heather (*Calluna vulgaris*) seems slowly to be deteriorating. This may be due to disease or to a slow change in climate, but lack of correct burning is certainly the cause in some areas. Periodic spring burning, systematic in terms both of areas burned over and of intervals of time (some fifteen to twenty years), is part of the skilled management of the heather moors if they are to be used profitably as sheep or grouse lands. Since both these uses have declined, neglect is inevitable and the heather fails to regenerate itself. Bracken often supplants the dying heather and in some parts the ground has reverted to birch scrub.

Bell heather (*Erica cinerea*) is abundant, and in the damper heaths the cross-leaved heath (*Erica tetralix*) with its delicious scent is plentiful. White-flowered ling, in clumps or in single sprigs, can be found in surprising quantities in young well-established growths on the drier hill slopes, once the eye of the searcher has become trained in the search. White bell heather is scarcer.

SHORES AND COASTS

The lowlands and the coasts have their own kind of plant life, often determined by the influence of salt-laden winds or sea-spray. Mull has relatively little *machair*, the small patches of shelly, sandy soil that lie between the low-lying peat and moorland areas and the sandy beaches. The *machairs* are usually cultivated, but where they are not they carry short sweet grass and they can be a riot of blossom in summer. The sandy *machair* at Calgary used to carry a carpet of wild pansies but these have now disappeared —probably through the depredations of day visitors to the beach there. The yellow iris grows freely in Mull, especially along grassy flats just above the shore.

On the rocky coasts sea pinks grow in profusion, along with bladder campion and yellow and pink stonecrop. On some of the rocky beaches are found two typical salt-loving plants, sea holly and sea lungwort. The blue flowers of the lungwort (*Mertensia maritima*) carpet certain beaches of the Treshnish Islands, and isolated plants grow in the shingle of some of the coves around the headland of Treshnish on Mull itself.

SEAWEEDS

Seaweeds about in wide variety, sometimes within vertically narrow zones where the rocks drop steeply into the sea, sometimes spreading in descending order over the whole tide-washed depth of a shallow bay. Highest in these zonations are the lichens of spray-soaked rocks at the upper limits of the tides, a no-man's-land where neither sea creatures nor vegetation can grow freely.

Next come the wracks where barnacles also begin, to be followed in descending order by limpets, whelks, and mussels. Below the wracks at low watermark come red algae, merging into the laminaria weeds; one of these with large swelling fronds is aptly likened by Fraser Darling to 'coarse tripe turned inside out'. The sequence of seaweeds, and even the presence of seaweed at all, at any point depend on many factors—steepness of the shore, depth of water, salinity, currents, character of the bottom, whether mud, sand or rock. The western and the eastern coasts differ in their seaweed vegetation.

Two varieties can sometimes alter the appearance of the rocky and shingly lower beaches. They are the bladder wrack (*Fucus ceranoides*) and the knotted wrack (*Ascophyllum nodosum*), which attach themselves to individual stones. When the plants are mature their lifting power can float small stones away, maybe to be carried considerable distances by wind and tide. Another peculiar type is the *Chorda filum*, a thin string-like weed which can attain a length of eight feet and which also attaches itself to small stones and pebbles. It is prolific in Loch na Lathaich, off Bunessan, where it can wrap itself round the propellers of small craft and immobilise them.

Two forms of red algae found at very low tides are dulse (*Rhodymenia*) and carragheen (*Chondrus crispus*), both of which are edible, with a rich, salty tang.

The spring harvest of wrack and laminaria is still a useful fertiliser for many shore crofts and farms on the light, sandy *machairs*, where, after it is ploughed in, it improves the organic content of the soil.

Scrambling along the rocky shores at low tide can be as rewarding as searching the hills for white heather, for there is an immense variety of things to be seen or discovered : the different species of seaweed, the creatures of the rocky pools, the beauties of empty shells, the flotsam of sea life along the shore, or the artistry of the sea where waves have carved rocks of contrasting character.

Ashore the blossoms are richest in late spring and early summer. At first the undergrowth in the damp woodlands and thickets is carpeted with masses of wood anemones and wood sorrel, with primroses, wild violets and wild hyacinths. Great quantities of

50

toadstools grow among the deep mosses and on the rotting wood of old birch trees. On the plantations, the delicate sheen of the fresh green shoots of the larch trees contrasts with the darker spruce. Some of the farm pastures carry a rich harvest of mushrooms. Summer has the fragrance of the fragile dogrose and wild honeysuckle; everywhere in the boglands the unforgettable scent of bog myrtle and bog mint is carried on the wind. Autumn brings the purple of the heather, blending with the rich hues of wide expanses of bracken. The eye is caught by the rich colourations of birch leaves against the silver of the trunks, backed by the autumn tones of woodlands and plantations. Wild fruits are plentiful—brambles, raspberries and strawberries, the last growing to the size of a large hazel nut, with an acid sweetness more delicious than that of the cultivated strawberry. Hazel nuts too are plentiful in autumn.

BIRDS

The Treshnish Islands are a natural bird sanctuary where there are established colonies of kittiwakes, puffins, guillemots and gulls. Fulmars, Manx shearwaters and storm petrels are also found there. In winter barnacle geese congregate to graze on the rich grass.

One of the commonest birds to be seen round the shores is the cormorant, locally called scart (gaelic *sgarbh*). Oystercatchers and redshanks are found all round the coasts and their high-pitched piping echoing from the rocks adds an atmosphere of remoteness and loneliness. A similar feeling of desolation is conveyed on the moorlands by the characteristic calls of the mergansers and duck, especially of the vocal mallard. The great northern diver takes toll of the trout in lonely hill lochs.

Golden eagles are returning to their old haunts, now that a more enlightened view is taken of the nature of their prey and they are less frequently destroyed. Buzzards are very common in Mull, as well as ravens and hooded crows. The hoodies are hated by shepherds for their bold attacks on weak lambs and injured sheep; they are the most cunning of the scavenging birds and hardest to keep down.

Among the smaller birds, the cuckoo is common and sur-

51

prisingly tame. Seven or eight have been counted within a few hundred yards in early summer, each with its attendant meadow-pipit foster parent. The corncrake, common at the beginning of the century, has almost disappeared.

Ptarmigan, which don white winter plumage, are still found on the heights of Dun da Ghaoithe and neighbouring hill tops, but the blackcock died out after the first world war. Grouse, once plentiful, are still found in isolated coveys. The new woodlands being established by the Forestry Commission may attract new species of birds and help to expand the small stocks of pheasants. The capercailzie, Scotland's largest game bird, might return, along with various mammals, such as squirrel, pine martin and polecat.

ANIMAL LIFE

The largest native mammal on the island is the red deer (estimated at 3,000 head in 1965); they are found in all the corners of the hills though concentrated in Torosay, in the Ben More deer forest and the Laggan peninsula. The deer can be a nuisance in winter, at lower levels, where they nibble growing crops, or among the plantations, where they will graze on young tree shoots. They cannot always be kept out by expensive high deer fences. Some interesting observational research could be done on the herds to compare their habits in this island habitat with those of mainland herds, of which Fraser Darling gives detailed account in *A Herd of Red Deer*.

Brown and blue hares (the latter growing a white coat for winter) are common. They were unaffected by the disease of myxomatosis which almost wiped out the hordes of Mull rabbits in the early 1950s. No one knows when the first rabbits appeared on the island; Dean Munro wrote in 1549 that they were present in great numbers in Mull and Inch Kenneth. Tradition has it that they were first observed on the sandy *machair* above the beach at Calgary, where the sight of these strange beasts aroused apprehension and curiosity among the people. They spread over all the smaller islands around Mull, the porous soils developed on the basalt rocks and the sandy *machair* suiting their burrowing habits admirably, and the fine grasses their appetites. As elsewhere in the country they became a major liability to farming,

Page 53: Two examples of volcanic dykes of the 'Mull swarm': (*above*) at Calgary a vertical dyke cuts through lava flows and stands out on the cliff face between a raised beach and the present shore. The walls of the old pier shed were built on to the bottom of the dyke; (*below*) at Carsaig a dyke projects above the level of the wave-cut sandstones on the shore

Page 54: (*left*) The 700ft high cliffs west of Carsaig Bay, with sandstones overlain by thick basalt flows: (*right*) Eas Forss, a waterfall on the north side of Loch Tuath, tumbling directly into a deep sea-pool covered at high tide

fouling the ground around their extensive warrens and ruining the grazings for livestock.

On one single hill farm the stock of young cattle has been increased by 50 per cent since myxomatosis took its toll of the rabbits, and were in better condition than when rabbit infestation was at its height there. Cattle are now grazing freely on the fine young grasses covering old rabbit warrens that were formerly a place to be avoided. Of course, rabbits used to be a useful—if monotonous—addition to the islanders' diet. In illustration of this there is a story of a visiting minister, who had enjoyed a meal of stewed rabbit, calling on the man of the house to give thanks after eating. The words of the grace feelingly summed up the man's attitude to rabbits:

'Rabbits young and rabbits old;
Rabbits hot and rabbits cold;
Rabbits tender and rabbits tough,
I thank the Lord I've had enough.'

Unfortunately, the rabbits are again breeding on the island.

Up to 1800 there were no moles in Mull. According to the Statistical Account of 1845, the first pair were accidentally brought into the parish of Kilninian when a smack over from Morvern discharged a load of earth ballast. They too have spread all over the island. By the year 1800, on the other hand, foxes had disappeared from Mull. Stoats and weasels are common, and the polecat has re-appeared since 1950. Wild goats are found on some of the high coastal cliffs at Ardmeanach and along the south coast of the Ross. They are descendants of the domestic goats kept by former generations, which either escaped or were released when the clearances began.

In the warm damp summers there is a vast amount of insect life, especially around the margins of the lochs, and ranging from the dragon fly to the midge. The latter is a very real pest to both man and beast from mid-June onwards. Their most favoured place is probably along the line of decaying seaweed at the high spring tide limits, but in windless weather they are everywhere except on the higher hilltops and far out on the water. It is advisable to go out suitably protected, whether with proprietary creams, a headscarf or a tobacco pipe. House flies and horse flies

D

are also plagues to man and animals. The attention of the clegs is responsible at times for the movement of the deer from one grazing area to a higher one.

Mull has its share of reptiles. Frogs and toads are everywhere, forming the principal food of adders, and slow-worms are quite common. Iona is free of both snakes and frogs: according to tradition St Columba banished them from the island. The adder is the only species of snake on Mull, the largest ever seen by the author measuring 32in in length. They may sometimes be seen basking on sun-warmed rocks or on top of heather or growing bracken, and it is advisable to carry a stick when walking through heather or bracken.

The enthusiastic angler will find that in Mull's streams there are no freshwater fish other than salmon, sea trout and brown trout.

All the coasts of Mull, but especially along the Sound of Mull, are frequented by the common seal, while the Treshnish Islands has a breeding colony of grey seals. There the flat basalt platforms just above sea level round some of the islands and skerries form hauling-out places for the grey seals, which gather for breeding and mating from August onwards.

3   THE PEOPLING OF THE ISLANDS

THE prehistoric peopling of Mull was accomplished by folk who were part of the successive waves of early migrants from the southern and central European mainland, mostly by way of the Atlantic sea route between Ireland and south-west England. Piecing together the story can be done for the island as for the other western isles through the interpretation of the nature and distribution of archaeological finds both on Mull and in surrounding districts. The absence of archaeological evidence does not, of course, mean that particular stages of prehistory were not represented on the island. A comprehensive and systematic survey of Mull has never been carried out, and much remains to be discovered and confirmed. The Royal Commission on the Ancient and Historical Monuments of Scotland is undertaking a survey of its ancient monuments.

During the 7,000 years or so since men started to reach these western shores, much can have been destroyed, washed away, buried, while some cultures would leave little trace anyway. Moreover the dating of the various cultures on the island can be but estimated; archaeologists and students of prehistory themselves hold different opinions about precisely dating the finds. Anyone familiar with prehistory in more southerly parts of Britain must bear in mind that, for the earlier ages at least, the waves of prehistoric migrants reached the western isles and highland coasts much later than they made their first landfalls in southern Britain.

Man and animals spread north following the retreat of the ice over a long period during which Britain was still connected to the mainland of Europe and when sea level fluctuated. After Britain became an 'island' about 5,000 years before Christ, there grew a steadily increasing flow of migrants via the Atlantic sea

57

route as far as the Hebrides and beyond, right up to the time of Christ. In trying to reconstruct Mull's prehistory one has to remember that, as elsewhere in the western isles, the island was probably occupied intermittently at times, and that, when settlement became more continuous, new arrivals, whether arriving peaceably as colonisers or traders, or coming as pirates or in war, commonly became intermixed with the aboriginal and then indigenous folk. Thus one finds a slow change in cultures, as new technologies were brought in; and a gradual intermixing of racial types of people, of their habits, customs, religious beliefs and language. Such assimilation would be of greater or lesser degree, depending on the dominance of the peoples concerned, but it was likely to continue even after the later Celtic and the Norse invasions.

THE EARLIEST SETTLERS

The first man to set foot on Mull may have belonged to a family of late Stone Age hunter-fisher folk whose crudely worked tools of bone, antler and stone and whose kitchen middens of limpet shells have been unearthed in two cave shelters near Oban, at a former beach level when the sea stood 25ft higher than it now does. Similar finds have been made in south-west Scotland and on Oronsay, but no tools and no kitchen middens have so far been found around the 25ft raised beaches on Mull to corroborate this conjecture. Professor R. J. C. Atkinson (in *The Prehistoric Peoples of Scotland*) has concluded that the mesolithic population of Scotland was probably exceedingly sparse, and indeed one family group, hunting seals, seabirds, wildfowl and deer, collecting shellfish and wild berries, and themselves a prey to wolves, may have been the only inhabitants of the shores around Oban and the adjacent islands. They lived by strand-looping—sailing from one bay to the next.

The first settlers on the island, therefore, were more likely to be neolithic colonists, arriving during the third millenium BC—perhaps they found a few aboriginal savages still inhabiting that part of Scotland's western seaboard. Neolithic settlement can be assumed to have continued on Mull, quite possibly with some temporary breaks, for as much as 1,000 years, and gradually to have given way to a more advanced way of life as the use of metals became widespread. Mull itself contributed no mineral resources to this development, but traders and new settlers, many of them from Ireland, would introduce the fisher-farmers of the island to tools, weapons and ornaments made from copper, gold and, later, bronze. The island may have seen a fair amount of traffic during those two thousand years or so up to the centuries before Christ—though little evidence has been unearthed to prove it in detail. But the island must have had some attraction for the Bronze Age peoples; its basalt soils were richer and less acid than those of the outer isles, even though workable sites may have been limited to a few lowlands, and moreover it stood near the south-western entrance to the Great Glen, a very early trade route across north-west Scotland.

The way of life of Mull's small settlements during this period would be based on a combination of cattle raising and crops, varied by fishing, shellfish collecting and hunting of wild animals such as deer, horses or wild ox. Small family groups would be settled on the favourable bay-head sites—near Calgary, for instance, or Salen or Glen Forsa mouth—cultivating with primitive tools the light sandy *machair* of these areas to produce summer crops of emmer wheat, bere (a kind of barley) and maybe flax. Although there was a climatic amelioration during this time, they would still be prevented by climatic conditions from using the soil at higher altitudes for crop raising. The cattle, a greatly valued asset and possibly a cross-breed of the domesticated cattle of the time, with wide-spread horns, with the native wild ox, would be pastured on the surrounding rough grasslands. Sheep were kept for meat, milk and wool. As time went on and herds grew in size, more distant pastures at greater altitudes would be brought into use, developing a kind of transhumance whereby some members of the family would stay with the grazing herds on the uplands for some weeks or months in the summer. With the onset of winter and the dwindling of the pastures animals, including many calves, which could not be fed on the limited resources around the lowland settlement would be slaughtered—this was a characteristic feature of the economy of the period.

It was undoubtedly a demanding way of life that required a fairly high level of organisation, however primitive the tools and techniques may have been, and although nothing discernible remains of the settlements—the dwellings and byres were probably constructed of turves and some timbers, and possibly of stone—there are in Mull several relics of that cultural organisation, in the form of megalithic sites of various kinds. Over a broad span of time, roughly between 2000 and 1500 BC, there spread over western Britain and into the islands a cult that involved the building of stone monuments, circles and cairns, of which the landmarks of Avebury in Wiltshire and Callanish in Lewis are well known. The origins of this, like those of Mull's crop cultivation, probably lay in the Middle East, arising from the Egyptian cult of the dead, for the cult spread via the Mediterranean and south-west Europe, through Brittany to the north-west, through the activities of a priesthood that was both mobile and vigorous. The megalithic monuments and the attendant rituals that the missionaries introduced to the Bronze Age settlements were doubtless acceptable since they would meet both the religious needs of these early folk and their need for a seasonal organisation of their economy, thus giving the priesthood control over the native peoples.

Several sites in Mull have been examined and recorded by Professor A. Thom, who lists their localities and form as follows:

Quinish (alignment)
Dervaig (three sites: two alignments and a group of three stones)
Glengorm (—)
Tobermory (alignment)
Ardnacross (alignment and two stones)
Duart (menhir and stone circle)

Ross of Mull (menhir)
Dail na Carraigh (cairn, alignment and two stones)
Ardalanish (two stones)
Uisken (cairn or tumulus, menhir)
Loch Buie (stone circle, possibly a cairn or tumulus)

None of these (Thom gives the O.S. map references to the sites in his *Megalithic Sites in Britain*) has proved to be one of the elaborate gallery or passage tombs that have been excavated elsewhere; they are mostly composed of standing stones and stone circles, some sited on remote parts of the moors, others near contemporary settlement sites on the lowlands. Most of the stones are deeply embedded in the turf; others are quite hidden under accumulations of peat; many have been removed as convenient building material and can be found built into the walls and buildings and in drystone dykes. One such stone can be seen in the east wall of the cemetery of Kilmore, above Dervaig. Of the two stone circles at Loch Buie, one is 44ft in diameter, the other just under 22ft.

In his very detailed analysis of the British megalithic sites Thom shows that there is wide variety in the actual shape of the 'circles' and he reminds us that there could have been ancillary structures of which no trace remains—wooden structures, platforms, roofed portions, sighting posts and fences. The arrangements of the standing stones and the stone circles are shown to be in accordance with observations and sightings of various heavenly bodies—sun, moon and some first-magnitude stars—such that they provided a calendar, accurate and permanent, for fixing the dates of the solstices, the passage of 'months' and even of hours. They also incorporated a unit of measure, the megalithic 'yard' that, it is suggested, has a relationship with the Spanish unit of linear measurement of that and later periods. Conclusions as to the purpose and use of the monuments are less easily proved, but they may reasonably be assumed to be connected with rituals concerning worship, death, the farming calendar, such as seed-sowing, animal slaughter and fertility. Research elsewhere has shown that similar cultural practices involving elementary geometrical construction existed in Stone Age times, in the building of earthen bank circles and mounds (though none has been recorded in Mull); and also that the megalithic monuments continued to be used long after the Bronze Age had been overlaid by the new technological developments of the Iron Age, by the Celtic druid-priests.

An interesting sidelight on this continuity of use is suggested by Mr A. M. Davie who has carried out a great deal of research and survey on the topic. Below Craig-a'Chaisteal, a mile west of Calgary Bay, there is a flat piece of ground below the road, known as Druids' Field. It extends to the edge of the cliff and must once have been surrounded by a very stout wall, the sunken remains of which can still be traced. In the field are two boulders whose west-facing sides are covered with cup-shaped hollows about two inches in diameter. According to Mr Davie the stone markings on at least one of the boulders is a 'map' of megalithic sites in north-west Mull. In his field work, based on the projection of the lines joining the hollows and of their intersections, he claims to have located the actual sites of the standing stones of the area, and also of a number of hitherto unrecorded stones, deeply embedded and almost invisible in the turf. Even some of the much later duns, or fortified sites, of the area appear to have been sited on the map system on which the stone 'plan' is based. These boulders are not included in Thom's list of megalithic sites on Mull, and their provenance and the age of the markings upon them remain to be substantiated.

The megalithic sites may be seen as a reminder of Mull's relationships within a widespread cultural organisation that encompassed almost the whole of Ireland and the western coasts and islands of England, Wales and Scotland well over 1,000 years BC, and also of the high level of intellectual achievement of the missionary-priests who attached themselves to the existing settlements and came to dominate them. No similar inter-related system of landmarks was laid on the country until the Ordnance Survey imposed its network of triangulation across the landscape in the nineteenth and twentieth centuries AD.

The individual settlements of Mull were self-supporting, scattered communities, tied to the lowlands and evolving under the influence of newcomers and traders, and exploiting to the full their local environment. Many of the archaeological finds related to them were probably connected with burials (cremation was then the practice). Amongst these are gold ornaments found at Torloisk, including a penannular ring and a dress fastener with ornamental ribbing, and a sun disc in copper, three inches in diameter, with engraved lines in dots and circles. Thin, knife-like blades of bronze were found at Callachally in Glen Forsa among sepulchral deposits. Pottery sherds have also come from lower Glen Forsa. The lowlands around Salen have produced several finds, including a flat axe of the early Bronze Age. A cist found there was associated with flint blades, bronze fragments and parts of a string-marked pottery beaker. Another cist at Quinish contained an urn or food vessel five and a half inches high, with string-marked ornamentation, and at Sunipol, near Calgary, a similar urn held a skull and a stone axe. Stone axes and flint arrowheads have also been found in that vicinity. Such archaeological finds may be seen in Mull houses or inns but no museum as yet exists on the island. The survey of Mull by the Royal Commission on the Ancient and Historical Monuments of Scotland may in due time find more evidence of these first permanent settlers.

Another kind of archaeological evidence, the remains of crannogs (or lake-dwellings), probably also dates from that time period known as the late Bronze Age, and serves to remind the observer that peasant refugees were known in Britain—and in Mull—in the centuries before Christ. Crannogs were a highly developed form of settlement, with a high standard of living, around the Swiss lakes, about 1000 BC. A worsening of the climate in subsequent centuries led to the need to abandon the lake dwellings, as the water level rose, and these peoples, with their domestic animals, families and belongings, became involved in the tremendous movements of people across Europe that were then developing, with the spread of iron age cultures and the increase of warrior tribalism. Some were driven beyond the European shores to seek refuge, along with other migrants, in Britain, and they re-established their culture in the south, around the Thames and in the meres of Somerset. It has to be guessed whether some families eventually migrated as far as the western isles or whether the *idea* of living in a crannog, which was a semi-defensive form of settlement, was passed on by them to other migrants coming to the north-west.

From the evidence available in Mull neither the cultural levels nor the ages of the crannogs there have been established, but here is witness of the arrival of refugees amongst the original settlers on the lowlands, whether peaceably or violently. There are at least six lake habitations, in the lochs Ba, Assapol, Poit-i, Frisa, Sguabain and na Mial (two miles south of Tobermory). Some are of the stone cairn type, an accumulation of stones sunk in the loch until they reached the surface, on which an artificial island was built. They were usually connected with the shore by a zig-zag causeway of submerged stepping stones likely to mislead or discourage intruders. Others were built on a framework of logs lashed to piles driven into the floor of the loch, with an infilling of brushwood and stones. Some of the islands are quite large—up to 85ft long. When Loch na Mial was partly drained in 1870, not only was the crannog exposed, that had previously been unsuspected, but also there were found the causeway leading to it, under 4ft of silt, and two dug-out canoes, one of which was 17ft long, with a beam of 3ft 6in.

THE COMING OF THE CELTS

The building of the crannogs may have heralded the next, more violent stage in the history of Mull's people, and fore-shadowed the building of defensive structures of a new type. Already incursions of Iron Age peoples from central and southern Europe were reaching southern and eastern Britain, pushing before them many peoples whom they had ousted from their settlements. This was a time of intense pressure on living space, when populations grew rapidly and iron implements made easier both the clearing of new land and the fashioning of more effective weapons. It is also the period when the Celts, as peoples, enter the local scene. The crannog builders may well have been related to them ethnically, sharing their racial characteristics and basic language.

T. G. E. Powell, in a chapter on the coming of the Celts in *The Prehistoric Peoples of Scotland*, reminds us that they were a trans-Alpine people known to the Greek and Latin Classical writers as early as the late sixth century BC, one of the barbarian folk admired by the Romans and recognisable by their charac-teristics in appearance, arms, manners and customs. In terms of customs they were iron-using farmers and stockraisers; they were widespread across Europe, powerful and warlike. With growing populations everywhere creating land hunger and with the political and military upheaval that accompanied the growth of the Roman Empire, Celts became involved in the outward migrations and reached Britain as invaders bringing new iron age cultures. Scotland they reached both by land from the south and by sea on east and west, and Mull may then have received its first hostile invasions from the east as well as on its seaward coasts. While it is known that the Celts fused with the indigenous bronze age settlers whom they overran, much as earlier migrants had done, they were a dominant element, stamping their language and way of life on the territory they took. No one can now tell whether any of Mull's existing population survived the incursions of the first Celts to reach there at some time during the few centuries before Christ, though on an island of this size one imagines that the well-armed and bold invaders could swiftly take possession of the farming settlements and establish themselves as masters of a subdued population; the natives might have been forced to retire to less hospitable dwelling sites on the upland moors—but again no evidence on this has yet been unearthed. The megalithic monuments probably continued to be used for their ritual purposes, for, at the dawn of recorded history, as Caesar accounted, a Celtic druid-priesthood existed. Their religion was by now probably a compound of ancient bronze age beliefs and other practices added in more recent times, but it may have provided something of a unifying force among the invaders and the invaded.

Pictish Celts who occupied Argyll were driven out gradually by strong invasions of 'Scots' from Dalriad in northern Antrim, the Cruithni, themselves a blend of Celtic iron age tribes and bronze age natives who spoke an archaic form of the Celtic tongue known to linguists as Goidelic. Thus in the middle of the fifth century AD the Gaelic language was introduced to Scotland, along with a legacy of Celtic institutions that were to persist into medieval times. The first colonies of Irish Scots were probably planted in Mull during the early part of the second century AD; by the fifth century the island was part of the Scots kingdom of Dalriada, embracing Argyll. About this time of Celtic assertion from Ireland towards the east and north, the Romans had come and already departed, in southern Britain Arthur was defending the Celtic way of life against the Anglo-Saxon invaders, Britain had moved from prehistory to history, and the Celts themselves were adopting Christianity.

As evidence of the warlike events in Mull during the iron age incursions, there remains a number of defensive works in strategic positions around the coasts. What may have been prehistoric permanent settlements, visible today as ruins almost level with the turf—for example, Reudle, a little inland from the north-west coast of Loch Tuath, and Suie, near Bunessan—are attributed to the period. At Suie, many rings of standing stones can be seen.

There are some three dozen duns or forts which probably served as defensive watch towers beside settlements, or as strong points where attackers could be delayed while the people and their livestock withdrew inland. Most of the duns, forts and caisteals are close to the sea, though a small fall in sea level since that period may have changed some locations to appear to be inland. Many stand within sight of each other, and warning signals by fire could easily be transmitted. Some, like Dunara at Glengorm, were occupied up to medieval times.

The ruin of a once massive fort stands at Dun Aisgean, about a mile west of Burg, Torloisk. About 35ft in diameter and circular in shape, its walls were 6 to 8ft thick, with narrow horizontal openings at regular spacing. It stands on a boss of rock rising from the 100ft raised beach above Loch Tuath, with a convenient inlet below for a haven. It had good arable ground around it that is now given over to sheep and bracken. If one looks down from its walls early in the year, before the bracken growth has started, one can see the outlines of some dozen old buildings; their age can only be conjectured, for this was a settled corner of Mull up to the middle of the eighteenth century.

A simpler type of construction on a crag at An Caisteal, between Bunessan and Loch Assapol, has been described in some detail in the *Proceedings* of the Society of Antiquarians in Scotland for 1927. The flat top, 200ft above sea level, is 35ft across and strongly protected by drystone walling on the exposed flank, a typical iron age fortification. The wall is up to 13ft thick, with traces of a gallery and cell within its width, and an entrance 5ft 6in wide. It is so much overlooked from nearby positions within range of bow and sling that its threat must rather have been from sword and spear at close range. Hidden completely from low ground, it has a perfect view of the sea approaches from east round to north-west. It was probably no residence but a look-out post and strong-point, a fighting platform without upper defensive walls or breastworks as in other duns. Attackers fighting up the steep slopes and walls would be met at the edge of the platform by spear thrusts from above. Much of the stonework has been plundered for local building and this area, including the ruins, is now under accumulated peat up to 14in deep. Excavations have revealed two small sherds and fragments made from very coarse clay, an upper rotary quernstone of mica schist, very much worn, nearly 14in in outer diameter, and a triangular piece of mica schist some 6in across with a cup-shaped depression, thought to be the upper bearing stone of a drill.

Dun Muirgheidh is a different type of fort, about two miles from Bunessan and less than half a mile from the main road to Kinloch. It stands on a promontory on the south side of Loch Scridain. On the landward side it was defended by three walls built from cliff to cliff, with a central passage. The inner defensive wall was 17ft thick, with a check and bar-hole at the entrance. There is evidence in it of a passage and a mural cell. The final defence was a light wall. In south-west Ulva the defence of the dun of Glacandaline is a crooked underwater causeway. This isolated fort, its outer walls still quite well preserved, stands on a steep, high rock; the causeway is uncovered at low tide.

A characteristic form of iron age dun was the Gallic fort, in which the dry masonry is bound with timber lacings, and it has been suggested that the 'vitrified' forts that have been found are Gallic forts with their stone walls fused through the burning, either accidentally or intentionally, of the timber. Vitrified forts are not common, but one has been identified in Mull, a mile north of Tobermory beside the Glengorm road, Dun Urgabul.

Brochs are rather specialised structures, rare outside the territory of the broch-folk of the northern highlands and islands. They are towering structures of stone, with stairs and chambers within the thickness of their walls and an open court within, their design described by Jacquetta Hawkes as 'proclaiming them the strongholds of a people bred to raiding and fighting by sea and land', though there are other opinions as to their use and origin. It has been suggested that two forts in Mull are brochs. Dun nan Gall, Fort of the Stranger, stands on the north shore of Loch Tuath, on a low rock washed by the tide at the southeastern end of Ballygown Bay, about three miles west of Ulva Ferry. Its internal diameter is 35ft and the walls average 11ft in thickness. The 4ft wide entrance is on the east, landward side, expanding at a depth of 4ft to a door check and bar-hole. On the south side an interior doorway gives access to a stairway 3ft wide in the thickness of the wall, where a few treads remain. There is evidence of another interior door in the north-east, 2ft

6in wide, leading to a guard chamber. The broch is surrounded by a gallery, the outer wall of which has disappeared.

An Sean Dun, the Old, or the Bewitched, Fort, stands at the high north-west end of a ridge sloping up from the moors between the head of Loch Mingary and Glengorm Castle on the north-west peninsula. Here a wall 10ft 6in thick enclosed a space 32ft in diameter. The entrance on the south-east side is 3ft 6in wide, with a door check 3ft within, and an opening that may have led into a guard room. A gap in the inner wall may have been a doorway to a stair room. Although no stairs have been preserved, there are traces of their existence in the west-north-west side. Outside the entrance, to the south-west, a structure of poor masonry has been added at some time.

When the kingdom of Dalriada was first established a line of demarcation between the Scots and the older, probably Pictish inhabitants was laid down; in Mull this frontier is believed to have passed through Glen More and thence north-westwards between the two northern Treshnish islands, Cairnburg Mor and Cairnburg Beag. Both the islands have fortifications from medieval and later days built upon much earlier structures. In Glen More there are two cairns, Carn Cul Ri Erin and Carn Cul Ri Alabyn—respectively the cairns with their backs to Ireland and Scotland (Alban, the land of the Picts, later became Scotland).

There are also, of course, many other standing stones and cairns whose origin is not prehistoric. Some pagan stones were taken over in early Christian times, adapted by the incision of crosses and used as markers along the pilgrims' way to Iona. Many cairns are of much more recent provision, connected with some folk-lore tale or tradition.

It is clear that the investigation of new finds in Mull could throw new light on the island's prehistoric inhabitants and possibly on the history of the settlement of the western isles. As recently as 1968 the excavation of a large stone, 5ft by 3ft square, near the pier at Grass Point revealed that it is apparently supported by four or five other stones, themselves resting on a deep stone platform. This 'structure' was buried almost entirely in the accumulation of peaty soil. Its age and purpose remain to be discovered. A mile to the south, at Port Donain, there lies a mound which has yet to be excavated.

4   CLANS AND CASTLES

THE historical record of Mull may be said to start with Columba's coming to Iona about AD 563, a story that warrants treatment in a separate volume, even though the island is part of the Mull group. But the existence of the monastery in Iona in some measure affected Mull's own history, because of the attraction that its manuscripts, relics, precious ornaments and caskets, and more practically its stores of food, had for the Norse pirates who about this time began to harass the western isles. The Norse invasions of the north-west Scottish coastlands and islands, which were intensified after about AD 800, were probably at first largely raiding parties, intent on plunder and perhaps the capture of slaves and womenfolk. Iona itself is recorded as being ravaged six times between 793 and 986, though the community contrived to continue its existence through this time. It is probable that the small farming communities on Mull, especially those in the western promontories, were also periodically raided, plundered and burned.

No evidence has yet been unearthed in Mull as to the extent of Norse settlement there, though the existence of Norse elements in place-names suggests that it certainly occurred. About this time there was land hunger in some Norwegian coastal settlements as well as other factors that drove some Norsemen to settle permanently in Scotland's northern and western isles. The survival and dominance of gaelic place-names and speech indicates that these incomers did not overrun the island and it is probably a fair guess that the raiding invasions gave way to landings for trading and for settlement, in due time peaceably, where land was available; and that ultimately gaels and norse were blended through intermarriage. The discovery and excavation of settlements of this period, that may now be hidden by undergrowth or peat, could throw light on both the type and the extent of the integration of the two cultures. Some gaelic speakers used to hold that the dialect of the people around Loch Scridain had an apparently Scandinavian intonation.

MEDIEVAL MULL

In the western isles Norse colonisation continued to be domi‑ nant from the eighth to the thirteenth century and Mull shared this very formative period of cultural history. During this time the family-tribal organisation evolved into the clan system, with patriarchal clan chiefs living like minor kings in their territories, united in a confederacy ruled by the Norse King of the Isles, a right won by the King of Norway from the Scottish Crown in 1098. After the battle of Largs, 1263, the Scottish kings were at last able to check the Norse threat. The Norse kingship of the Isles ended and, as part of the Hebridean isles, Mull came under the administration of the lordship of the Isles, subject to the Scottish Crown. The title Lord of the Isles survives to this day, when the present holder is Charles Prince of Wales. Independent, powerful and unruly, the confederacy of clans, under the leadership of MacDonald of Islay, Lord of the Isles and Earl of Ross, was eventually forced to submit by James III in 1476. The Celto-Norse overlordship was thereafter abolished, though the individual chiefs continued for some time to be troublesome subjects of the sovereign of Scotland.

Since the eleventh century Norman lords had advanced northwards into Scotland and were even granted land by Scottish kings, displacing native chiefs. It is even possible that feudal Norman influence reached Mull. One branch of the Beaton family, the famed doctors of Mull, originated in Bethune, France; their history is treated more fully on pages 163-4. Certainly Mull was relatively close to the southern edge of the highland zone and accessible to the advancing frontier of Norman conquest. It lay in a region in which many defensive castles were built during the medieval age of romance that saw the rise and fall of the Lords of the Isles. To this age of clan culture and ceremonial are attributed many of Mull's tales and legends.

Page 71: (*above*) The remains of Dun Aisgean, an iron age fort near Burg, Torloisk, surrounded by dense bracken. In the middle distance lie the narrow waters between Ulva and Mull and, on the skyline, the central mountains; (*below*) Cup-marked boulder in Druids' Field below Craig-a' Chaisteal, near Calgary Bay

Page 72: (*above*) Grimly carved slab in Kilninian churchyard, probably covering the grave of a Maclean chief of Torloisk. Showing kilt and broad-sword, it is typical of carving done by the monks of Iona at the Nuns' Cave, Carsaig; (*left*) The shaft of a cross standing in Pennygown chapel, carved with Virgin and Child and an inscription (now illegible); on the reverse is carved a very fine design of a galley with furled sail, vine leaves and tendrils

Castles

Duart Castle was the home of the Chief of the Clan Maclean. The clan's loyalty to the Macdonalds in their bitter feuding with the Campbells and later their support for the Stuart cause cost them dear. They were dispossessed in 1692 and the castle, already partly destroyed by Cromwell, fell into ruins. It was purchased back in 1912 by the Chief of the clan, Sir Fitzroy Donald Maclean, restored and re-occupied.

Standing on the dark headland of Duart (Dhu-Ard) Point, a few hundred yards from the sea, it dates from the thirteenth century. From its commanding position its cannon could sweep the whole width of the Sound of Mull—it is the first point of the island passed on the way from Oban through the Sound. The thirteenth-century tower is the oldest part of the buildings, with walls of ten to fourteen feet thickness. The castle is in two flats entered from the great central quadrangle, and has 100 apartments.

Since 1968 the castle has been opened to the public during summer months and on certain days of the week. Access is by a private road branching off the main road about two miles south of Craignure. Its embrasured battlements, stout walls and prominent site stand as reminders of dark and stormy days of the island's history.

The ancient keep of Aros Castle stands commandingly at the edge of a bold bluff north of Salen Bay, between eight and nine miles from Tobermory and close to good arable ground. It can be reached by the farm road that branches towards the sea just above Aros Bridge. With the consent of the farmer whose buildings lie 200 yards from the ruins, visitors may drive along this approach. Although it is reduced now to a few walls and masses of rubble, it was obviously a place of considerable size. The remaining walls are very thick, ten feet or more, but they are massively rather than skilfully built. There are traces of a fosse or ditch on the landward side, and the remains of outbuildings, one of which resembles a chapel. Built by the Lords of the Isles in the early fourteenth century, this was their main stronghold in Mull, and the vast dining hall, whose outlines can clearly be traced, must have witnessed some rousing scenes of clan ceremonial.

E

Moy Castle, the old stronghold of the MacLaines of Lochbuie, was built in the fifteenth century. The MacLaines are descended from the Clan Maclean through the fourth Chief of Duart. It stands four-square on a low rock just above the shore at the head of Loch Buie, backed by the fertile plain of Magh (Moy). One can still see where boulders were rolled aside on the beach below the castle to allow galleys to be run up. Walls, windows and dungeon are still complete, and there are three tiers of compartments. The line of a fosse, which formed the outer line of defence, can still be traced. The floor of the castle is formed of solid rock, levelled for the purpose, in which a spring of pure water rises into a basin carved four feet deep. Strangely enough, it never overflows, yet when emptied it soon refills. The castle was occupied up to about 1750, but the main door is now kept locked and casual visitors are not allowed access because of increasing danger from loose stonework in the ageing masonry.

The fortress island of Cairnburg Mor, in the Treshnish Islands, was an impregnable sea-girt stronghold, built on earlier fortifications. Pennant's *Tour* of 1772 states that in 1249 Jon Dungadi was appointed by Acho, King of the Nordeneys (the northern Hebridean Norse territory) to defend the two Cairnburg islands. He faithfully held out for a long time against pressure from King Alexander III of Scotland, even after the Norse rulers had been expelled from the Hebrides. In those days it was known as Kiarnaburgh or Bianaburgh. In 1608 it was recorded as having held out against the punitive fleet under Lord Ochiltree, sent to subdue the rebellious clan chiefs. Maclean of Duart held the stronghold in 1715, and during the Jacobite rising it was taken and retaken by both sides.

The massive upper walls, added about the sixteenth century, had defensive slots tapering inwards through which light cannon could fire from built-in emplacements. From the one difficult landing on the island a steep path climbs to the island summit, narrow and contained by high smooth walls. This path was a deathtrap for attackers, down which the defenders could roll boulders from a stockpile kept at the top. The defenders were accommodated in a narrow gully on the island top, which was roofed with timbers and turf. There was even a little chapel, for Cairnburg Mor was also a refuge—or a prison as the case may

74

be—for several personages in the days of the clan intrigues. As in Moy Castle, there is a spring of fresh water flowing into a small rock basin, called in gaelic the 'Well of the Half Gallon', for it holds that quantity and no more. When emptied it refills exactly to the same level, and it never overflows.

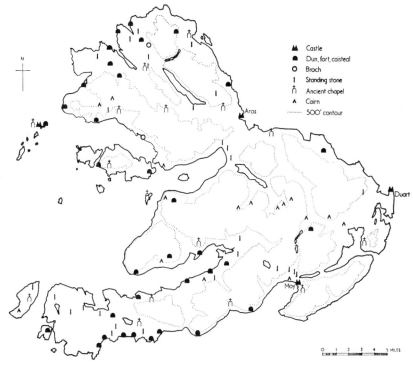

Sites of prehistoric and medieval remains in Mull

There was formerly grazing for a few cattle and sheep on Cairnburg, but they are no longer kept there; the walls of the fortress, remarkably well preserved, are surrounded by tall, tough nettles growing in the enriched soil. Cairnburg Mor might be one of the most rewarding places for archaeological research. It is reputed that books, manuscripts and relics were hidden there by monks fleeing from Iona; and although Cromwell's men and the Reformers are supposed to have searched the place and destroyed everything they found, precious objects may still lie hidden.

75

Remote and well guarded by the sea, Cairnburg Mor may be slow to yield its secrets.

Chapels

An old chapel, church or cemetery can be looked for wherever the prefix Kil- appears. Kil (gaelic *cille*) was originally the cell or habitation of the early missionaries and came to describe the surrounding ground. Ancient chapels—all ruinous except for that of St Oran's in Iona, which is restored—are scattered all over Mull in seemingly haphazard fashion. When they were in use they

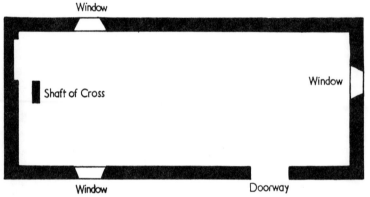

Plan of the remains of Pennygown Chapel, typical of medieval chapels in Mull. The chapel is 39ft 9in by 17ft

would be conveniently sited in relation to the many scattered communities of that time, when people thought nothing of walking many miles to attend worship. They were built mostly between the twelfth century and the Reformation and were constructed mostly on a simple plan, of which Pennygown chapel is a typical example.

On Inch Kenneth are the remains of a church of the first pointed period, about 40ft by 20ft in area, with a piscina and, in the southeast, a ruined sacristy; the windows are deeply splayed lancets. Outside the north-east corner lies the grave of a medieval chief, Sir Allan Maclean, covered by the most elaborately carved slab in Mull. The effigy, in high relief, is in quilted armour, the right hand grasping a ball; a broadsword and dirk are worn; the left hand bears a plain shield and under the helmet the hair is long and curly. By the side of the head are the figures of a monk and a nun in attitudes of prayer. A hound lies at the foot. Old crosses and stones stand in the vicinity of the chapel.

The chapel of Pennygown, surrounded by an old burying ground, stands beside the main road three miles east of Salen. Only the walls remain, built of basalt and felsite blocks; mortar of calcined seashells was sparingly used. The sides of the entrance have recesses for bars and hinges. Three narrow windows with rounded heads and the door are faced with sandstone from Gribun or Inch Kenneth. There is a recess about three feet square in the east wall. On the grassy floor of the building lie many plain flat tombstones of slate and schist, some covering a collection of human bones, doubtless taken from the cemetery. Close to the east wall stands the lower shaft of a broken celtic cross of mica-schist, possibly fourteenth century and brought from Iona. It is intricately carved with, on one side, the Virgin and Child and on the other a lymphad or galley with furled sails surmounted by a design with foliage. Outside the south-east corner of the chapel lie two very old carved slabs, said to cover a chief of the clan Maclean and his wife. The way into the cemetery is over steps on either side of the boundary wall—a device to prevent cattle from straying into it.

Tombstones

Such carved recumbent tombstones dating back to between the thirteenth and the sixteenth centuries, sometimes even older, are to be seen in several of the older churchyards in Mull; they are an attraction in Relig Oran beside Iona cathedral. The material used was often slate or schist slabs imported from the mainland, but in the Nuns' Cave at Carsaig (which had also been used as a workshop by the monks of Iona) many stones were shaped from sandstone slabs cut from the quarry on the shore below. On the walls of the cave itself can be seen what appear to be 'trial' carvings and holy symbols, and the trade marks of individual craftsmen.

Old tombstones were carved to a pattern which identified the person interred, or his pursuits. The Cross and holy symbols are common to most. Sword and galley indicate a clan chief; the sails of the galley are often furled to show that a voyage has ended. A huntsman was represented by a dog in pursuit of a hare, or symbols of fishing or falconry. A woman has shears, mirror, comb or harp on her tombstone, while clergy are marked by chalice and bell.

Besides those already mentioned at Pennygown and on Inch Kenneth, others are to be seen at Tobermory, Kilninian, and elsewhere; too often they are neglected and covered with moss or grass.

A symbol carved on the wall of Nuns' Cave, Carsaig, is considered by the Ancient Monuments Commission to be the trade mark of a mason or monk who worked there, possibly in early Christian times

Standing stones adapted to Christian use as markers along the pilgrims' way through the Ross of Mull to Iona have already been mentioned. In south-eastern Mull there were several landing places, and sections of old faint tracks may be seen. They seem to start and end without connection, but they were old paths connecting with the pilgrims' route. Names like Port nam Marbh (Port of the Dead) point to alternative landing places, where the bodies of the dead were landed, for transport overland to Iona.

THE CLAN SYSTEM

By the end of the fifteenth century the Celto-Norse inhabitants of the western isles lived entirely within the clan system, the gaelic social-cum-military organisation, which is widely documented elsewhere. Suffice to comment here that within the complex social hierarchy of the clans the chief held the clan territory in trust for his clansmen, who were bound to him in ties of kinship. Families and family groups worked the inbye land, sometimes in common, and shared a communal grazing area on the hill ground. The chief was adviser, judge and protector of the clan and to him the clansmen owed, amongst other customary duties, that of military service, which was called on in the many inter-clan feuds over territory and livestock. This obligation and the kinship ties were features of the gaelic society that survived the breakdown of the system itself, as is witnessed by the response in later centuries to army recruiting calls in the islands under the chiefs now turned lairds or landlords, and by the clanship and recognition of chiefs today.

The clansman would lay down his life for the chief, obeying his slightest wish, not in servility as might the serfs and villeins of feudal society, but as members of a family obeying a patriarch. Boswell related a story in illustration of this: a clansman in Iona was suspected by Sir Alan Maclean, his chief, of having evaded an order to provide some rum, and was pointedly reminded of his chief's powers of summary justice. Hurt by this lack of trust the man confided in Boswell, 'Had he sent his dog for the rum I would have given it. I would cut my bones for him.'

After the abolition of the lordship of the Isles, and the weakening of the MacDonald's power, the Macleans became the principal clan in the Mull area. They were of very ancient lineage, claiming descent from the kings of Ireland. Through intermarriage with the family of the Lord of the Isles, they were granted extensive lands in Mull and their territory included the whole of the island, Morvern, Coll and other extensive possessions. They were a noble clan—there was reputed to be only one bad chief—and their tradition has many stories of great deeds. Neil Munro summed it up thus: 'The MacDonalds were warriors, but it was the Macleans that were the gentlemanly fellows.'

The Macleans suffered first through their support of the Royalist cause during Commonwealth times and later through their strong Jacobite leanings. Their dispossessed lands were handed over to the Campbells, the Dukes of Argyll, under whom in the eighteenth and nineteenth centuries much good work was done to encourage industry in Mull though without great success. Financial pressure obliged the Argyll family to part with most of their Mull lands by the middle of the nineteenth century.

The island of Ulva was clan territory of the MacQuarries for 800 years until they were forced by economic necessity to sell the land at the end of the eighteenth century. Besides the MacDonalds other clans on Mull were the MacKinnons of Mishnish, formerly of Gribun; the McArthurs, of piping fame; the Rankines, hereditary pipers to the Macleans of Duart; the McFadyens, MacGillivrays, MacEacherns, Livingstones and Beatons. The MacLaines of Lochbuie were an early offshoot of the Duart Macleans.

The way of life within the clan system was a pastoral one, based on the breeding of beef cattle, which were the only form of wealth that could be realised in cash through export to the mainland. Cattle drovers undertook the herding of beasts along established traditional 'roads' across the island, collecting also stock brought in from the outlying islands of Coll and Tiree, and from Morvern. The cattle were driven on the hoof as far as the Trysts (sales) at Crieff and Falkirk and to fairs at Carlisle. Apart from the periodic income gleaned from cattle sales the islanders supported themselves by growing a few subsistence crops and keeping some sheep for their wool and milk. Oatmeal was the basis of their diet and in general existence was bare. Bad harvests or some other natural calamity could cause famine and hardship to the small isolated communities, and feuding over territory or livestock was prevalent.

THE EIGHTEENTH CENTURY

The supremacy of the chieftain's power in some measure maintained a balance between the clansfolk and their territory. The clan chief could withhold a man's right to marry until he was able to demonstrate that he had the substance and stability to undertake the responsibilities of a wife and family. But the sixteenth century saw the beginning of the disintegration of the clan structure of the gaelic society of Scotland and power and control of clan life were gradually removed from the chiefs by the Crown and the government, most forcibly after the 1745 rebellion.

With the natural growth in population came pressure on the available land resources and by the mid-eighteenth century a marginally balanced economy became a precarious one. The introduction of potato growing at that time eased the food shortage but in turn contributed to the rising rate of population growth. There was no accompanying provision of new employment or expansion of the arable area. Indeed in many townships the old communal system of run-rig crofting gave way to independent holdings on the arable land, which became more and more fragmented with division amongst the family.

The islanders were not practised in any industry other than their pastoral farming and its ancillary occupations like cattle droving and fishing, and in the material terms of the national economy of the time they were extremely poor as well as overcrowded. In spite of the terms of the Treaty of Union of 1707 the Scottish coinage was debased and unreliable, and the islanders chiefly had barter as the only means of exchange. Stevenson worked the poignant facts of the shortage of money into fiction in *Kidnapped*, in which David Balfour, making his way through the Ross of Mull after being shipwrecked, had to resort to the house of a 'wealthy man' in order to obtain change for but a guinea piece with which to pay for a night's lodging.

Five and a half miles along the Glen Aros road from Dervaig there was an open-air market, near the watershed and about 200 yards left of the road, at an important focus of drove roads. This was Druim-tighe-mhic-gillie-chattan (the ridge of the descendants of the Cattanach fellow)—probably the longest place name in Mull. In rough huts of turf and around low turf tables, whose outlines can still be traced on the moorland, domestic goods were exchanged or bartered for, without money entering into the transaction.

Commerce came in really only at a higher level towards the century's end, as landowners began to grasp opportunities to get a higher return for their land than crofting rents produced. This led in turn to the incautious and wasteful exploitation of both the land and its people, even though some lairds were more thoughtful about their tenants' welfare. Human need and human greed are inextricably mixed in the unhappy events of the later eighteenth century and the nineteenth century. Famine and pesti-

81

lence there had been many times before, but in earlier times the people were resilient; they had land; their community life helped them to recover. Those days were now long gone and there followed the historical processes that are reflected in the island's present-day difficulties.

Mull's population rose to over 8,000 by 1801, probably well over a two-fold increase in a century and that despite the large numbers of those who emigrated in the 1770s to join the flow of people from the highlands and islands to North America, and of others who were recruited into the army.

5   MODERN HISTORY

DURING the eighteenth century ideas about higher standards of living and a new materialism spread north and west through Scotland and filtered gradually to the upper strata of island society. The lairds, formerly the leaders and protectors of their island kin, became used to a new and more extravagant way of life that required to be financed in some way, while the crofter-peasants became a more and more depressed class. Some lairds sold out their land to incomers or to absentee landlords who had neither sympathy for nor understanding of the way of life of the islanders. In the course of the evolution from 'clan chief' to 'landlord', the crofters' position was weakened by their failure to obtain any security of tenure, whether of the inbye crop land or of the communal hill grazings.

The kelp-burning industry developed towards the end of the eighteenth century—its rise and decline are recounted in a later chapter—and about this time flockmasters from the Southern Uplands were moving north and west in search of new grazing lands for their sheep, offering cash rents for leases, a return that was irresistible to many of the new generation of lairds. Mull, like the Hebridean islands, offered a very suitable environment for grazing Cheviot sheep and to make space for them many of the landlords began to withdraw the rights of the traditional tenants to the use of the land, knowing that those tenants had no legal claim to invoke. By 1810 lowland sheep flocks had become established over the Mull grazings, displacing the crofters' cattle and sheep stocks. The kelp burning for a time absorbed some of the surplus labour and around the coasts produced a bare living for some of the islanders, though at a dreadful cost of living and working conditions.

The island population continued to increase, reaching 10,612 by the time of the 1821 Census, a number that included soldiers returned from the Napoleonic wars. The names of 116 officers alone are recorded as having come from Mull to fight in those wars. There must have been hundreds of men in the ranks, now returned to find the old way of life largely gone, their homes threatened by eviction and their future livelihood in jeopardy. By 1825 the kelp burning industry had collapsed. For the rest of the century, as the living standards of the islanders fell, the size of the population dropped steadily, largely through massive emigrations as the clearance of the land continued.

THE CLEARANCES

The turning over of the crofters' grazing and inbye lands to rented sheep grazing was no less than blatant confiscation of the tenants' right, and it was frequently accompanied by cruel eviction. It was also an ignorant (if unwitting) misuse of the land, for the sake of high profits for the time being, for sheep grazing both required more extensive areas per head than did cattle grazing and caused cumulative damage. The sheep were allowed to overgraze the land, even though it was burned periodically in order to encourage regeneration of the vegetation. Gradually large areas reverted to peat land or bracken-infested moors, a condition from which they have not yet been recovered.

Houses, settlements and cultivated lands that lay in areas wanted for sheep grazing were taken over, at the laird's estimate of compensation, but often without any recompense; the tenants were evicted and the houses razed to the ground. Many ancient settlements disappeared for all time. From the top of 'S Airde Ben the ruins of old houses can be seen, level with the heather on the moorland below. Inside each is a bright green bank of nettles, a sure sign of vanished habitations and livestock.

As a boy the writer was told by an old man that he remembered well when he was a child, being carried on his father's back out of the family cottage in Ulva, which had been built by his forefathers. The factor and his men were standing outside the door with blazing torches in their hands. As soon as the people were out, the torches were thrust into the thatch; their home was burned to the ground together with those of their neighbours.

This was the common story of events wherever land was taken for the sheep, but in those days the inhumanity and injustice were not reported throughout the whole country as they are likely to be nowadays. It was not until nearer the end of the century that evidence was assembled in official reports. One of these was prepared by the Royal Commission (Highlands and Islands) 1892, which was convened 'to find out what the desire of the people is in the way of land, and to ascertain what land there is available for crofts and other small holdings'. The proceedings make sad reading. Witnesses were examined, usually in the gaelic tongue and through an interpreter. The testimony of one man alone presents a shocking indictment against the landowners; his evidence related to the north of Mull but similar destruction of a way of life took place over much of the island.

According to his evidence, twenty crofters and three townships were cleared in Mishnish in 1842. Sorn (now Glengorm) had a long record of earlier clearances, which were rounded off by James Forsyth in the middle of the century with wholesale clearances of cottages and townships. In Calgary, four populous centres were cleared by the Marquis of Northampton in 1822. Treshnish had three fine townships cleared in 1862. He told how Ulva and Gometra saw perhaps the most wanton destruction of all. From what was the finest arable ground in or adjacent to Mull, 100 people were evicted by the owner, F. W. Clark, between 1846 and 1851; they were soon followed by most of the remaining inhabitants of the islands, out of a total population of 800.

The treatment of the tenants in Dervaig, on the Quinish estate, was both harsh and contemptible. Established in 1799 by Maclean of Coll at the head of Loch Cuan, Dervaig consisted of twenty-six houses built in pairs, each with its own garden, and an ample outrun of soumings, or grazing lands, on the hill behind, common to all the people for the support of their livestock, on which their livelihood depended. In 1857 the new proprietor, James Forsyth, induced twenty-four crofters to sign a new lease; but he failed to explain to those trusting tenants that they were signing only for the tenancy of the houses and gardens, but no longer for the outrun, which reverted to him. This was a double gain for the unscrupulous laird, who now was receiving both the former rents, and also the use of the grazing lands. All that was left to support the people were the small vegetable gardens.

One exception among the larger Mull landowners was the Argyll family, especially the fifth Duke at the beginning of the nineteenth century. With an earnest desire for the welfare of his tenants he spent a considerable amount of money in encouraging new industries, such as fishing, and the growing of flax for spinning into twine for nets. Although his experiments were not very successful, nevertheless, as long as the land remained in the hands of the Argyll family, the incidence of clearances and emigration was much less than in those of other landowners.

It is not commonly known how Glengorm Castle received its name. The owning of sporting estates in the highlands and islands became fashionable for the gentry in the second half of last century, when neglected land could be bought fairly cheaply. James Forsyth, the same laird of the clearances in that area, built himself a fine new house on his estate, one of the Victorian mansions erected in Mull at that time, and he sought to call it Dunara, after an ancient coastal fort on the estate. It was pointed out to him that this was not very appropriate, as the dun lay quite a mile away. He then asked an old woman of the estate for her advice. With bitter memories of the recent clearances she replied, 'Call the place Glengorm'. The delight of the laird at this beautiful name would have been shortlived had he realised that its meaning—the Blue Glen—was commemorating for all time the cruel days when the glen was indeed blue—with the smoke from burning townships.

In the early days of the clearances Mull was certainly already overcrowded in relation to its land resources and the pastoral economy. The exodus of surplus population, already started during the preceding century, was bound to continue but it is sad that the evictions that precipitated massive emigrations were so callous, and that this callousness extended even to the exploitation practised by the owners of emigrant ships.

Destitute families migrated to Tobermory and other larger settlements in search of a living and shelter. A meagre Poor Relief was accepted with shame; some found work making new roads. But poverty was widespread and many were in effect homeless. Famine added to their desperation after the failure of potato harvests in the 1840s, which caused a loss of what amounted to four-fifths of the food supply. In 1862 the Poorhouse was built, near Tobermory.

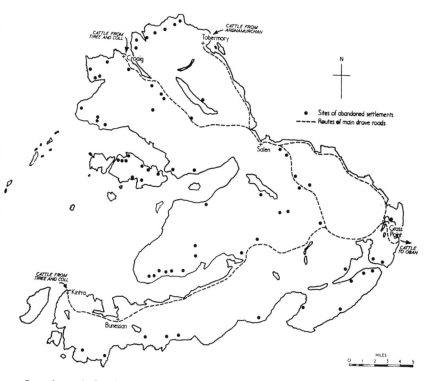

Locations of abandoned settlements in Mull. The routes of the main drove roads are shown; subsidiary tracks that connected settlements with these can still be traced and followed on the ground

In the fifty years up to 1871 the population of the island fell by a half and it continued to decline steeply until the turn of the century, many families emigrating to Canada and other pioneer outposts of the Empire. In contrast to some of the outer Hebridean islands, Mull's peak of population was reached early in the century (1821), possibly because the island is located closer to Glasgow and the opportunities there for employment—or for transport overseas. The trend of population changes in Islay and Skye was similar to that of Mull.

87

DEER STALKING AND DISCONTENT

In due time the sheep grazing boom for the landlords declined, partly because of competition from the mainland and oversea meat and wool trade but also, more significantly for the future of Mull itself, because of the mismanagement of the grazing land and the consequent decline in its yield. Through the Victorian fashion for hunting and shooting large areas were turned over to deer stalking estates during the latter part of the nineteenth century, again a land use that contributed no real improvement in opportunities for employment for the islanders and bringing in new landowners with even less knowledge of and less interest in the island's social life than their predecessors.

The discontent of the people of the highlands and islands—for they had all suffered as Mull had—eventually roused the government to take action. The sporadic rioting that occurred in some areas did not arise in Mull, though there was good reason for it to do so. The Crofters Acts of 1886 and 1892 were intended to remove their grievances, chiefly by preventing arbitrary eviction and establishing security of tenure and protection against excessive rents for the small tenantry. Because the selling and buying of holdings among themselves were also precluded by the terms of the legislation, however, these measures effectively prevented the small holders and crofters from establishing farms of a size better suited to the requirements of farming in the present century, even though their hill grazings were adequate enough or actually increased; an increase in the arable area and the consolidation of the tiny, fragmented holdings were the real needs. Thus the legislation intended to improve crofting conditions did in fact create a rigid system and obstruct progress. Grimble sums up the situation thus : 'It has frustrated every attempt to solve the Highland problem during this century.'

THE TWENTIETH CENTURY

In Mull these measures may have had some beneficial effect; there was a temporary halt in the rate of depopulation around the turn of the century. But since 1911 the trend has been continuously downwards as the people have drifted away to urban

88

Aros Castle, Isle of Mull.

Page 89: (*above*) Ruins of Aros Castle, from a picture made about 1800; (*below*) Duart Castle, stronghold of the Macleans of Duart

Page 90: *(left)* Kilmore Church, Dervaig, with pencil steeple; *(right)* Moy Castle, formerly the stronghold of the MacLaines of Lochbuie

life and employment in mainland Britain and commonwealth countries. An additional—and depressing—fact is that the age and sex structure of the population has become unbalanced. Women outnumber men and the proportion of people in the older age groups is too great to support balanced economic progress. The deserted cottages and bracken-infested moorlands that we see to-day illuminate the fact that the island's inhabitants now number fewer probably than they did at the beginning of the eighteenth century.

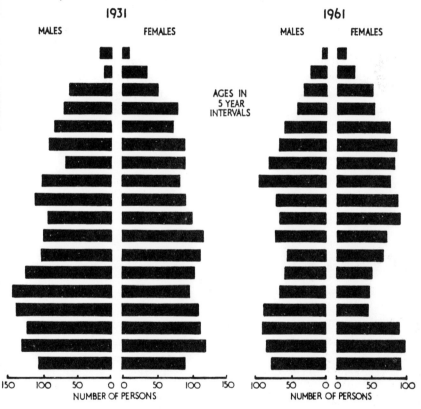

A comparison of the age structure of Mull's population in 1931 and 1961 illustrates the increasing imbalance. The number of persons in the younger age groups and of those of effective working ages have become disproportionately low, reflecting the emigration of people born in Mull in the inter-war years and the consequent low birth rate of an island in a state of depopulation. In the vertical scales the youngest age groups are at the bottom

F

Crofting as such, with common grazings and common arable, is now mostly confined to part of the Ross of Mull; in the north it has given way to individual small holdings. The chief change of scene in the twentieth century has been wrought by the Forestry Commission, starting in 1924 and now advancing its plantation boundaries rapidly on ground acquired through lapsed farm leases and the toll of taxation on overburdened estate owners.

In recent years the government, faced with the need to devise means whereby the highlands and islands can be helped to develop economic progress and to restore life to decadent communities, has brought in legislation (the Crofters Act of 1955) and established the Crofters Commission (1955) and the Highlands and Islands Development Board (1965). The efforts of these agencies have yet to bear fruit. Mull is 'a microcosm of the whole' region and the survival of the island and of its remaining people depends on the achievement of such economic progress and social restoration.

6   MULL AND THE SEA

THE traditional highway of the islanders of Mull was the
sea, and to the voyagers of the western waters through the
ages, Mull offered a safe harbourage, at Tobermory Bay,
a fine natural harbour thirty miles nearer to the Hebrides and the
open sea than Oban. Sea power and territorial power were closely
bound together during the six or seven centuries between
Columba's time and the subjugation of the Norsemen, and fighting ships and sea warriors must have terrorised the small communities on the island just as the Viking invaders terrorised the
eastern shores of Britain. But commerce also played its part in
the history of these and later times, and for Mull this also meant
sea transport, both for trading locally with nearby communities
on the mainland and other islands, and for more distant exchanges. The whole economy of the island is still, naturally, controlled by the availability of sea transport.

EARLY SHIPS

The earliest boats of which relics have been found are the dug-
out canoes discovered in Loch na Mial, near Tobermory. These
were tree trunks, roughly hollowed or burnt out, and rudely
shaped, and they are assumed to be of an age with the lake
dwellings where they were found—probably made by late bronze
age people some centuries BC. The Celts used coracles, unwieldy
frameworks of wood and wattles covered with stretched skins.
These were certainly used at the time of St Columba (sixth
century AD) and were much larger than is popularly supposed.
The coracle in which St Columba and his companions landed in
Iona is believed to have been 60ft long.

When the Norsemen came sweeping along the coasts in their
galleys, their fine seaworthy craft set a new pattern for boat-

93

building in the Hebrides. A typical Viking galley of the tenth century displaced about twenty metric tons and measured 76ft in length by 17ft beam. With high, carved prows and sterns, their draught was under three feet, and amidships their freeboard was no more than three and a half feet. They were clinker built (that is, each strake overlapped the one below, and both were riveted together through small iron rooves), and their seams were caulked with cords of animal hair saturated with tar.

A representation of the lymphad (gael. *long fhada*) or galley of the Hebridean and maritime clans was rendered in simple terms for heraldic purposes, on coats of arms (here of the Clan Maclean) or shields and tombstones of the island chiefs

Sixteen pairs of oars were carried, made of pine wood, and of differing lengths, designed to strike the water at the same time. The rudder was a large special oar blade on the starboard ('steer') side aft, and the mast, which carried a square lug-sail, was amidships. Normal crew for a long voyage numbered about three dozen, but for local expeditions there were two or three men for each oar and an additional fighting crew.

The Viking ship was the prototype of the craft used afterwards in the Hebrides for hundreds of years; this was the galley, or lymphad, or longboat, and the smaller birlinn. The lymphad appears as a distinctly unseaworthy heraldic device on the shields and the tombstones of the island chiefs, especially the clan chiefs of Mull. The Hebridean galley was fitted with a rudder instead of a steering oar, however, and was designed for two dozen oars. The birlinn carried up to sixteen oars.

After the Norsemen were subdued in the thirteenth century, and Mull came under the domination of the MacDonalds of Islay, these Lords of the Isles required a fleet of galleys to control their widespread possessions. About 1480 hundreds of galleys met in the rival fleets of Angus Og, in a struggle against his father John, Lord of the Isles, and his allies. This was the bloodiest naval battle ever fought in Hebridean waters, and the bay where it was fought, just north of Tobermory, is said to have run red with blood—hence its name, Bloody Bay. Only a few years ago, in a tidal cave under the cliffs which encircle Bloody Bay, skulls and human bones were found which may well have been the remains of some survivors of the fight.

In the next century, foreign ships began to appear; but none more impressive than the few storm-tossed survivors of the Spanish Armada which called in at points on the Mull coast to refit. The most famous of those was the galleon, *Florencia*, which sheltered in Tobermory Bay in October 1588. According to documents in the possession of the Duke of Argyll (in whom is vested the ownership of the wreck) she carried pay chests of the Spanish army which was to have invaded England. On the point of departure from the bay the ship was damaged by an internal explosion, the cause of which is the subject of various legends; she sank 300 yards off what is now the New Pier. Attempts to salvage the treasure catch the public imagination from time to time—though Sacheverell, Governor of the Isle of Man, is reported to have recovered much of the lost bullion on the first salvage expedition, in 1688.

The determination of the mainland government to subdue the clansmen played its part in the evolution of the maritime craft of the western seas. The sea was the quickest and safest medium for transporting troops to police the western isles during troublesome times in the seventeenth and eighteenth centuries, for mainland roads in the west of Scotland were few and primitive. In 1609 (it is recorded in the *Register of the Privy Council of Scotland*, Vol VIII, 1607–10) Lord Ochiltree was ordered to proceed with a punitive fleet to subdue certain 'Rebellious and Insolent persons inhabiting the northern and western isles of the Kingdom committing certain barbarous villainies on each other without reference to God or Law'. Lord Ochiltree was further ordered to destroy enough of their galleys, birlinns, and lymphads, and every other aspect of shipping, to restrict their future raidings and insurrections. The expedition achieved its objectives by enticing the principal chiefs in Mull and the surrounding district to come on board the flagship, which was anchored in Aros Bay, near Salen, and sailing away with them to the courts of the south, where they were placed on probation. They obtained their freedom only by signing the Statutes of Iona, measures by which the Scottish Crown intended to bring the western isles under greater control.

In the greater security that followed these events there was freedom for commerce to develop. Larger and more seaworthy ships were required. Sloops, smacks, skiffs and fishing boats were built. Up to the mid-nineteenth century Mull fishing boats were undecked, which made them more controllable on the exposed rocky coasts where the larger east coast boats were unhandy in use. But in competition with the experienced fishermen from the new fishing communities on the eastern seaboard of Scotland— professional fishermen, unlike the crofter-fishermen of Mull—the islanders found themselves outclassed, and fishing never became a major industry in Mull.

The smack, up to forty-five feet long, was the maid-of-all-work of the eighteenth century. Around Mull these boats carried passengers and cargo—livestock, potatoes, fish—covering long distances in all weathers. The skiff, much smaller and lighter, was used on sheltered inshore passages.

A pattern of regular transport routes began to emerge around Mull and Tobermory emerged as an important harbour. Even in October, 1773, when Dr Johnson and Boswell visited Tobermory, they found it a busy place, though only twelve or fourteen ships were at anchor where there had been up to seventy. Some of these vessels traded as far away as the Clyde, Newcastle, and even foreign parts. By 1797 there were thirteen sloops based on Tobermory engaging in coastal trade around the coasts of Mull itself.

For centuries Mull people have travelled far to seek steady employment, adventure, or perhaps a fortune. Before speedy and reliable transport came in they were travelling regularly to Glasgow and the south in sailing smacks and skiffs, long journeys in overcrowded boats across wide stretches of the open sea. The lighter skiffs were rowed or sailed to Crinan, and from there, like the galley of King Haakon the Viking, they were hauled and manhandled across the isthmus to the sheltered waters of the Firth of Clyde. The larger boats faced the stormy passage round the Mull of Kintyre to their destination at Greenock, which was then the port of Glasgow.

The traffic was seasonal. As many able-bodied people as could be spared left the island to seek work on the rich harvest fields of the Scottish Lowlands for three months of the year. The return of these temporary migrants, and of others returning with them on routine visits to their families, were times of great rejoicing, for family ties were strong; the traditional *duthus* or hearthstone of the home was a magnet for the sons and daughters who had ventured over to the great world across the Firth of Lorne. In August 1822 Iona and the Ross of Mull suffered their greatest calamity of the nineteenth century. The smack *Mary*, of Iona, with a full complement of workers bound for the harvest fields, foundered after being run down off Greenock by the steamer *Hercules*. Only four people, a woman and three men, were saved, and the victims were buried in the old cemetery at Greenock. The loss of over forty breadwinners and people in the prime of life was a tragedy felt for generations in the Ross of Mull.

THE COMING OF STEAM

When steamboats appeared in 1821 sailing craft began to be superseded, for the obvious advantages of the steamboat in these waters could not be denied. With the introduction in the twentieth century of the internal-combustion engine, the small hardy old inshore craft were beached for the last time, and their disintegrating timbers can be seen above high-water mark in many a bay and inlet around the coast of Mull.

The friendly and utilitarian 'puffer', or steam lighter, even yet pushes its blunt nose into many a corner of Mull with assorted cargoes, a vessel highly suited to this locality. Its advantage was its ability to manoeuvre through intricate channels between reefs into such tiny slipways as Croaig, near Dervaig; or to be beached high and dry on its flat keel at low tide on hard beaches where formerly carts and now lorries could come alongside and load up. A consignment of coal brought in the puffer for individual houses in a local community would be carted away and dumped in separate piles for the people to collect at their leisure.

The inelegant puffer, which so faithfully served Mull and the rest of the islands, was little more than a floating hold, with an engine aft, and one mast forward carrying a stout derrick. Its name arose from the sound made by the early type of propelling machinery, and the noisy exhaust from the steam winch (the modern puffer is equipped with diesel engines). It was of 105–120 tons, with a length of 66ft and a draught, fully laden, of under ten feet, dimensions which were standardised to fit canal locks, for the craft were mostly built at Kirkintilloch, on the Forth and Clyde Canal a few miles north of Glasgow, and, in the Hebridean trade, used the Crinan Canal across the isthmus at the head of the Kintyre promontory. In *The Vital Spark*, in which he captures the authentic atmosphere of island harbours, and even the speech and idiosyncrasies of the people, Neil Munro relates the humorous background of the puffer.

THE SEA ROADS

Many sea roads were regularly followed around Mull. The nearest corner of the island to Oban is Auchnacraig, better referred to as Grass Point, with a sea passage of only seven miles; so Grass Point, on the south side of Loch Don, naturally became a focal point on Mull. Here in the old days converged not only the livestock of Mull, but also of Coll, Tiree, Morvern and Ardnamurchan. From the first two islands cattle were conveyed in open boats to Kintra, near Fionnphort, or to Croaig or Calgary in the north-west. From Ardnamurchan they were ferried over to Tobermory, and from Morvern to Salen.

A short but treacherous ferry lay across Loch na Keal, between Gribun and Ulva or Torloisk, on the main north-south route for people moving between the Ross and the populous parish of Kilninian and Kilmore. This was the Ulva ferry which features in the poem by Thomas Campbell, when Lord Ullin's daughter (daughter of Sir Allan Maclean of Knock) was overwhelmed by a storm when eloping in the ferryboat with a young MacQuarrie chief to his island of Ulva. No trace of the old Gribun ferry is to be seen today, and the modern Ulva Ferry is a stretch of water 150yd wide, between Ulva and the Torloisk–Salen road, with which it is connected by a half mile of side road. There is a good slipway on each side of the ferry, and visitors to Ulva may summon the ferryman (who lives on the Ulva side) by tolling a bell fixed above the slipway on the Mull side. Casual visitors to Ulva are not encouraged, but those with a genuine interest in the island are welcomed by the owner.

There was also a regular ferry from Fionnphort to Iona, where motor boats now run frequently. From the little piers at Carsaig and Lochbuie there were sailings to Oban, Easdale and Crinan. In 1773 Dr Johnson and Boswell embarked at Lochbuie for Oban after their tour of Mull and Iona, and it was there that the formidable doctor was for once reduced to speechless indignation when the bluff laird of Lochbuie greeted him: 'Are you of the Johnstones of Glencro, or Ardnamurchan?'

After 1812, when steamships appeared in the western isles, a more regular pattern of routes began to emerge, which was well established by the twentieth century. A daily mailboat service ran between Tobermory and Oban, leaving Tobermory (where the boat tied up overnight) about 7.30 in the morning, to shuttle along the Sound of Mull, calling at Drimnin and Lochaline on the Morvern side, Salen and Craignure on the Mull side, and arriving at Oban in time to connect with the noon train for the south. The boat left Oban about 1 pm (after the arrival of the mail train from the south) for its return trip to Tobermory, with the same calls along the Sound of Mull.

Between 1 June and 30 September each year the popular

99

Staffa and Iona steamer operated from Oban, leaving there daily (except Sundays) at 8 am, proceeding by Iona, Staffa and Tobermory (afternoon call) on Mondays, Wednesdays and Fridays, following the reverse order on alternate days, with the morning call at Tobermory instead of the afternoon, and returning daily to Oban by 6 pm.

Then there was what was called the 'islands' boat based on Oban, which left there early on Mondays, Wednesdays and Fridays, sailing direct to Tobermory and continuing to Kilchoan, in Ardnamurchan, and thereafter as far as Barra in the Outer Hebrides. She returned to Oban on the alternate days, calling at Tobermory in the later part of the day.

A large passenger/cargo boat run by MacBrayne sailed weekly from Glasgow, calling at Tobermory on its outwards and inwards trip to the Outer Isles. This overlapped somewhat with a sailing by McCallum Orme's two boats, MacBrayne's only opposition in the Hebrides, which called at Bunessan as well as at Tobermory. (This amalgamated with MacBrayne between the wars). There were also casual sailings by smaller cargo boats serving Lochbuie, Bunessan, Ulva, Tobermory and other ports around Mull, while in summer occasional excursions were run from Oban, as well as special runs for collecting wool, sheep, or cattle.

Nowadays MacBrayne run a regular service between Tobermory and Kilchoan. There are short excursions by private boats from Tobermory along the sea-lochs in the district, and from Ulva Ferry round the Treshnish Islands and west central Mull. The old ferry at Grass Point still runs, with a small fleet of motor boats in the summer and at least one in winter, catering for small assorted cargoes, school children returning from Oban at the weekends, tourist parties and special runs.

The importance of sea routes is borne out by the number of piers and slipways that exist. The two main piers are at Tobermory and Craignure. Salen pier was built originally by a private company, the Salen (Mull) Pier Company Limited. The present structure, now privately owned by the local landowner, is the third to have been built. Adverse winds and currents led to the abandonment of the first two, the fragments of which can be seen in their old positions.

There are also piers at Calgary, Bunessan, Carsaig, Lochbuie, and Grass Point, with smaller slipways at Croggan, Kintra, Tiroran, Ulva Ferry, Croaig, Iona, Fionnphort and elsewhere. There are three piers at Tobermory; the small estate pier at Aros, the 'Old Pier' built before 1800 (which can handle only puffers and small craft), and the 'New Pier' built by MacBrayne in 1864 and extended in the 1930s. A still older slipway at the mouth of the Tobermory burn is now disused.

MACBRAYNE AND THEIR SHIPS

It was Neil Munro who said that he was over twenty years of age before he realised that not all the ships in the world had red funnels! The familiar black hulls, white upperworks and red funnels of the MacBrayne fleet stand for well over 100 years of transportation maintained between all the scattered communities of the Hebrides and the mainland, in the face of geographical and increasing economical difficulties. The house flag is a blue pennant carrying intertwined red and blue crosses. The funnel colours go back to 1840, when they first appeared on the *Shandon* belonging to Robert Napier, one of the companies that combined soon afterwards to form MacBraynes. Still later there was a link with the Cunard line through the Napier-Cunard-Burns connection, on the strength of which the famous Cunard black hoop or hoops were added to the colours, though this was discontinued in 1906.

The first steamship to appear in the Mull area was the famous *Comet*, designed by Henry Bell, which began to sail between Greenock and Fort William in 1812. Other companies were soon formed; for instance, in 1836 the *Tobermory*, a wooden paddle ship of eighty tons, was built for 'a body of enterprising gentlemen consisting of landed proprietors, tacksmen, and merchants connected with Mull, Morvern, and Ardnamurchan'. Two years later the sailing of the *Glen Albyn*, of 200 tons, was sponsored by the Glen Albyn Steamboat Company of Tobermory, a group of merchants and landowners in the district. This was a much larger and more powerful boat.

In July, 1838, the *Rob Roy* began to sail from Oban to Staffa and Iona every Tuesday and Friday, returning on the evening following. Regular summer sailings on this run, beginning in 1855, have ever since been one of the most popular sailings in Europe. After Queen Victoria included the highlands and islands in her Grand Tour of 1847 there followed an unprecedented expansion in the tourist trade of these areas.

1880 was a turning point in the history of David MacBrayne and in the communications of Mull, for in that year the Caledonian Railway was extended from Callander to Oban. Mull and the Hebrides were now in touch with Glasgow and the Lowlands at speeds hitherto unknown. Oban became known as the 'Charing Cross' of the Highlands, and Mull, sharing something of the new order, was finally drawn on to the map.

Two developments followed the opening of the railway, first, MacBrayne received the whole of the mail contracts for the western isles; second, a daily mailboat service was opened between Tobermory and Oban which was to continue until 1964. In 1906 a Post Office was opened on the *Grenadier*, the paddle steamer on the Oban-Staffa-Iona run at that time.

Mull people agree that the Sound of Mull run between Tobermory and Oban was the sailing which has left the most nostalgic memories. They recall the delays on the days of the Oban markets, when sheep were given priority over passengers, and the Glasgow train might be caught with only seconds to spare. They remember sharing the already limited passenger space with a packed woolly cargo of over 1,200 sheep, damp, smelly, and filling the air with their protests. The shepherds who accompanied the flocks were dressed for the occasion in blue suits and black boots, a hazel stick in their fists, a raincoat slung over the shoulder on a piece of rope; their collie dogs swarmed at their heels. Loading against time at every port of call, captain and mate would be everywhere, screaming imprecations in the gaelic. It always seemed to be raining at the time, with a half gale blowing up the Firth of Lorne off Lismore Lighthouse, and conditions 'tweendecks in the mixed aroma of sheep, frying kippers in the galley, and later of diesel oil, may be imagined.

The *Pioneer*, a paddle steamer of 200 tons, was the first boat to take up this regular run in 1881. In 1893 she was replaced by the *Carabineer*, of 299 tons, also a paddle steamer. This boat was previously on the Portsmouth–Isle of Wight run for the railway company until bought by MacBrayne for the Sound of Mull run.

In 1908 the *Lochinvar*, of 216 tons, succeeded the *Carabineer*. This was the third motor vessel built for the company, and one with a long and interesting history. At the start she had one tall, thin exhaust-funnel near the stern. This was exchanged at a refit for a triangle of three narrow unsightly deck stacks, one for each engine; at a later date these were finally led into one stumpy funnel over which the electric crane was free to swing. She took about three-and-a-half hours, including all calls, to cover the thirty miles between Tobermory and Oban. Except for short absences for routine overhauls she served continuously until 1955.

In spite of criticisms of the scanty accommodation provided for passengers, who were separated into 'cabin' and 'steerage' classes, she gave dependable service over the years in the specialised job for which she had been designed. In spite of her fine lines she was a sturdy little craft. There was one occasion in the 1920s when she aroused the anxiety of the whole Mull community. Held up in Oban one winter afternoon by a howling gale blowing up the Firth from the open Atlantic, she ventured out at last during a short lull. Caught in the open by darkness and a fresh onset of the storm, and unable either to carry on or to return, she was obliged to turn tail to the wind, and vanished into the maze of islands, narrows and sea-lochs of Loch Linnhe. Partly by luck, partly by magnificent seamanship, she somehow passed though, over and under the obstacles, and dropped anchor at last in sheltered waters. At daybreak she found herself anchored almost at Fort William, thirty miles north of Oban. There was relief and jubilation on the island when she was reported safe, manned as she was by a crew hailing chiefly from Tobermory.

A few years later, in a thick fog, she cut clean through a fishing boat which had incautiously dropped anchor in her path off Craignure. There was no loss of life, although the sharp bow of the *Lochinvar* had cut the other boat in halves, sinking her in minutes. The mailboat herself was little the worse of the encounter.

After 1955 her place was taken by the *Lochearn*, of 540 tons. The *Lochinvar*, after serving as relief ship based on Oban, was transferred to the Portree (Skye) run, though she did not prove to be very popular with the Skye people. After a farewell run from Tobermory to Oban on 28 May 1960 she was sold into the hands of a company operating in the Thames estuary, where she ran until 1963. Laid up until April 1966, she was sailing north to take up duties as a cruise ship between Inverness and Invergordon, on the Moray Firth, when the 58-year-old boat was caught too close to a lee shore in a North Sea gale and was wrecked with the loss of all hands at Donna Nook, south of the Humber. Her bell, binnacle and steering wheel are now kept at Duart Castle by Sir Charles H. F. Maclean.

The *Columba*, 2,100 tons, service speed fourteen-and-a-half knots, designed to carry 600 passengers (400 in winter) and sixty motor cars, took up the new Craignure-Oban run in 1964, when the old Tobermory-Oban run ceased with the opening of Craignure pier. She is the crack ship of the specialised car-ferry fleet operated by MacBrayne in the western isles. She handles very well with the additional help of a bow propeller and stabilisers.

The *Columba* also serves as a small floating hotel, mobile by day, but tying up at Oban every night.

The more exposed Staffa and Iona sail round Mull has of necessity seen a number of fine seaworthy ships during the last 100 years. The *Grenadier*, a two-funnelled paddle steamer of 350 tons, took over from the *Chevalier*, of 300 tons, in 1885, and sailed during the summer months until 1927. In that year she was partly destroyed by fire one night when tied up beside Oban pier, with the loss of several lives, including Captain McArthur, who had commanded her for many years.

She was succeeded by the *Fusilier* (140 tons), an older and smaller paddle boat, until she in turn was replaced in 1931 by the *Lochfyne*, a modern motor ship of 750 tons designed to carry 1,200 passengers. The boat now on the run is the *King George V*, a two-funnelled motor vessel of about 900 tons which was added to the fleet in 1936. She uses about eight tons of oil fuel (£62 at 1968 prices) for her daily run compared with the eleven tons of coal (£14) consumed by the smaller *Grenadier* in the 1920s.

Twelve of MacBraynes ships, totalling about 5,000 tons, saw war service between 1939 and 1945; among them the *King*

George V had a distinguished record. When acting as tender on the Clyde, her duties were interrupted by the evacuation from Dunkirk. She made no fewer than six trips to and from the beaches in May 1940, narrowly escaping aircraft attacks and shellfire, and Captain MacLean and Chief Engineer W. MacGregor were each awarded the DSO, and the bo'sun, Mr MacKinnon, the DSM. Her wartime duties ended in 1945 and she returned to the Staffa and Iona run in 1947, where she still continues in the late 1960s.

One recalls also the graceful clipper bow of the old *Claymore*, and the lines of the *Chieftain*—the large passenger-cargo ships based on Glasgow; or their modern counterpart, the new *Claymore*, and many more humble units of the fleet.

Two world wars cost David MacBrayne Limited dear in inflated running costs and overheads. In fact, without government intervention and subsidies (about £600,000 in 1969) the company could not have carried on. New ships had to be built to replace obsolete craft if an effective service to the islands, and an effort to maintain their economy, were to be continued. The financing of such ships was beyond the capital resources of MacBrayne, so the government stepped in, built the ships, registered them in name of the Secretary of State for Scotland at the Port of Leith, and leased them to the company on long-term charter. However, from the point of view of the travelling public, such a ship as the *Columba* is always regarded as a MacBrayne ship in the old traditions.

The company, which Magnus Magnusson has described as 'a legendary scapegoat of island ills', has a difficult problem. Their ships have to be economical in size to handle such a diversity of small consignments, and to call at so many places where shallow draught is essential. Maximum tonnage (unless for specialised purposes, such as car ferries) cannot exceed 1,000 tons, and a 16ft draught is the upper limit. The company owns Tobermory, Lochaline, and other piers, but elsewhere dues are payable at privately owned piers, which add to operational charges. The tourist season is short, and dependent on the weather.

In 1969 Coast Lines Limited, who had in 1928 acquired a 50 per cent shareholding in MacBrayne, sold their interest to the Scottish Transport Group, who already held the balance of the shares in MacBrayne. The Group now own this old company in its entirety, but under single ownership it is expected that there should be easier working conditions as regards administration, quicker operational discussions, and better area planning.

CRAIGNURE PIER AND THE FUTURE

Prior to 1964 passengers and goods for the south of Mull had to be ferried in small boats in all weathers between the small slipway at Craignure and the daily mail boat. As far back as 1865 strong recommendations were being made by the local lairds to have an adequate pier built, but it was not until 1962, 100 years later, that Argyll County Council decided to alter the priorities of their pier-building programme to allow a pier to be built at Craignure to coincide with the introduction of a car ferry. Thanks to the generous gift of £50,000 received from the late Neil Cameron, of Tobermory, the project was completed even earlier than programmed, and a modern structure was formally opened in 1964.

As a result of this MacBrayne was able to remodel its whole transport system to and within Mull. The Tobermory-Oban mailboat was discontinued, and in its place the new car ferry *Columba*, based on Obon, provides a regular daily service (except Sundays) of three or four return trips (fewer in the off-season) between Oban and Craignure, taking forty minutes each way, with one or more trips extended to Lochaline pier on the mainland shore of Morvern. From Craignure pier motor coaches convey passengers north to Salen and Tobermory, and south to Fionnphort and Iona ferry. Passenger fares in 1969 were, for the return journey Oban-Craignure, about 11s, plus 12s by coach to Tobermory, 22 miles distant. The return fare Tobermory-Oban by the former daily mailboat was about 16s.

Since the opening of the Oban-Craignure car ferry service in 1964 there have been significant changes in the numbers of passengers to and from the chief destination points on the island during the summer peak period. This is an indication that the availability of convenient car transport to the island rapidly gives rise to greater daily or short-term mobility of the islanders, attracts many more visitors (and thereby creates new internal

106

Page 107: (*above*) Sheep farm house at Burg, Torloisk; (*below*) Crakaig, Treshnish, a deserted village

Page 108: (*top*) The SS *Grenadier* at Tobermory Pier, about 1926; (*centre*) the TSMV *Columba*, the 2,100 tons car ferry; (*below*) the MV *Lochinvar*, on the Tobermory-Oban run until 1955

problems concerned with roads and accommodation) and, through stimulating greater interest in the island, brings more passengers to the other ferry and sailing services. The following statistics— the only ones of this nature available for Mull—have been supplied by Messrs David MacBrayne Limited and illustrate these conclusions. They relate to the total number of passengers, both incoming and outgoing, during the four-week summer peak period (mid-July to mid-August). Before 1964 the main service was provided by the once-daily Tobermory-Oban mailboat run. Iona passengers, during the summer season, are conveyed both by the direct run (Oban-Staffa-Iona cruise) and by the Oban-Craignure car ferry, but the figures below include only the car ferry passengers.

Passengers from and to:	Four-week summer peak period in:				
	1962	1963	1964	1967	1968
Tobermory	6,300	4,400	3,700	4,000	5,000
Salen	1,600	1,500	300	10	20
Craignure	1,200	1,100	10,000	38,000	46,000
Iona	700	800	800	1,000	1,500
Total	9,800	7,800	14,800	43,010	52,520

Before the building of the new pier the drivers of motor cars leaving or going to Mull had the hair-raising experience of driving from the level of the piers at Tobermory, Salen or Oban, on to the congested upper deck of the *Lochinvar* across two narrow planks tilted up or down according to the state of the tide. On other ships car loading was done by the normal method of a wide-mesh padded sling and the ship's derrick. These were slow methods and the number of cars was limited by the very restricted deck space. However, thanks to the skill and care of the crews, no accidents ever seem to have occurred.

The opening of the new pier and the car ferry brought a massive invasion of cars to Craignure and Mull, as the following annual statistics show. Again, the pre-1964 data refer essentially to the daily Tobermory-Oban mailboat service (which ran throughout the year).

	1951	1960	1961	1962	1963	1964	1967	1968
Total motor cars ferried:								
	454	1,131	1,336	1,220	1,514	5,344	17,496	20,483
Total passengers ferried:								
	24,000	36,000	40,000	41,000	43,000	68,000	199,000	233,000

There have been local complaints in Mull on the scale of freights charged for motor cars. Between Craignure and Oban the return freight charge for a small car of the Morris 1000 type is about £6. The concession rate for Mull motorists who are obliged to make frequent journeys to and from the mainland is held to compare unfavourably with the single day-tourist rate. Those Mull motorists who can afford it leave their cars at Craignure and keep another garaged at Oban.

Charges are based on a rate per foot of car length. In the case of an 11ft car this works out at 4s. 10d per foot for a normal single journey (£2 13s 2d), 3s 11d per foot for five return journeys £21 8s) and 3s 8d per foot for ten return journeys (£40). These charges include 2s each way for dues payable at both Craignure and Oban piers (levied on MacBrayne by the local authorities) and the current rates may be considered to be not so unfavourable as is generally supposed. A comparison between MacBrayne's passenger fares and those of many other coastal and continental ferries around Britain suggests that the local situation is not one of exorbitant charges. Nevertheless, fair though passenger and freight charges may be on the face of it, the extra costs enforced by the sea passage represent a considerable extra burden on the economy of the island. A resident in Tobermory has to pay £1 3s for a return journey by motor coach and car ferry to the railhead at Oban (about 30 miles). In the Lowlands of Scotland the return fare for a journey of the same distance by rail is 9s (day return) or 12s (single ticket each way). The return figure for travel by motor omnibus over the same distance is also 9s. From Oban to Glasgow (about 110 miles) the period return fare is £2 16s. by rail.

It is unfortunate that when the *Columba* was designed and the pier planned it was not at that time possible to incorporate the modern roll-on, roll-off principles for loading, with a variable-level ramp designed as an integral part of the pier, instead of building a car lift into the ship, which raises a maximum of six

110

cars at a time from the car deck to the pier level. The additional cost (for the pier) would have been about £50,000, but the advantages of the system are massive, for it allows an uninterrupted flow of cars onto and off the ship, speeding up loading and unloading operations and turn-about times, and therefore allowing more journeys to be made. Before 1964 no pier of this kind existed in the western isles, nor even a pier which catered for a car ferry with the loading point aft of centre of the ship. This method of car handling on ferries ought certainly to be introduced to the western isles early in the next decade.

Attention has been drawn to shortcomings in the Craignure service when compared with the private facilities provided by another company, Western Ferries, between the mainland of Argyll and the island of Islay; on this ferry, boats run on the Norwegian principles of low-cost design, a higher frequency of services (giving the islanders a feeling of being less isolated, of being more a part of the mainland), and bulk shipments of cargoes which avoid the amount of handling and trans-shipment involved in MacBrayne's services. As a result, Western Ferries are able to operate below the freight rates of MacBrayne, and, according to some reports, there has been a general drop in farming and industrial overhead costs in Islay.

Nevertheless, it has to be borne in mind that MacBrayne is not a free agent, but is under the bureaucratic direction of the government. It cannot lay down the design of piers, or pick and choose its business. For years its plans for a complete revision of its services to Islay were repeatedly held up; in the interval, Western Ferries, uninhibited by statutory restrictions, stepped in with ideas and a scale of charges on much the same lines as those envisaged by MacBrayne, and only recently has a scheme been approved which would allow all kinds of commercial traffic to be handled economically and expeditiously to a standard which the Islay islanders should expect.

If other ferry companies are encouraged to enter widely into competition with MacBrayne in Mull and elsewhere, selecting and creaming off the more remunerative traffic, a breakdown of the whole transport services in the western isles could result. The government has appointed MacBrayne to provide approved transport services of all kinds for a large and uneconomical area, and

111

the company can survive only by averaging the profitable with the unprofitable.

As far as Mull is concerned, Craignure pier should be one of the first to be converted to the roll-on, roll-off system. The pier is in any case inadequate to handle the peak output of the Mull Forest when this reaches full production, for its timber storage capacity is only 100 tons. Moreover, the pier lacks pens for livestock on a scale which would allow any great increase in the island's livestock production. The necessary modifications, with the addition of some smaller ferry-boats, with more frequent sailings, the possibility of bulk shipments, and a simultaneous and comprehensive improvement in Mull roads, offer the only solution to Mull's freight and transport problems—unless government subsidies to MacBrayne were to be substantially increased.

After 1964 MacBrayne organised a distributional system of lorries to handle imports from the mainland. These amount to 120 tons weekly maximum during the peak tourist season, 40 tons during the off-season. The existing 8 ton load limitation on Mull roads is a great handicap; not only does it confine distributional services to the main Tobermory-Salen-Craignure-Fionnphort road, inhibiting the carriage of economical loads across the island, but it has also forced MacBrayne into the expense of acquiring specially designed passenger vehicles. However, the car ferry does allow the transport of loaded lorries (subject to the 8 ton limit) direct from the mainland which can then make deliveries on the island.

Tobermory is still MacBrayne's main storage centre on Mull, for the town is still served by the direct cargo boat from Glasgow. But its location in the extreme north of the island adds to internal delivery distances and handling costs. There is a fair concession for lorries conveyed on the car ferry with loads of animal feeding stuffs and fertilisers. Such vehicles, which seldom carry any return load back to Oban, are charged a flat rate of £1 10s for the return part of the journey.

The design of the *Columba* has been criticised for unduly limiting vehicular space and headroom in favour of the extra passenger, cabin and luxury accommodation the ship provides. Yet this same passenger space has been the chief factor in attracting tourists, who are bringing up to £70,000 extra revenue in

112

the season to Mull hotels and restaurants. It is clear that a formula for sea transport must be found which would cater simultaneously, and with greater convenience and economy, for both the island's industry and tourist-visitors.

PLEASURE SAILINGS

The Craignure car ferry connects a pleasant cruise from Oban for day visitors with organised motor-bus tours round the island. There are also attractive sailings available locally. At Tobermory a fishing boat has been refitted to comfortable standards to accommodate fifty passengers on cruises lasting from an hour or two to a whole day, depending on weather and choice of route. One popular sail is up Loch Sunart, a long, calm picturesque sea-loch whose entrance lies just opposite Tobermory across the Sound of Mull, and which divides Morvern from Ardnamurchan. Another enjoyable sail in clear weather is round the cliffs of the north of Mull to the open sea and the Treshnish Islands, with the blue outlines of the Hebridean islands standing out boldly on the northern and western horizon.

The Treshnish Islands and Staffa may also be visited by arranging or joining a trip in the cabin cruiser which is based on Ulva Ferry, whose owner is licensed to carry parties in the holiday season. A feature of this sail is that time ashore is allowed on some of the islands, if desired, subject to weather conditions. Smaller boats can be hired at a few other points in Mull for short trips, and of course the ferry boats at Grass Point cater for holiday parties.

MacBrayne run a small passenger and light goods boat daily from Tobermory to Kilchoan, a useful link between Mull and this western point of the mainland.

YACHTING

The Hebrides and west coasts of Scotland can be a yachtsman's paradise, or the reverse. In fine clear sailing weather, with a fresh north-westerly wind, nothing can be more invigorating than the whip of the keen salty air, the long lift of the rollers whose reach extends far out to the limits of the Hebrides, and the incredible blues and purples of the islands. But when a depression is blowing up and the visibility is cut down by rain and mist, then the coasts become cruel and menacing. There is no place for inexperience once a yachtsman sails west of the peninsula of Kintyre. However, by keeping to the lee of the islands and following such sheltered channels as the Sound of Mull, a great deal of safe and enjoyable sailing can be done.

There are many well-charted anchorages for yachtsmen round Mull. Care must be taken in studying the direction of the wind, for a sudden change can convert a safe anchorage into a highly dangerous one. Islets, reefs and skerries abound, especially round the south-west and west coasts. A favourite bay is the Bullhole, half a mile north of Fionnphort, which besides being safe, is central for visiting the attractions of Iona. Another excellent place is Loch na Lathaich, Bunessan. Neil Gunn's book *Off in a Boat* describes conditions around Mull, certainly from the angle of a small party cruising in an old motor boat.

Tobermory is the perfect centre for yachtsmen, with its wide safe sheltered anchorage, offering a welcome return to civilised amenities for crews who have been living under difficult conditions for days. Fifty or sixty yachts and cabin cruisers of all sizes are to be seen in the bay any day in July and August when the weather is fine. In such ideal surroundings it was inevitable that a local yacht club should come into being.

The Western Isles Yacht Club was formed in 1936. In 1969 it had 90 full members and 30 cadet members. About fifteen of the local members own yachts varying in size from dinghies to forty-footers, and there are also five dinghies owned by the club for the use of cadet members. The club runs a regatta each August; this event was a local fixture which was started in the early 1900s, until the organisation was taken over by the Yacht Club. It also shares with the two Oban clubs the running of the West Highland Yachting Week. Of course members run many afternoon and evening dinghy races throughout the season.

THE LIFEBOAT SERVICE

A lifeboat was stationed at Tobermory between 1937 and the late 1940s. It was manned by a volunteer crew with a full-time engineer. The boat was named the *Sir Arthur Rose* and gifted in his memory to the RNLI by the late Miss Lithgow, of Glengorm. However, it is perhaps a tribute to the safety of the local waters that the boat was withdrawn. In fact, it was stationed rather far from the area of potential danger, and its services were seldom required. The lifeboats stationed at Port Askaig (Islay), Mallaig and Barra Head now cover the area quite adequately.

7 COMMUNICATIONS WITHIN THE ISLAND

NEARLY up to the end of the eighteenth century there were no real roads on Mull. The scattered communities were linked by rough ridge tracks and footpaths, and by the cattle droving routes. Without wheeled vehicles the method of transportation was by creels or panniers carried on the backs of the islanders themselves, or slung across the tough little garrons, the Mull ponies, which were smaller than their counterparts on the mainland, and could carry no more than a hundredweight and a half. The garrons were often harnessed to light wooden sledges for such work as dragging stones off cultivated ground; the sledges might be forked tree branches or rough planks, rather like the American Indian *travois*.

When the spoked wheel came into use rough tracks were formed for the passage of carts, which were at first no more than rough boxes on wheels. These demanded a heavier breed of horse, and by the end of the nineteenth century, with more and better roads and new farming methods, there were heavy draught horses for agricultural work, garrons for hill work (as on the sporting estates), and medium breeds for drawing passenger vehicles.

The people used the gig, or dog-cart, holding up to three passengers. The heavier hiring vehicle, with more comfort, was the 'machine' or wagonette, carrying seven or eight, drawn by one or two horses. On the steepest hills passengers were often obliged to alight and walk to the summit to ease the load for the horses; indeed, the short cuts used by the walkers can still be traced across many of the acute bends. A useful small commercial vehicle of the delivery type was the spring cart with low sides, much used by travelling salesmen and tinkers.

116

DROVE ROADS

Old grassy tracks marking former lines of communication can be seen crossing many of the moorlands. Some of these end at peat banks, where the fuel was once dug and carted home, but others pick their way across a saddle of the hills into the next valley. They all connect with old ruins and townships, and usually merge somewhere into the modern road system.

Many of these tracks were drove roads. Cattle from Coll and Tiree were landed at Croaig in the north-west, and were driven via Dervaig and the Glen Aros route to Salen. At Drumtighe, at the head of Glen Aros, other tracks come in from the glen above Kengharair, leading from Treshnish and Torloisk. Salen was the focus also for drove roads from Tobermory and district, and for stock ferried over from Ardnamurchan. Thence the track continued by Craignure to Grass Point.

A smaller branch came in from Glen Forsa, and a main branch began at Kintra, at the tip of the Ross of Mull, another landing place for cattle from Coll and Tiree. It traversed the Ross, and after passing through Glen More it was joined by a track from Lochbuie.

At Salen, the focal point for north and central Mull, fairs, games and markets were held at seasonable times, and to this day the Mull and Morvern Agricultural Show, established in 1832, is held there annually in August. From Grass Point the cattle were shipped to Kerrera, the island which shelters Oban Bay, whence they were made to swim across the narrow channel to the Oban shore to begin their long weary journey to the markets of the south. For the crossing they were secured to the stern of a small boat by a length of rope tied round the horns, and, swimming behind the boat, were towed across.

ROAD DEVELOPMENT

At the beginning of the nineteenth century the only road in Mull capable of taking a two-wheeled vehicle followed the coast between Salen and Grass Point. In 1790 the Duke of Argyll contributed £350 towards the making of this road. By 1807 it had been extended to Tobermory in the north and Lochbuie in the

117

south, and it was about this time that a stagecoach was brought over to the island to prove that the road was indeed passable. The vehicle was taken back to the mainland immediately after this exacting experiment. Road construction on Mull lagged behind that on the mainland, even behind that of the island of Skye, where more government aid was forthcoming. Early travellers to Mull, Dr MacCulloch, Dr Johnson and many others, were unanimous in their complaints. In 1773 Dr Johnson hired horses to carry him by tracks and bridle paths the twenty miles from Tobermory to Inch Kenneth, a route on which the rivulets, to which Boswell referred, could, in times of heavy rain, turn into swollen torrents, unbridged and dangerous to cross.

Up to 1840 there was very little expansion of the road system. The Statistical Account of 1845 criticised it severely; the roads, it said, 'are extremely bad and the improvement proceeds but slowly—the funds allowed are so disproportionate to the extent and surface and to the expense requisite that unless aid from the government is obtained to assist proprietors in their laudable exertions to benefit the community in opening up new lines and repairing the old, there is no hope of anything of an improvement for many years to come'. At the beginning of that decade an interior road was extended from Grass Point through Glen More as far as Kilfinichen on the northern shore of Loch Scridain. It was financed by the public-spirited proprietors of the island, aided by grants from the rest of the country, and it linked the populous west-central part of Mull with the eastern area, giving them greater access to the fairs and markets of Salen and Grass Point. An important bridle path led from Salen via Loch Ba across the ridge of Mam Chlachaig on the shoulder of Ben More, descending to Glen More near Kinloch.

The natural expansion of this road through the Ross of Mull to Bunessan and Fionnphort followed within ten years, and thereafter other roads spread throughout the island. Fortuitously enough, once the clearances began there was no lack of cheap labour. For many able-bodied people work on the roads removed the threat of abject poverty and allowed them to maintain some measure of family life.

Before the days of bitumenised surfacing the job of the roadman was quite specialised. He was something of a craftsman, wise

118

in the selection of hammers of the correct weight and length for the job, and something of a practical geologist, too, for he had to assess the correct texture of the rocks he prised out of the quarries by the roadside for breaking down into smaller blocks. These in turn were knapped down into specified sizes. Wages were based on piece work. The expert roadman has now disappeared from the rural scene and one can no longer watch him, wearing his dark protective eye-shields, scuffed heavy boots, chipping away all day with a minimum of effort, adjusting his strokes to the texture and cleavage planes of the stones.

Motor cars first shattered the pace and peace of Mull roads about 1909, introduced by one or two of the landowners. By the start of the first world war motor cars were quite common on the island. The steep hills, acute bends and numerous humpbacked bridges demanded robustness rather than speed. One could easily overtake those early, chain-driven Albion vans as they ground their way up the hills, and if he was daring a lad could swing on behind (unknown to the driver) and enjoy an exciting, if precarious lift home. The Albion car was followed by the Model T Ford, whose reliability and simplicity introduced a new conception of transportation to the public in Mull, as it did in the other remote districts of the highlands and islands.

Neil McDonald, of the McDonald Arms Hotel, Tobermory, a respected local gentleman now long dead, was one of the early motoring pioneers. He drove with a fixed concentration which involved him in many small mishaps, but his slow speed and the sturdiness of the car ensured that neither he nor the car suffered much. Any broken signposts were attributed to him, for it was only necessary for a passenger to query the choice of a road to cause him to transfer his attention and concentration to the signpost—with dire results.

MODERN ROADS

Mull has plentiful resources of road metal. There are small grass-grown quarries every few hundred yards along the roadsides from which the road makers used to work. Some of these supplied the hard whinstone, others the softer 'rotten rock' used to bind the sharp surfacing, the whole being levelled and con-

119

solidated by the wheels of passing traffic, or by the horse-drawn roadroller.

The increasing use of motor cars demanded more and better roads. In Mull bitumenised surfaces were introduced in the 1930s, and brought to an end the choking clouds of dust which up to then had marked the passing of a vehicle in dry weather. Specially prepared surfacing material is now brought in to convenient piers by small coasters from mainland dumps, such as Loch Etive, north of Oban, in loads of up to 300 tons. This is distributed by motor lorry to the various road gangs throughout the island.

Argyll County Council is now responsible for the upkeep of 144 miles of classified roads in Mull, including a few short stretches within the Burgh of Tobermory, and two-and-a-half miles in Iona. The only Class I road is the 49 mile coast road from Tobermory via Craignure and Glen More to Fionnphort. It is nine miles longer than the alternative road via Gribun. There are about 51 miles of Class II roads, and 34 of Class III. Increasing lengths of private roads are being built by the Forestry Commission; others have been constructed by the Department of Agriculture and handed over to the county for maintenance.

In 1963 the amount of traffic recorded just failed to reach a figure that would justify the construction of two-track roads. As the car ferry statistics (page 110) show, more recent figures would prove the urgent need for such roads. It has been estimated that even with passing-places at every 100 yards or oftener, and allowing for a minimum of seventy vehicles per hour, the journey from Tobermory to Fionnphort takes half-an-hour longer than it would on double-tracked roads.

The Motor Taxation Department of Argyll County Council does not separate vehicular registrations into districts, so the figure for cars 'domiciled' in Mull can only be estimated. From personal observation it is suggested that in 1969 there must be at least 300 motor vehicles domiciled in Mull, including private, agricultural, forestry, goods, passenger, postal, etc, and a small number of motor cycles. This gives a ratio of about one vehicle to seven of the population.

There are only half-a-dozen or so motor vehicles in the island of Iona and it is hoped that no local car ferry will ever bring an influx of transport to this quiet little island, with its negligible road mileage, although such an idea has already been considered. Cars belonging to visitors to Iona are parked at Fionnphort in a large modern car park provided by the County Council.

Although narrow and hilly, with many dangerous corners and old-fashioned bridges, the roads are generally well surfaced but lack firm bottoming. Sharp dips and undulations develop above soft peaty stretches, and although they are a deterrent to speeding they are too often a danger to the suspension of heavily-laden vehicles, thus requiring the imposition of a maximum weight limit of eight tons. This restricts economic weight loads, whether of timber, livestock, or goods, which on mainland roads are commonly 20–30 tons. Unfortunately Argyll County Council is heavily committed elsewhere, and improvements to the roads of Mull can only be on a long-term basis.

However, passing places and lay-bys are being constantly extended and sight-lines improved on blind corners: but most important, a fine modern road, starting at Fionnphort, is being built through the Ross of Mull and Glen More to Craignure. Completion of the final stretch from Loch Sgubain (halfway along Glen More) to Craignure is steadily proceeding, and the project should be completed by the early 1970s. In time this road will be further extended from Craignure along the Sound of Mull to Tobermory. While it follows the line of the existing road wherever possible, many completely new sections have had to be constructed to eliminate loops and dangerous stretches.

A highly spectacular coastal road at Gribun winds under the high crumbling cliffs, cutting in places through the solid rock, with unprotected drops to the sea far below. About a mile of this route presents problems, as the area is subject to landslipping. Under conditions of heavy rain, or after frost, rock avalanches are frequent. On one occasion a postal van was immobilised for days when one rockfall came down just in front of it and, before the postman could reverse or turn back, another came crashing down at his back, effectively cutting off the van. Even in summer, boulders can come bounding down and across the road, started off by minor slides dislodged by sheep grazing far up on the ledges.

Perhaps the most important of the Forestry roads is the service road branching off the main Tobermory-Salen road a mile above

Aros Bridge, cutting through the new woodlands to Loch Frisa and Lettermore. If this route were extended along the length of Loch Frisa to meet the Tobermory-Dervaig road below the Mishnish Lochs it could become a useful tourist road and open up the excellent angling possibilities on Loch Frisa.

By and large, Mull is a place where—subject to considerate driving—a motorist can relax. There are no double yellow lines, no parking meters, no traffic lights—only two or three white guiding lines in the whole road system, including the Burgh of Tobermory. Some of the narrow sideroads still have a line of grass, or worn-down oily rushes, along the centre of the road, reminding the motorist that he is indeed far from mainland speed-tracks.

Nevertheless extreme caution and concentration are demanded from drivers. Early cars could average no more than 12–15mph in Mull. On the steadily improving roads the modern car can average 25–30mph, the performance of a car being restricted by local conditions. For strangers accustomed to fast mainland highways, driving on the island might be hazardous, or frustrating. The 50 mile run from Tobermory to Fionnphort can take up to an hour and three quarters—rather less with the completion of the new road through the Ross of Mull; the seven-mile miniature Alpine road from Tobermory to Dervaig can be covered safely in twenty minutes.

PUBLIC TRANSPORT

Mull is not well served by public transport, though without it the island community cannot function effectively. Apart from MacBrayne's motor-bus services from Craignure to Tobermory and Fionnphort, one or two private contractors, and several vans running on Post Office private contracts, travellers have to make their own transport arrangements. During the off-season passengers from Iona intending to sail to the mainland in the morning are obliged to spend the night in Mull, as the amount of traffic does not justify an early morning run by the Iona-Fionnphort ferryboat in time to connect with the car ferry at Craignure.

Minibuses are used to convey pupils from scattered homes to

and from school. These vehicles might be integrated into a more general service for the travelling public. In addition, the suggestion could be followed up to use Post Office vehicles for carrying fare-paying passengers, as well as for delivering parcels and light goods; passenger-carrying facilities already exist on the Tobermory-Dervaig run. Under existing conditions, if it were not for the fine service provided by private travelling shops, living in some of the remote corners of Mull, especially for elderly people, would hardly be possible.

In the tourist season MacBrayne and one or two private hirers organise coach tours round the island, to Iona, and to the fine beach at Calgary, twelve miles from Tobermory. This might be turned to greater advantage by retaining a nucleus of the service during the out-of-season months, using smaller buses with a more frequent service. Under present conditions, however, this could hardly be a paying proposition.

AIR TRANSPORT

An air landing strip exists at the mouth of Glen Forsa, on the Sound of Mull, two miles east of Salen and close to the small hospital and old folk's home there. Opened for regular flights by Loganair on 13 September 1966, it was built as an exercise by sappers of the 38th Engineer Regiment, on behalf of Argyll County Council, in fifty-four days, at a cost stated to have been £6,000, a fraction of what it would have cost as a commercial venture. The runway is grass over gravel, 3,000ft long by 90ft wide, and the work of levelling involved the moving of 50,000 tons of earth and the clearing away of 1,000 trees. The airstrip is only thirty minutes' flight from Glasgow Airport via Ganavan, beside Oban, which is just five minutes' flying time from Glen Forsa.

Mull will fit into the extending lines of local flying services being developed by Loganair (now a subsidiary of the Royal Bank of Scotland) in the Hebrides. There are regular flights between Mull, Oban and Glasgow on Fridays, Saturdays and Sundays; but as an outcome of the increasing convenience of air travel (there is some limited commuting by business men with interests in the south), Loganair anticipates that this will become

123

a daily service. The record times for flights so far are : Mull to Glasgow Airport, 22 minutes; Mull to London Airport (changing planes at Glasgow), just under two hours. Passenger fares are : Mull to Glasgow, £5 15s; Mull to Oban, £1 5s. (for a single journey). Special arrangements are made for air charters, aerial photography and pleasure flights from Glen Forsa. Freight is carried at a charge of sixpence per pound, minimum five shillings. Air freight transport is especially useful for high-value perishables produced locally, such as lobsters.

POSTAL SERVICES

On his visit to Mull Dr Johnson was on tenterhooks at the idea of missing a sailing boat that would carry his correspondence over to Easdale. In those days, mail depended on fortuitous transport to the island.

The question of a post office was first raised in 1776 by the factor of the Duke of Argyll; but it was not until 1791 that a Customs House and Post Office were set up in Tobermory. About 1801 a small packet boat began to sail between Croaig and Tiree carrying letters and passengers every Thursday, weather permitting. The Post Office paid the Duke an annual subsidy of £5 for this service. Tenants of the Argyll Estates in Mull were obliged to use this boat to transport their cattle and goods. The organisation of postal services within the island did not develop until the 1840s. MacBrayne received their first mail contract in 1852, but this may not have included the Mull district. In 1845 there was a thrice-weekly mail service between Grass Point and Oban, probably run by a private contractor.

Up to this time charges had been graduated according to a mileage chart based on London as the centre, but under the new regulations the Penny Post was set up for deliveries over any distance. Postage stamps had to be cancelled by an impression showing the identity, but not the name of the office of posting. In Scotland this took the form of a heavy square of horizontal bars with a rectangle space in the centre which bore the national number of the office, each office being allocated a different number. Reference to early editions of the London Post Office Directory (1844–5) and later Guides (1856–7 onwards) shows

Page 125: (*above*) Tobermory: the main street and the old and new piers; (*below*) Tobermory at the end of the eighteenth century. All the buildings, except the high-roofed one on extreme left, are still standing. The building at the pier entrance was the Mull Hotel; that next to it is now the post office

Page 126: (*above*) Central Mull: a shepherd's lonely cottage beside the old road through Glen More, looking west towards Ben More; (*below*) North-west Mull: the quiet village of Dervaig

when post offices were first opened in different parts of Mull. Their importance varied with the movements of population and improving transport.

Place	Number	Year first mentioned	Notes
Aros (Salen, Aros)	23	1844–57	Altered to 669 in 1906
Auchnacraig (Grass Point)	21	1844–57	Vacant in 1874; restored in 1887; vacant 1892–1906
Tobermory	325	1844–57	Vacant 1874, but restored
Salen	315	1887	Originally Strichen number; vacant in 1887
Iona (Isle of)	446	1887	
Bunessan	48	?	Originally Bonawe number; vacant 1874; restored 1887
Carsaig	559	1892	
Craignure	541	1892	
Fionnphort	637	1892	
Grenadier (Steamer)	666	1906	Staffa and Iona cruise boat

In 1883 the cancellation system was replaced by the composite double circle (the principle of our modern franking system) showing the name of the post office instead of the number.

Tobermory was the chief post office for Mull, Iona, Tiree and Coll, until November 1964. As a result of transport rearrangements it has been reduced to a sub-office under Oban, which is now the chief office for the Mull district. There are now in Mull fifteen sub-offices, including Tobermory and Iona, with a total

H

staff of thirty-two. Carsaig and Grass Point, once important centres, are now only small sub-offices. Throughout the island there is generally one delivery and one collection daily, carried out by official mail vans, motor cycles and private mail contractors. Mails now converge on Craignure and are carried by the car ferry to Oban.

Deliveries in Mull can be as complex as on the remoter islands of the Hebrides. For instance, the farms at Tavool and Burg on the south side of Ardmeanach are isolated from the main road by a five-mile track which crosses the high shoulder of the hill by fierce gradients and is liable to be cut by wash-outs after heavy rain. The mail for these farms first travels the nineteen miles by van through Glen More from Craignure to Pennyghael. From there the postman takes the road by Kilfinichen Church, delivering to scattered houses as he goes, thence by the side road to Tiroran, where he leaves his van. From here he walks up the rough track to the summit, where (until recently) he kept a bicycle padlocked to a telegraph post (even distant Burg has a telephone). After four miles of walking and cycling he reaches the end of his round at Burg. Now that the road has been slightly improved, the postman can pick a cautious way by motor cycle. Distances on the island may not be so very great, but the terrain can make communications difficult.

Even the case of the postman to Burg can hardly compare with that of his counterparts at the end of the nineteenth century, when mails from Oban were still being handled from Grass Point. The complexities of mail deliveries and collections in the Ross of Mull in that era seem to have been much more than a half-century away from the present-day postal developments of the mainland. At that time the postman covering the ground between Pennyghael and Grass Point lived at Salen. He began his round by walking the three miles to Knock, below Loch Ba, then seven miles up the side of the loch, over Mam Chlachaig across the shoulder of Ben More, and down to the Glen More road east of Kinloch Inn. There he was met by the local postman who had already walked from his home at Pennyghael to Bunessan to collect the mail, and then all the way back to the meeting point—a round journey of over twenty-six miles. The mail container they were concerned with was no more than a foot square, which could carry the whole mail from the district in those days.

The outgoing mail was then carried to Grass Point through Glen More by the Salen man, still on foot, who thereafter completed a reversal of the earlier procedure in order to achieve the delivery of the incoming mails. The timelessness of the system and the fitness of the letter carriers are to be marvelled at. Even when the letters on this route finally did arrive at Bunessan, this was by no means the end of the story, for there were no local deliveries. Letters might lie for weeks in the little post office until someone living near the addressee happened to call, and agreed to hand the letter to its destination.

At the Iona end of Mull in the early days of the twentieth century the mails were delivered from Oban three times a week by the steamers *Fingal* and *Dirk*. From Iona the steamers continued to Fionnphort, Bunessan (where they tied up overnight), Tiree, Coll, Tobermory, Salen, Craignure, and back to Oban. There was also a road service then by horse and gig from Craignure to Pennyghael. The first man regularly engaged to deliver mails in Iona was still alive in 1967, aged eighty-four.

When the parcel post was introduced, it offered a real shopping medium for the islanders. Few houses were without their catalogues from the warehouses of the cities, and everything from trout flies to Sunday suits came by post. Commercial travellers were a common sight in Mull with their cases of samples, which brought the glamour of the shop windows to the distant farms and cot-houses of the island. The recent enormous increases in parcel post rates has almost priced this service out for some of the less well-to-do islanders.

TELEGRAPH AND TELEPHONE SERVICES

Mull was first connected with the mainland by submarine telegraph in 1871, when a cable 6·4 nautical miles long was laid between Ganavan Bay (Oban) and Grass Point. This was connected on the island with telegraph offices at Tobermory, Dervaig, Calgary, Craignure, Pennyghael, Tiroran, Fionnphort, Bunessan and Iona.

The new telegraph posts and wires sang a strange and lonely

129

note along the empty roadsides and across the moorlands in the strong sea winds. On some of the grouse moors the wires were hung every few yards with squares of metal ('spectacles') about six inches by four, pierced by two round holes, to warn off low-flying birds, which sometimes dashed themselves against the unseen strands. This custom has been discontinued owing to a reduction in the numbers of game birds. During the last war certain lines were transferred to underground conduits, namely the Tobermory–Dervaig–Calgary lines, the Craignure–Auchnacraig route, and locally in Tobermory, Craignure and Dervaig.

The service was particularly appreciated by the merchants of the island; and in this connection a story has come down from the days of war-time restrictions and regulations. A butcher had just called at a Mull post office and sent off a telegram. After he had left, the postmistress turned to another local man who had just come in, and in that happy spirit which characterises certain confidential transactions in out-of-the-way places, she remarked, 'Now, isn't that a funny message for him to be sending to the suppliers in Oban—"Don't send meat, am killing myself!"' The man pondered this seriously for a long time and then agreed, 'Yess, inteet; it iss a stupid message; I'm sure he knows fine he cannot be killing himself without a licence.'

The first telephone exchange was opened in Tobermory on 12 December 1931 with one call office and twelve private subscribers, mostly business men. At the same time an omnibus circuit was provided within the island connecting the post offices at Iona, Fionnphort, Bunessan and Pennyghael, while another connected Coll and Tiree with Tobermory, through Dervaig and Calgary. The cable to the islands dipped into the sea at Calgary Bay, connecting Mull with Scarinish, Tiree, twenty-five miles away. The original operator who was present when the first exchange was opened, was in 1967 still faithfully carrying on her duties as caretaker-operator.

In 1934 this Mull internal telephone system was at last connected with the mainland by a submarine cable following the line of the former telegraph cable. By the end of the 1960s the service had expanded to include 410 subscribers, with twenty public call boxes and kiosks operating through eight telephone exchanges. The Iona exchange, opened in June 1935, serves

130

forty-four subscribers, with two public call offices. Even Gometra House, one of the remotest corners of the area, was connected in 1958. The poles run from Ulva Ferry for six miles along the rough road in Ulva, then over a narrow bridged channel of the sea to the island of Gometra, with a further mile to the end of the line.

The linesmen in Mull are faced with many a difficult problem of maintenance, especially when the storms blow in unchecked from the Atlantic. In November 1966 one particularly fierce gust caught a road contractor's hut with two men sheltering inside it, lifted it bodily into the air, and blew it into a bed of sixteen telephone wires. The poles here are twenty-four feet above the ground, which adds a grain of truth to a statement made afterwards by one of the men that for the duration of the flight he had been affected by air-sickness!

NEWSPAPERS, RADIO AND TELEVISION

Daily newspapers reach Mull (Craignure) with the first ferry of the day. The *Glasgow Herald* is probably the most popular for general and business information, with the *Scotsman* a close second. 'Hot news' is provided chiefly by the *Scottish Daily Express* or *Daily Record*. Local and district news comes weekly in the *Oban Times*, which has been printed and published (in Oban) since 1861, and the *Peoples' Journal*, a weekly paper printed in Dundee which provides more general news of the highlands and islands. Sunday newspapers are brought over from Oban by a special morning run by the little Grass Point ferryboat, there being no public ferry service from the mainland on Sundays.

As in the rest of the country, evenings are now spent far more frequently at home, watching television or listening to the radio. The quality of television reception is poor on the whole because of the shadowing effect of the hills and the distances from relay stations, the nearest of which are in Skye and Oban. Mull people may well contend that, badly placed as they are in comparison with the accepted standards of television reception in the south, they should be classified as a marginal area with a concession in the amount paid for licence fees.

131

SOCIAL CONDITIONS

HOWEVER beautiful the western isles are at times, in comparison with the more sheltered parts of Britain they offer a harsh environment for human occupation. Life on Mull can never have been easy and over the centuries, as it has become more economically and socially complex, the islanders have had to face many frustrations and seeming injustices which have arisen both because their home *is* an island and because of their incorporation into a larger society that enjoys greater material advancement. As for most of the highlands and islands region, Mull is nowadays actually struggling to remain a viable economic unit, with a year-round life cycle, and not merely a summer-time tourist resort. The island's problems may best be seen against the background of its internal social development.

HOUSING

In Mull, where wood was scarce and stone abundant, buildings survive for a long time. Hence Mull appears to have a very large number of settlements, for the stone lasts until it sinks into the ground; even then building lines can be traced on the surface. In other places where wood and not stone has been the building material, traces of former habitations have completely disappeared.

From the seventeenth century, when the population began to increase substantially, settlements began to be established all over the island. In most cases they were sited near the sea, near running water, and adjacent to arable ground. With the passage of time and as mainland influences grew stronger, housing standards were slowly improved, but it was not until the second half of the nineteenth century that the more primitive types of houses were vacated, or rebuilt to improved standards.

The oldest type of house conformed to the general pattern adopted in the Hebrides—double-walled, with a drainage space filled with rubble or dried peat between the walls. Wooden cabers (thin tree trunks or rafters) were stretched across the inner walls and angled to form a roof, which was thatched with barley straw, heather, or turf, and held down by ropes of twisted heather weighted with stones. The rain ran off into the space between the walls. On later buildings the cabers were extended to cover the whole width of the walls.

While buildings of this sort can be found in many corners of Mull (nearly all are marked on the Ordnance Survey maps) the two deserted townships of Crakaig and Glac Gugairidh, which lie within a few hundred yards of each other, are typical examples. They lie in a sheltered hollow (The Hollow of the Dark Grazings) above the cliffs overlooking Loch Tuath, between Treshnish and Torloisk. Up to the middle of the nineteenth century they had a total population of close on 200, catered for by a blacksmith and other tradesmen. The last members of the dwindling community left just before the end of last century. There is a large walled communal garden and a sizeable sheep fank (fold), all with high drystone walls. The houses were set down to no regular plan. They varied in size from 20ft by 12ft (interior measurements) to tiny cot houses, all of them with walls three feet thick. They were built by natural craftsmen who used hardly any mortar except round doors and windows. The mortar they used was made from calcined sea shells, hard and enduring, still to be seen in the window facings of the ancient ruined chapels; the art of making mortar must have been handed down from the days of the monkish craftsmen. Houses had one doorway in the long side and up to four windows. Inside and out the surfaces of the walls are faced with stone blocks chipped to a uniformly smooth surface, and the outside corners are evenly rounded. The whole pattern is snug and streamlined, with a pathway of large flat stones laid outside the walls.

One particular house style is believed to have been peculiar to Mull. This is the house built with one square and one round gable. Towards the gable end an open tilted bucket-type chimney

133

was built into the thatch; not so much a chimney (none of the houses has a built-in chimney) as a vent through which the dense smoke escaped from the fire of peats kept burning all the time in the middle of the floor. The floor itself was beaten earth, strewn with fresh rushes, straw, or heather. Against the walls were low platforms covered with blankets over a foundation of springy heather tops, which served as beds; shelves were easily fitted into the stone-work of the walls.

Below the permanent layer of smoke the air was reasonably clear, which accounts for the low-set design of seats and chairs used by earlier generations. The thatch became so heavily impregnated with soot that it was removed periodically and dug into the ground as a very effective fertiliser; fresh thatch was substituted.

Peat smoke was thought to be a fumigant which lessened the risk of disease. Domestic animals, the cattle and sheep, often shared the same roof as their owners, entering by the same door and being separated from them by a low partition, or simply haltered at the other end of the room. This way of life has been described by the Scottish expression 'the clartier (dirtier) the cosier!' Before one condemns old dwellings like this as insanitary hovels, it must be remembered that outside them lay the fresh open moorlands over which blew the strong cleansing sea winds, and the people themselves were engaged in heavy, healthy work in the open air. They were in fact very different from the miserable, congested and ill-ventilated slums of the lowland cities —and even from the seventeenth- and eighteenth-century houses of the nobility along the Royal Mile in Edinburgh.

The style of Mull house described above is called a 'black house' today; they were originally so named not as a reflection on their appearance or sanitation, but to distinguish their dry-stone walls from later styles of building. The expression *tigh dubh* (black house) is suggested by Dr Sinclair to have been correctly *tigh tughath*, or 'thatched house', the confusion having arisen through similarity of pronunciation.

Nowadays Argyll County Council, and the Burgh of Tobermory within its own boundary, are responsible for the housing programme on Mull. A high standard of building has been set throughout the island, nearly always including full services— cleansing, sewers, electricity, and mains water. Building costs are high, and the Council pays 40 per cent more for a standard council house in Mull than in, say Dalmally, outside Oban, and nearly double the cost of a house in a Lowlands county such as Ayrshire—£5,000 against £2,500–£3,000 for a four-apartment house. Private builders find that prefabricated houses cost 25 per cent more than in Oban, 60 per cent more than in Perth. Repairs are very expensive and are aggravated by lack of local labour. The crippling effect of freight charges is obvious; for instance, the cost of bringing to Mull a load of bricks for the foundations of a prefabricated house is £15 by puffer, £57 by car ferry, even at the off-peak period.

Private owners who want to build are at a disadvantage. Of necessity, many of the sites—on outlying farms, or by the seashore—are in locations where services such as water, drainage and electricity are not available. Sanitary facilities in Mull compare most unfavourably with the rest of Scotland, and there are still far too many houses with no running water laid on. Improvements and modernisation can be undertaken by an owner only at prohibitive cost, which would mean an exorbitant economic rent if the property were not owner-occupied. More realistic grants should certainly be allowed by the government, for the County Council gives such cases every possible assistance.

The price of houses has naturally soared in recent years as a result of demands by non-residents for holiday accommodation, though such property, lying empty for most of the year, does not improve or contribute much to local amenities. Moreover, residents with limited means can hardly afford to buy and restore houses for retirement in competition with incomers investing in holiday accommodation. Small cottages, often lacking in modern amenities, are sold for £3,000 and over. Alterations and improvements to modernise the building can bring the total cost to £4,000–£5,000. There are now at least 150 holiday houses in Mull and Iona.

FUEL AND LIGHTING

Peats were of course the staple fuel, supplemented by coarse heather and any wood cast up on the shores or buried in the bogs. Care had to be taken in the appropriation of driftwood, for the ownership of valuable timber cast up was vested in the

Superior of the ground, as is recorded in old records of the Argyll Estates. Coal was far too expensive for the ordinary people when it was first brought in by the early nineteenth-century ships. It sold at 10s to 12s per ton. Later, and up to the present day, coal came into common use, delivered around the island shores by 'puffers'. One cart load of coal (approximately one ton) was equal to between twenty and forty loads of peats, depending on quality.

The quality of peat varies according to the composition of its constituents. Mull has not, on the whole, the same depth or high quality as the fine hard black peat found in some of the other Hebridean islands, but it was a quite adequate fuel. Concessions were held by the people of Iona and some neighbouring islands to cut peats over in Mull. Cutting was hard work, in which the whole family joined. The initial clearing of the surface was particularly tough, formed as it was of matted roots of heather, bog myrtle and coarse grasses. Below that the peats were cut with a spade specially designed for the purpose and made by the local blacksmith. The peat blocks varied in size and shape in different regions. In Mull they did not exceed eighteen inches in length by four inches square, and they were cut at an angle of about sixty degrees from the vertical.

The stockpile of peats, neatly stacked to allow the rain to run off, used to be a familiar sight outside every cottage; an average household would burn about 15,000 peats a year, a requirement that meant at least fifteen days' cutting, and countless days of turning and drying in little pyramids and cromlechs through which the wind could blow, for peat, when freshly cut, contains up to 95 per cent water. Thereafter it had to be stacked up for transport home from the moors, and all the work was dependent on good weather and drying winds.

Occasionally the bogs supplied roots of resinous bog-fir which are the remnants of ancient forests. These, when dried and split, were used to light the houses, being held in iron sconces fixed into the walls, and also for kindling. Another form of lighting, which added to the miscellaneous odours, was provided by 'cruisies', or little iron containers, filled with fish- or seal-oil and fitted with a wick formed from the dry pith of rushes. All these iron implements (which are now sought as curios) were made locally.

The nostalgic tang of peat smoke is now rarely met; peats are cut only in a few outlying districts. Paraffin oil lamps were succeeded by pressure types fitted with incandescent mantles, which are still used where electricity is not available. In modern kitchen cookers coal is gradually being replaced by oil, now that small oil tankers can be transported bodily on to the Mull roads. For years paraffin stoves provided quick cooking facilities but now, where electricity is lacking, bottled gas supplying more convenient appliances is generally used, with the small solid fuel kitchen range or cooker in the background. The gas, in special containers, is stocked by a few agents throughout the island.

Some of the larger houses such as the estate mansion houses used coal gas for domestic purposes, generated on the premises and stored in a miniature gasholder. In 1865 Torosay Castle used fourteen tons of gas coal in the year, priced at 20s per ton, and sixty tons of domestic coal at 11s to 13s, part of which was a perquisite of some of the estate workers. Some houses used acetylene gas generated from calcium carbide. All these have now been largely superseded by electricity and oil, and the luxury of central heating has found its place on the island's domestic scene. Some large isolated houses, such as Inch Kenneth or Ulva House, use a paraffin-diesel generating plant to provide their own electricity.

FOOD AND DRINK

Up to the middle of the eighteenth century, when potatoes were introduced—and at first treated with suspicion—the diet of the people was rather limited. Barley and oats of poor quality were grown and ground into a coarse meal in hand querns, and later by water mills. This meal was used for making bannocks and gruel, thickening kail soup, and similar dishes. Kail (a kind of cabbage) was the only green vegetable grown, at least up to the early nineteenth century, but as it had a high Vitamin C content it helped to balance the monotonous diet.

Fish, fresh, dried, or salted, was an important item of diet. Although the Mull fishing industry never prospered, the crofter-fishermen could always meet the needs of the maritime townships. Shellfish, too, must have been eaten in abundance, to judge from the heaps of shells still lying beside some of the old houses. Edible

137

seaweeds, such as dulse and carragheen, were a healthy dish. The last-named was made into a kind of blancmange by boiling with milk.

Meat was scarce, little more than the flesh of goats, or a braxy sheep—one that had died from natural causes that did not affect the flesh. Beef was seldom seen; cattle were too valuable to be slaughtered for food, the best animals being exported, the poorest kept for breeding. Through lack of winter fodder the stock was weak and emaciated by the time spring came again. In times of real scarcity those animals were bled (still further weakening them) and the blood mixed with oatmeal to enrich and eke out the store of food. Sometimes a deer might be killed, or wildfowl.

Seabirds and their eggs were also important. Young birds were captured in the early summer and salted down in barrels for use in the winter. Puffins and gannets (said to taste like salt beef) added to the menu; cormorants as well, which were edible after being buried for a few days in soft earth which absorbed the strong fishy flavour.

It was not until about 1840 that the use of such luxuries as tea, sugar and wheaten bread became more general, and by that time potatoes were plentiful. The food was natural and un-adulterated. The essence of the grain was retained, and the vitamin content high. Evidence of this is seen in the tall stature and well-preserved teeth of past generations.

The drink of the ordinary people was, as elsewhere, ale. The start of whisky distilling dates from the sixteenth century. The imposition of Excise Duty was bitterly resented, and a wave of illicit distilling swept the island up to the early nineteenth century. In 1780 whisky sold for 10d a quart! Of course, the chiefs and leading families could obtain ample supplies of luxuries like wines and silks, which were easily smuggled into the islands and main-land coasts, whose remoteness and difficult terrain made it almost impossible for preventive officers to carry out their duties.

HEALTH

However healthy one may think the mode of life in the open air and in the black houses, the fact remains that islanders shared with mainland folk the risks and the incidence of disease of past centuries. Apart from endemic diseases the people were tall, active and of good physique. However, life was hard and exacting; child mortality was high and expectation of life low according to modern standards.

Severe outbreaks of smallpox, cholera and typhus occurred through ignorance of health principles and lack of hygiene. The incidence of tuberculosis was heavy until modern times. The various forms of rheumatism were common.

The installation of proper sanitation came about only slowly. In spite of the ample supplies of good fresh water available from springs, lochs and hill burns, a private supply of piped water is still lacking in many of the older houses lying outside the modernised urban centres of the island. In fact, Mull is below the Scottish average, even below that of the whole County of Argyll, in its domestic supplies of piped water. It is related that in the early days of plumbing, one man who had proudly laid a sewer from his house was found, when moving to another house, to be lifting the drainage tiles, arguing that the sewer was part of the moveable fittings.

Relatives coming home from distant places often carried infection that hit these isolated communities with particular virulence. Smallpox, especially, was regarded with almost superstitious horror, and the victims were sometimes entirely isolated, food and drink being left where they could be collected. Volunteer nurses were few and far between, and the sick were often left to live or die. As late as 1891 there was a local outbreak of smallpox in the Ross of Mull. Shunned by neighbours, the occupants of the two houses involved were cared for by a complete stranger, a travelling pedlar, who nursed them through their illness. Resuming his rounds with his pack on his back, he found that he himself had been infected with an attack so virulent that he died by the roadside. He was buried, along with his pack, on the spot where his body was found, a place now marked by a little cairn surmounted by a simple iron celtic cross, beside the Pedlar's Pool on the river Lussa.

In the days when culture reached its highest standards under the Lords of the Isles, and later under the Macleans, covering a period of 400 years from the fourteenth century onwards, a form of medical service was provided in the Hebrides by the Beatons, the famous Mull doctors, to whom fuller reference is made on pages 163-4. The art of medicine died out in Mull partly through the general decline in culture which followed the breakdown of the clan system, partly because of the specialised teaching and increasing skills in medicine that were developing in the Lowlands of Scotland.

In modern times Mull has, of course, come under the provisions of the National Health Service, which is administered by the Oban and District Hospital Board. There are three doctors, stationed at Tobermory, Salen and Bunessan; although there is a pharmaceutical chemist at Tobermory, each of the doctors has to dispense most of his own prescriptions, which gives rise to duplicated visits and waste of time. There are six district nurses, based at Tobermory, Salen, Dervaig, Lochdonhead, Craignure and Bunessan. For dental treatment Mull people have to travel to the mainland.

The health authorities are faced with problems arising from the disproportionate number of elderly people who need specialised attention. A medical centre and home, known as Dunaros, was established at Salen in the early 1960s, and proved to be so successful that in five years it was upgraded to the status of Small Hospital and an X-ray unit was provided. There were then seven geriatric and five sick-bay beds; further enlargement of the hospital is contemplated.

There are emergency arrangements in force, for use by day, of an air ambulance from Loganair using the Glen Forsa airstrip (two miles distant), but night ambulance flights are not yet considered practicable because of the mountainous approach to the airstrip. A type of fast sea ambulance, based on Oban, might be a desirable amenity, but the efficiency of this would depend on better public transport throughout the island.

ADMINISTRATION

The need to provide publicly for the general welfare of the islanders arose only after the clan system had broken down, for up to that time the clan was a large family unit under the care and jurisdiction of the chief. After the seventeenth century the island society might have been completely demoralised had it

140

not been for the steadying influence of the church, acting through the Kirk Sessions which were administered by the most responsible of the people. Through the period of the clearances and evictions there was plenty of provocation for revolution, but being God-fearing and law-abiding, the ordinary folk became amenable to the new order. In fact, minor offenders against society were in greater fear of the wrath of the Kirk Sessions than are their more numerous modern counterparts of the Courts of Law.

Up to the time of the Reformation Mull was composed of a number of small parishes centred on the various churches. After the Reformation these were amalgamated into the single parish of Mull; but in 1688 the area north of Loch na Keal became the parish of Kilninian and Kilmore, the rest of Mull being the parish of Ross. Forty years later the Ross was subdivided into the two parishes of Torosay, and Kilfinichen and Kilviceon. Iona was decreed a *quoad sacra* parish in 1828, but was included in the civil parish of Kilfinichen and Kilviceon. These parish divisions remain up to the present day.

Mull is included in the Parliamentary Constituency of Argyll. The whole of the island, except the tiny Burgh of Tobermory, is under the landward administration of the County of Argyll, whose council directly controls major services such as roads, housing, cemeteries, education, etc. Minor services are run by the local District Council, successor to the former Parish Council.

The island sends three representatives to Argyll County Council, one from the north, one from the centre and south, and one from the Burgh of Tobermory. A councillor's duties are onerous, for it can take up to three days to attend and return from a meeting at Lochgilphead, where the administrative offices are situated. Moreover, in Argyll, where distances are long and travelling involved, meetings are sometimes held at other centres in order to average out the inconvenience for attending members. Air travel, when fully developed, might ease the Mull councillors' lot.

EDUCATION

Provisions for local education were only slowly established on Mull, though the island was long influenced, even after the decline of the monastery, by the aura of learning that emanated

141

from Iona, whence St Columba sent out teaching missionaries far and wide across Britain, and even to the continent. At its height Iona was a centre of great learning.

In the days of the clans it was the prerogative of the families of the chiefs and the leading families to send their children to southern colleges for their schooling; there were no colleges nearer than in the southern cities. By the middle of the eighteenth century the influential islanders were becoming aware of the desirability of greater education and social polish. A convention of chiefs met at Aros Castle, then a place of some importance, to consider the possibility of establishing a centre where Highland youths could receive adequate education. Soon after this the rising of 1745 and the aftermath of Culloden destroyed those local ambitions and no college was ever established at Aros or anywhere else in Mull during the painful times that followed those events.

Leading Mull families engaged tutors for their children. For a time Thomas Campbell the poet served there in this capacity, and at Sunipol, near Calgary, he learned much of the island's traditions and folk lore that were to inspire some of his finest work.

After the Union of the Crowns in 1603 determined efforts were made by the Privy Council in Edinburgh to set up new standards of culture and education in the Highlands and Islands. One of the provisions of the Statutes of Iona (1609) was that sons of the unruly chiefs were to be sent for academic training to the centres of education in the Lowlands, and some success did follow this measure. It was followed in 1616 by a decree that a school should be set up in every parish. One of its objects was to discourage the general use of the 'barbarous' gaelic language, which was considered a barrier to culture and learning.

The General Assembly of the Church constantly pressed for the implementation of those measures; but it was only when the Act of 1616 was ratified in 1633, and more organised education demanded by the powerful Covenanters after 1638, that some improvement took place, although only in the more convenient districts of the mainland. Salaries of teachers were to be raised by levies on the owners of land, but for the next 200 years they were quite inadequate.

In common with the other Hebridean islands, the remoteness

142

Page 143: (*above*) A young descendant of the Highland kyloe; (*below left*) home-carved crooks exhibited at Salen Show; (*below right*) a very old leister (salmon spear), made by an island blacksmith

Page 144: (*above*) Weighing and boxing salmon for the Glasgow fish market; (*below*) shearing blackfaced sheep at West Ardhu, Dervaig

of Mull discouraged the early or easy establishment of state schools and it was principally through the effort of the Church that schools were finally set up. At first a few elementary subjects were taught, but almost entirely to boys. By 1795 there were in Mull three parish schools (one in each parish), one charity school, and four church schools ('for Christian knowledge'). There were a few girls' schools where simple domestic subjects such as spinning and sewing were taught. Later on, in the middle of the nineteenth century, these were quaintly described as 'schools of industry for young females'. The fact that one such school was conducted in the upper storey of Tobermory jail was no reflection at all on the young females; on the contrary, so many years had passed since the jail had been used for its original purpose that some of its unwanted space was turned over to the benefit of the public.

The earliest schools are described as highly unsuitable. Any hovel could serve as a school, and the teachers' emoluments were dishearteningly meagre. The Parochial Schoolmasters' Act of 1803 brought a much-needed improvement into a population which was becoming more socially conscious, and in 1824 a further advance was made when the General Assembly, acting through the local Kirk Sessions, began to finance and more actively establish additional schools. From that time a more effective co-educational system began to develop in Mull.

The confusion of schools which persisted throughout most of the nineteenth century—parish, church, gaelic, charity, etc—was regularised by the Education (Scotland) Act of 1872, whereby all schools, with a very few exceptions, were taken over by the State, controlled by locally elected School Boards, and financed by Parliamentary grants. From this the modern system of education developed, with amending Acts in 1918 and 1929 which transferred the control of education within each county into the hands of an Education Committee of elected councillors.

By 1845 there were seven state schools in Mull. It was unfortunate that at first lessons were taught in the English tongue, to the bewilderment of a gaelic-speaking community. However, this rule was wisely revised soon after then, though in any case the English tongue was slowly but surely replacing the native gaelic.

There were seventeen schools in 1900; today there are eleven, including the secondary school at Tobermory, and one in Iona. With the one exception all are junior schools. In common with other non-academic secondary schools, Tobermory was designated a Junior Secondary school in the 1940s. However, the title is misleading, for the school continues to be, as in the past, one of Higher Grade standing, with full academic courses including up to three languages. The former course of three years was raised to four in 1962; so Tobermory is now (1969–70 session) a four-year secondary school, with a staff of thirteen, presenting candidates for the Scottish Leaving Certificate 'O' grade. It is sometimes officially designated as a Senior Secondary school.

There are at present 125 pupils, of whom 60 are in the secondary department. It must be remembered that Tobermory school draws its secondary pupils from the northern areas of Mull which can be reached by a daily conveyance; for other pupils away from their homes lodgings are provided in the town, but not without some difficulty, as there is no school hostel. This explains the seemingly disproportionate number of pupils centred on a little town with a population of just over 600 and an average annual birthrate of nine.

In 1969 a fact-finding survey of intelligence of children in the western isles revealed an average intelligence quotient of 85, which is that of unskilled labour. Tobermory (and Mull as a whole) was no exception to this standard. It seems strange, therefore, that ex-pupils from Tobermory continue now, as in the past, to achieve university degrees, including first-class Honours. Teachers consider that this can be attributed to the more effective nature of the education received by continuous attendance at a four-year school for as long as possible, where in the case of Tobermory classes are smaller and individual attention much greater. This may be borne out by comparing education in the north of Mull with that in the south, where pupils at a comparatively early age have to go to Oban Secondary school for all their secondary education. Here they are accommodated in a school hostel, absent (except at week-ends) from the steadying influence of home life, and being taught in larger classes with less individual attention. Their chances of success seem to be less, for comparatively few pupils from Mull, outwith the Tobermory area, have attained a university degree in the last twenty years.

A former pupil of Tobermory school, Duncan Livingstone, who emigrated to Natal, left a handsome endowment of £2,500 to the school when he died in 1965. Besides providing bursaries for former pupils attending universities, it provides funds for use within the school, which is now thoroughly up to date with a television set, a record player, radio, tape recorder and a sailing dinghy, all of which are profitably used.

Attendances in other Mull schools show this uneconomic teacher-pupil ratio, and it may be for this reason, as well as the social appeal of Mull, that there is no shortage of teacher-applicants when a post falls vacant. Several isolated schools have been closed down, for example, the tall gaunt building between Ensay and Torloisk which once served the now deserted townships of Rhudle, Crakaig and the neighbourhood. The school bus now conveys the pupils from scattered farms and cottages to convenient centres. An example of this daily journey in the island is worth describing. It concerns the two children who used to travel daily to and from Pennyghael school from Inch Kenneth (the family left the island in 1968). They were up at seven o'clock, summer and winter, ferried across the half mile of sea to Gribun in the little motor boat, picked up there by the school bus, and conveyed along the wild coast road and through Glen Seoilisdair the seventeen miles to Pennyghael, on the south shore of Loch Scridain. The same route was followed when returning home every evening.

There is a proposal to establish a residential training centre at Aros, Tobermory, which, if achieved, would be of immense benefit to the youth of the island and of the adjacent mainland. Here they could be trained in arts and crafts, fishing, agriculture, forestry, etc—crafts and skills directly linked with the life of the island.

POOR RELIEF

There were no poor in Mull in the old days, when the people were self-supporting. Problems only arose when the economy became unbalanced, with immediate repercussions on the level of subsistence, as at the time of the collapse of the kelp trade, of the potato disease, or of the clearances of the mid-nineteenth century. In 1843, in the parish of Torosay alone, there was an average of twenty-seven cases of abject poverty, each receiving a grant of 12s.

Care of the poor and destitute was a service administered and financed at first by the Kirk Sessions. Collections for the poor were taken at the churches, and to this were added the fines imposed by the Sessions on people found guilty of immoralities, along with any charitable contributions. The Parish Councils gradually took over this and other secular services, and a more organised system of local administration arose. The District Councils, their successors, now carry on the work, although the main services are the responsibility of the County Council.

After the middle of the last century Tobermory had become overcrowded with dispossessed and destitute people, desperate for any work they could find, and living as best they could in huts and outhouses. Their plight became so bad that the authorities decided to build a central establishment somewhere near the town for the care of the poor not only of Mull, but also of Morvern, Ardnamurchan, Coll, Tiree, and Moidart. Accordingly, all these parishes co-operated in building what was called the Mull Combination Poorhouse, a huge, rambling building which stands in five acres of ground enclosed by a shining loop of the Tobermory river just over a mile up the Dervaig road.

Built in 1862 at a cost of £20,000, it was designed to accommodate 140 people in two large wings of two storeys, one for men, the other for women. There were fine offices, storerooms, kitchen, laundry, bathrooms, a joint dining hall—and even a pulpit provided there for the minister who conducted a service every Sunday afternoon. The buildings were surrounded by walled gardens and fields of arable ground; there were piggeries, a stable, henhouse, blacksmith's shop, etc, with all necessary tools —everything to encourage the will to work on the part of the inmates.

It was a well-run establishment; people were cared for, and even allowed little luxuries. However, the intensive depopulation of the islands and ultimately the introduction of the Old Age Pensions Act in 1911 caused the numbers of inmates to dwindle until in 1925 the six remaining—and they were all geriatric cases —were transferred to Oban, and the building was sold for £400 to a private buyer. Now it is partly demolished, partly ruinous, an eyesore in that lovely hollow, and an object of curiosity for strangers. Its stonework would be better used to widen the narrow and dangerous bends of the main road which runs beside it. Better still, it might be adapted to house new industries around Tobermory.

This is an attractive little town—as the local people like to call it—which rises in terraces above the finest and most picturesque harbour in the Hebrides. It must be about the smallest burgh in Scotland, administered by a Provost, two Baillies, honorary Treasurer, Dean of Guild, and four Councillors. Hampered by a low valuation and faced with constantly increasing expenditure, Tobermory has administrative difficulties which could be overcome by surrendering Burgh status and being absorbed into the landward area of Argyll county; but the town it not yet prepared to give up the prestige that goes with that status.

The town was created a burgh in 1875. In the petition to the Sheriff of Argyll it is interesting to note the appearance of such names as Yule and Noble, most unusual in Mull. They were the descendants of the east coast fishing families settled here by the Fishery Board soon after Tobermory was established as a fishing station by the British Society for Encouraging Fisheries in 1789 (referred to on page 190).

The impressive courthouse was built in 1862. Here the Sheriff held monthly diets until the early 1920s. It now serves as police station and District Council offices.

In 1882 a fine water supply was laid on from a reservoir built two miles above the town beside the Dervaig road at a cost of £6,000. The Mishnish Lochs, a mile further up the road, were tapped in 1967 as an additional source of supply, while the old pipes were renewed, and choked filters modernised, at a cost of about £100,000. The effect of this on the rates was catastrophic, requiring an increase of about 8s in the £, while the outstanding debts for capital works were practically doubled. Some idea of the cost of running this Burgh may be had from the figures of the County requisition for 1966–67.

Police £1,469; Roads and Bridges £2,629; Health £1,920; Education £15,944; Court House £8; Child Welfare £197;

National Assistance Act £500; Weights and Measures £69; Valuation, etc £318; Fire Service £402; Miscellaneous £209: Total £23,665.

To this has to be added the administrative expenditure of the Burgh itself, roughly £13,000. Before the impact of the new water development, the rates payable for 1966–67 were 16s in the £; in 1969 they were around 25s.

The Burgh owns sixty-two houses, and has plans to extend the housing scheme within the next few years. Considering its small financial resources, the public services in Tobermory are kept up to a good standard.

In 1969, to mark the fiftieth anniversary of the setting up of the Forestry Commission, the policies of the former Aros House

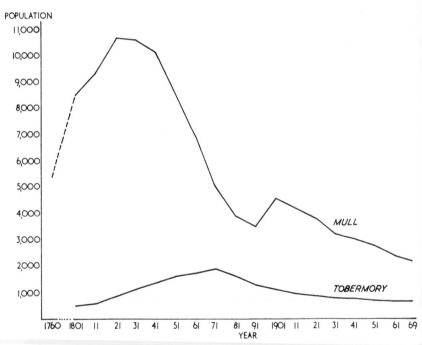

The trend of population in Mull and Tobermory from 1760 to 1969. The rapid growth of the eighteenth century reached a peak in 1821, after the return of soldiers from the Napoleonic wars. While the island's population fell steadily thereafter, the number of people in Tobermory itself rose to a maximum about 1871 as the evictions gradually cleared many of the country settlements

150

were handed over by the Commission to the Burgh of Tobermory as a public park. This site lies on the south side of Tobermory Bay, about a mile distant, with access along a picturesque path skirting the bay, and also inland from the Salen road to a new car park at the site. Within its amphitheatre of cliffs, and backed by a small lake, with a magnificent display of rhododendrons gathered over the years by four generations of the Allan family (former owners of the policies), this park is an attractive addition to the amenities of the town. About the turn of the century the Allan family gifted to the people of Tobermory the two-storey building known as the Aros Hall, containing library, reading and committee rooms, and a hall to seat 300.

Once a prominent landmark across the bay, the original Aros House (known then as Drumfin—white ridge—House) was built early in the nineteenth century by the Macleans of Coll, who used it as a winter residence. In 1860 it was bought by a land speculator (together with the whole Aros estate), who partly drained Loch na Mial in a fruitless search for bog iron. It was then sold to Farquhar Campbell, who resold it in 1871 to Bryce Allan, great-grandfather of Mr A. H. Allan, the present owner of the estate in 1969. The 'Lands of Arrois' extended from the Aros river (Salen) to Loch Frisa and the Mishnish Lochs, and included most of the town of Tobermory. Drumfin House was reconstructed in 1873–4 and its name changed to Aros House, which is often confused with Aros, the postal district of Salen.

Then in 1954 part of the estate, including Aros House and woodlands, was sold to the Forestry Commission. This fine house was finally demolished in 1962, and in 1969 the rubble was used to construct the car park for a new public park. Mr Allan resides at Linndhu House, which lies about a mile from Tobermory along the Salen road.

Tobermory's chief economic disadvantage—especially now that the harbour focus has been moved to Craignure—is its lack of small industries. Space for these is not lacking, and it may be that strong and urgent representations that have been made by the Mull and Iona Council of Social Service may achieve some supporting action by the Highland Development Board. From whatever angle one considers it, Tobermory is far too attractive a little town to be allowed to die. The rateable value of Tober-

151

mory in 1966–67 was £14,135; that of the rest of Mull was £28,168, and a penny on Tobermory's rates yields only £60.

The population of Tobermory has, like that of the whole island, fluctuated widely in the last 250 years. There were fewer than 200 folk there when it was established as a fishing port in 1789. The maximum population for Mull was in 1821, while in Tobermory, with rural depopulation, it came fifty years later.

	Population of the whole of Mull	Tobermory only[1]
1801	8,539	456
1811	9,383	550
1821	10,612	850
1851	8,369	1,540
1871	5,017	1,850
1891	3,465	1,265
1911	4,173	900
1921	3,754	850
1931	3,160	772
1951	2,693	693
1961	2,343	668
1969	2,100	610

[1] For years when census figures have been unobtainable estimates based on official reports and other sources have been used.

By the middle of the nineteenth century the number of people in Tobermory had soared with the influx of dispossessed families seeking locally in Tobermory what Mull people now emigrate to seek in the industrial south—security of employment. A witness before the Land Court at the end of last century said of the town :

'There is not a poorer place in creation than Tobermory; for when the people were swept away from their lands and houses they had to take refuge in barns and behind dykes; and all kinds of outhouses were brought into requisition to shelter the people driven away from their places.'

In 1892, in spite of the benefits of Poor Relief, there were seventeen families in Tobermory bordering on abject poverty. Like the rest of Mull, Tobermory was to see its population dwindle away through lack of work and the attractions of the mainland.

9   THE ISLAND CULTURE

T HE interchange of ideas and social intercourse with neighbours and strangers is naturally limited for island-dwellers by their confining sea barriers and by the restrictions of their economy. The people of Mull long since developed a distinctive character. Acutely aware of the supernatural, yet devout worshippers, they were in the days of the clans devotedly attached to the land and their chief. They are still good church attenders, but no bigots; not given to emotional display, yet highly sentimental; ostensibly polite and kind to strangers, yet basically suspicious and reticent, a trait perhaps inherited from the bitter lessons of the past. Any suspicion of patronage or 'talking down' condemns a stranger—and memories are long in Mull.

The mysticism of the ancient Celts, the quick change from depression to gaiety, the vivid imagination, all are still found in Mull as throughout the western isles. The islander's character was forged in fighting for survival against other clans, against disease, poverty and famine, even against the elements, and, seemingly, the worst struggle of all, during the eighteenth and nineteenth centuries, against the despair that both God and man were heedless of his existence.

As workers the Mull folk are slow, methodical and conscientious, with a belief in the elasticity of time that is typical of western folk of the British Isles; but only an unintelligent stranger would dare to describe them as lazy and shiftless, an insult that may arise from the curious belief that the industrial south has a monopoly of efficiency and hard work. Nevertheless, there is a regrettable lack of initiative in commercial development within the island. It is disappointing to find lacking in Mull many minor services which might profitably be carried on if only some commercial development would be encouraged and maintained, even as sidelines. For instance, fish has to be imported from the main-

153

land fishing ports; nearly all vegetables and soft fruits are imported; there are no commercial laundry facilities; there is no honey production, though the heathery moorlands could yield plenty. There is not even a barber's shop on the island, although in Tobermory there is a ladies' hairdresser whose services are much in demand.

One must recall that emigrants from Mull, a supposedly lazy and unprogressive environment, have in the past participated in the pioneer movements that established the first outposts of the British Empire. Compelled by social and economic privation to leave their island home, the ordinary crofting folk took their characteristic toughness and conscientiousness—and doubtless their insularity and pride—to help to found early settlements in inhospitable environments in Canada, Australia or New Zealand.

However, while there seems to be opportunity for more self-help within the island, its unusual lack of sophistication is in itself an attraction for the visitor. Perhaps there is something about Mull as an island which casts a spell on its residents, as happened in the land of the Lotus Eaters?

Mull people who live and work far from the island tend to congregate in order to preserve the atmosphere of home. This is a characteristic of the folk of other Hebridean communities, such as Uist and Barra, Skye, Islay, and elsewhere. In 1866 the Mull and Iona Association was formed in Glasgow (always a magnet for the islanders) with the objects of providing opportunities to meet, to foster the art, literature, and music of Mull, and to assist cases of distress among their people. In 1966 the Association celebrated a centenary of steady expansion and the full implementation of its objects. Generations of hard-working and enthusiastic office-bearers have included some of the most prominent people in Mull. The annual concert—the 'Mull and Iona'—is one of the most popular of the many clan society functions held in Glasgow, and many people travel all the way from the island to be there with their friends on that night.

GAELIC LANGUAGE

The gaelic language was, in times past, one of the distinctive characteristics of the highlands and islands, and, since speech and communication are so important in human relations, one of the most significant regional features. The progressive unification of the British Isles has involved the gradual elimination, or the suppression of regional social characteristics; in the case of gaelic speech, as of Welsh, it has survived longest, and relatively late in history, in the remoter western enclaves and islands. Through the intervention of political, religious and economic mainland influences on an island like Mull, there has been a change from the monoglot use of gaelic, through a stage during the nineteenth century of the English tongue being generally understood if not habitually used, to a present-day situation where gaelic is habitually spoken only by the older generation.

In 1881, 88 per cent of the population could speak gaelic; in 1961, only 38 per cent. In 1881 over 800 people could speak only gaelic; in 1961, only 2. The Burgh of Tobermory, as one might expect, has always shown a lower proportion of gaelic speakers —about 4 per cent below the average figure for Mull—through the presence of a larger ratio of residents not indigenous to the island and its traditional ways.

Census year	Speaking both gaelic and English	Speaking only gaelic	Non-gaelic speakers	Total population
		(Included in previous column)		
1881	3,395		431	3,826
1891	2,351	634	480	3,465
1901	3,293	454	810	4,557
1911	3,056	209	908	4,173
1921	2,595	83	1,076	3,754
1931	2,254	35	871	3,160
1951	1,281	15	1,397	2,693
1961	882	2	1,459	2,343

The most important factor that affects the language is the method of education, and the process of deterioration in the state of the gaelic language has been accelerated since 1872 when a national statutory system of education was established in Scotland, in which the English language was the medium of instruction. The acquisition of education has long been valued by the islanders, but in the question of language, the desire to learn has conflicted with their cultural heritage. Some fifty years ago it was considered a social offence to be heard talking in gaelic within the precincts of certain schools—a situation that left some of the

155

children almost tongue-tied. The paucity of modern literature, even of school books, published in gaelic, and the evolution of the English language itself in a time of technological change have added to the difficulties of survival for the gaelic language.

Since 1918, the official educational policy in Scotland has been to include gaelic in the school curriculum as a special subject for gaelic-speaking pupils, which nowadays usually means that it has to be taught in English like a foreign language. It remains to be seen how strongly, and for how long, the language can be preserved, and therefore to what extent the cultural heritage of the island, much of it shared with the other islands, can be opened to coming generations.

The gaelic language is described as plastic, copious, and expressive. Its finer shades of meaning are untranslatable, best summarised by the man involved in a heated discussion who averred in exasperation—'I would tell you what I thought of you in the gaelic, if I thought you had the education!' The spoken English of the island is soft, slow, lilting, and in childrens' voices fascinating to listen to. It is grammatically pure, subject only to lapses in construction caused by speaking a form of English which is basically translated gaelic, as for example, 'I will be going' instead of 'I'm going'.

It might be said that the people have the softness of the rain and sea mists in their voices. Exaggerated vowels—as in the 'o' or 'a' sounds—are quite absent; in fact, in Mull the substitution of diphthongs for straight vowels is regarded as affectation. So also is the misuse of the letter 'r', slurred, omitted, or intrusive, as in the case of southerners, who in turn consider the letter over-exaggerated by the islanders. The letter 's' is soft and sibilant; 'j' becomes 'ch'; 'b' is softened to 'p'. One might compare what a southern ear would hear in Mull speech : 'Hwen we gott outt off the poat, thèr wass the stack chust pesite the rrock', with what the Mull man would hear in an English voice: 'Wen we got aout ov the bowt, theh waz the steg jawst besyde the wock'.

STORY-TELLING

Besides its music and songs, Mull has a long heritage of story-telling, of which more is said in the chapter on folk-lore. Story-telling was a popular art and the variety of tales endless. Until the veneer of modern sophistication began to submerge the old ways of life there was also a very real background of superstition. Fairy people were believed to live in every dun (old fort) and mound; a water-horse or water-bull had its lair in every loch and deep dark pool.

The *ceilidh* was (and still is to some extent) a popular occasion, when neighbours met informally to join in the traditional story-telling, joking, music, dancing, and harmless conviviality. Dancing could almost be called a form of indoor athletics, for such energetic dances as the reel, schottische and strathspey were the rule.

Among the gaelic-speaking islesmen of Mull humour in story-telling and joking has none of the slickness and artificiality of the south. It is natural, spontaneous, literal, and closer to the things of daily life. The art of exaggeration is freely drawn upon. A story attributed to Callum-nan-Croaig, reputed to have been Mull's greatest raconteur (who lived about the end of the nineteenth century) illustrates this : 'I wass good at tieing the flies—for fishing, you know. One night I wass busy at the kitchen table getting some ready to go to the loch next morning. Well, ass fast ass I wass finishing one I would put it down on the table in front of me; but next time I looked up, it would be away. Aal right! The next one I made, I chust put it down, then sat back and lit my pipe and watched. Do you know, I wass tying them that good the spiders wass coming down from the ceiling to take them away !'

These stories are typically long drawn out, with lengthy descriptive asides which, if translated word for word into English, would lose their nuances and become simply tedious. The art of repartee is also well developed. Never be deceived by the apparent slowness of a Mull man; he is one jump ahead of you all the time. The Staffa and Iona cruise boat was one day lying beside Tobermory pier with a full complement of passengers. One of them leaning over the rail nudged his companions and, indicating a shabby uncouth figure standing vacantly at the edge of the pier, he remarked, 'Watch me take a rise out of that chap.' Pointing to the Marconi wireless mast (the 'Big Pole' of the wireless station which stood for many years above the village), the tourist called out, 'I say, my man, can you tell me what fruit grows on that

157

tree?' Back came the unhurried answer, 'Inteet yess, sir; electric currants'.

MUSIC

Mull folk have music in their blood, and few of the isles of the Hebrides have such a heritage; in the words of an old song, 'Morvern for sword play, Mull for a song.' The social evolution of the people is expressed more vividly in music than in the written word. At the national Mod, the annual festival of gaelic music and language organised by An Comunn Gaidhealach (The Gaelic Society), which is held in turn at various centres in Scotland, natives of the island have repeatedly been awarded the gold medal, the top award, not only as individuals, but also as families, such as the three MacMillan sisters of Dervaig, whose voices have enthralled audiences since the 1930s, and as composers and translators with a gift for expression, like the late Kenny MacFarlane, of Tobermory. In contrast, Mary MacDonald, of Brolas, near Bunessan, a simple country woman born in 1817, with no knowledge of written or spoken English, composed that lovely hymn that is translated as *Child in the Manger*. Greatest of all the songs of Mull is of course the anthem of the island, *An t'Eilean Muileach* (The Isle of Mull), a song from the heart by Dugald MacPhail, the bard from Strath Coil, written and composed when working in distant Newcastle. This was a favourite set piece of the famous but now disbanded Glasgow Orpheus Choir.

Naturally, the music of Mull has the sea in it, in all its moods, most forcefully expressed in the *iorram* or rowing songs, in which the rowers, swinging in unison, sing in a kind of undertone one of those exquisitely beautiful songs, half-recitative, half-melody, with a rousing chorus in which all the occupants of the boat join. It is almost oratory set to music—all in time with the swing of the heavy oars, the click of the thole pins, and the quick slap of wavelets against the bow. There are also gay and rollicking airs with mischievous wit, such as *Callum Bheag* (Wee Callum), a song of forty-six verses describing the highly imaginative voyage to Glasgow and back by a man who had never before been in a boat.

Music was the medium which used to lighten monotonous

158

manual work such as weaving, milking, butter-making, and wauking (shrinking newly woven cloth). The love songs have a wistfulness, the sadness of parting, while the dance music, gay and energetic, overlaps into another style of singing, the *Port-a-Beul*, or mouth music. This is a rapid, rhythmical, tongue-twisting, repetitive style of singing, imitative of the bagpipes, and formerly used as a substitute at dances where a piper was not available. This is now just another form of singing and no longer replaces the bagpipes. Wherever a Mull man finds himself he is transported back to the island in imagination by a few bars of one of its nostalgic songs—*Fionnphort Ferry, Mull of the High Cool Hills, I'll See Mull, Mull of the Mountains, Leaving Lismore, The Sound of Mull, Farewell to Fiunary, The Boatman*; in the words of Yeats,

'I hear lake water lapping with low sounds on the shore;
While I stand on the roadway, or on the pavement gray,
I hear it in the deep heart's core.'

The art of bagpipe playing has for long been associated with Mull. Bagpipes are a very ancient musical instrument—one early Greek coin bears the impression of a man playing an instrument that closely resembles the Highland bagpipes. In the great days of Clan history there was a pipers' college in Ulva run by the McArthurs, hereditary pipers to the MacDonalds, and second only in prestige to the famous MacCrimmons of Skye, where McArthur had his early training. The Rankines were the hereditary pipers to the Macleans of Duart.

In *The Lost Pibroch* Neil Munro says 'To the make of a piper go seven years of his own learning and seven generations before. If it is in it will out . . . if not, let him take to the net or the sword'. How often those words are recalled when one listens to the gifted family of pipers, the MacFadyens of Pennyghael, who over the last twenty years have collected an impressive array of trophies and awards for piping all over the country. Let the critic of the bagpipes put aside prejudice and prejudgement and substitute a measure of toleration and concentration—but above all, hear the pipes played by a first-class exponent in the natural setting—woodlands and the open air; then of a sudden he may 'stand at the start of knowledge, and leaning a fond ear to the

159

drones he may have parley with old folks of old affairs . . . stand by the cairn of Kings, ken the colour of Fingal's hair, and see the moon-glint on the hook of the Druids!'

Nowadays the violin and piano-accordion have ousted the bag-pipes at the dancing; old time dances are fewer in number, and the young folk conform to the fashions of the south. The island folk are no different in appearance from their mainland cousins. The kilt is not worn by the man-in-the-street as a regular article of dress; sometimes it may be seen worn by a rare enthusiast, either a visitor to the island, or one of the local lairds. Wireless, television, and an easier interchange of population have led to general conformity in habits, as in popular music and social activities.

DRAMA AND ART

Within the communities, social life has tended to become narrower. There are still occasional ceilidhs and concerts, and the activities of Church social organisations, the Womens' Rural Institute, and the Drama Group. In the schools, drama activities have been taken up with enthusiasm, and the children reach quite a high standard in open competitions.

A new theatre development was inaugurated in 1965 when the Mull Little Theatre was opened at Dervaig. The theatre houses an audience of no more than forty, and its summer programme of serious modern plays has been widely acclaimed throughout the country. All the parts are acted or spoken by the two princi-pals, sometimes with the aid of puppets and tape recordings. These two enterprising people, Mr and Mrs Hesketh, are both experienced in stagecraft and broadcasting—and additionally they run an adjacent boarding house. Initiative of this kind has met a real need for entertainment both among residents and visitors. Reorganised as a private limited company, the Dervaig Arts Theatre Limited has an ambitious programme for expansion.

On the other side of Mull, at Tiroran, a barn has been fitted up as a small cinema with modern seating and projection, and occasional shows are given. The travelling cinema also visits the island at infrequent intervals and presents films in the village halls.

In the superb setting of Carsaig Bay, among the trees over-looking the curving beach, a residential school of painting was opened in 1967 by Julia Wroughton, ARCA, ARWA, at her home, Innienore Lodge, where, between April and October, up to a dozen amateur artists are catered for. A small pottery was added to the school in 1969.

OUTDOOR ACTIVITIES

In summer, when time allowed, the men-folk used to compete in strenuous athletics, trials of strength such as weight-lifting, putting the stone, or tossing the caber. This last sport, now formalised at Highland games throughout the country, is supposed to have originated from the skill and strength needed to raise the 'cabers' or rafters when building the roofs of houses. Wrestling and running were popular—there was plenty of agility in the people of such a hilly island. According to *The Gael*, men of past generations are visualised as 'leaping from crag to crag and engaging in manly sports demanding brawn and muscle, or crossing dirks and claymores at the tiniest hint of a personal insult'. Dr Johnson and Boswell had as their guide in Mull Col Maclean (Maclean of Coll), who 'could run down a greyhound, adjusting his pace, which the dog would not'.

Formerly the young men of Mull were keen on the game of shinty, and exciting matches used to be held on New Year's Day and other holidays up to the turn of the nineteenth century. It is played very little now in the island, although in some other parts of the highlands, such as North Argyll and Inverness-shire, it is still popular. Matches in which teams compete for the *Camanachd* (Shinty) Cup arouse even more enthusiasm than football. Shinty is a free-style form of hockey in which the *caman* (stick, which is often home-made) may be raised to any height in hitting the ball. It closely resembles the Irish game of hurley.

Pastimes are now thoroughly sophisticated. Tests of strength are confined to the Highland Games held at Tobermory every July. In August the Regatta (Tobermory), the long-established Salen Show, and various sheep-dog trials are popular tourist attractions. Yachting has its local followers (there is an enthusiastic yachting club at Tobermory) and the attraction of the seas and lochs around Mull bring thousands of yachtsmen from all over Britain. Tobermory is the centre, but there are plenty of

K   161 anchorages in the many sheltered lochs and inlets. Increasing numbers of young people are coming to explore Mull, and a hostel, open all summer, has been set up in Tobermory by the Scottish Youth Hostels Association.

Fifty years ago there was a wave of interest in golf in Mull. Courses were laid out at Calgary, Glengorm, Salen and Craignure, in addition to the sporting little course at Tobermory, and one in Iona. Facilities on most of them were rather primitive, and the courses were all of nine holes or even fewer; however, enthusiasm was high, and for a few years inter-club matches were played. The Tobermory course, overlooking the harbour and the Sound of Mull, has one of the most picturesque situations in the Hebrides. Established in 1896, it was transferred for many years to the fields above the Poorhouse, a mile along the Dervaig road. It returned to its original site at Erray (above and north of Tobermory) in the 1930s, and is now the only course in Mull. A 9 hole course of 2,324 yards, with a Standard Scratch Score of 64, its many hazards make good scoring anything but easy. It is now run in conjunction with the nearby Western Isles Hotel, whose guests are entitled to free use of the course. Local membership is 60, and it is open to visitors in the summer months.

Angling enthusiasts will find plenty of scope in Mull, for every loch and burn has its indigenous stock of brown trout. The extent of salmon and sea-trout fishing is limited by the terrain, but some is readily available on private waters at a moderate fee. Far too much uncontrolled brown trout fishing is carried on in waters that are too readily accessible. Visitors often regard this sport as a free-for-all, and questionable methods of catching fish are too often used—such as bubble float bait fishing on lochs which should be reserved for fly fishing; as a result the quality of the fishings on such lochs has deteriorated. In common with similar areas Mull would benefit from stricter angling laws, and at local level, by the formation of angling clubs which would be of immense benefit to all concerned.

FAMOUS MULL PEOPLE

Natives of Mull have filled many important positions and entered most professions. Up to the seventeenth and early eighteenth centuries, Mull was famous throughout the Hebrides—and further, even to the Royal Court in Edinburgh—for its doctors, who were referred to as simply the *Ollamhan Muileach*, or Mull doctors. This was the Beaton family who lived at Pennyghael, where the enclosure in which medical herbs were once grown used to be pointed out by older residents. They were hereditary physicians to the Lords of the Isles, and later to the Macleans of Duart.

The Beatons traditionally passed on their medical skill from father to son. Medical manuscripts which are still preserved (in the Advocates' Library, Edinburgh, in the British Museum, and in a few private collections) not only record the ancient arts of medicine, but also have genealogies of the family. There are still Beatons in Mull, but no direct link can now be traced with the famous doctors.

After several years of research a history of the Beatons has been published. It was prepared by Dr G. H. Beaton, Willowdale, Ontario, and his father J. H. Beaton, who are descended from a Ross of Mull family which emigrated to Canada early in the nineteenth century. They have located two distinct genealogies which suggests that there were two branches of the Beaton doctors, one originating in Ireland, the other in France, who may have become connected through intermarriage. The Irish branch is traceable, through one or more of those old manuscripts, from the seventeenth back to the fourth century, to Niall of the Nine Hostages, King of Ireland. The other goes back through the Bethunes of Skye (also doctors in that island) to the Bethunes of Balfour in Fife, and much earlier to the Norman knights who came into Scotland in the twelfth century, when the name Bethune first appears. It is associated with Bethune in the Pas de Calais. A copy of Dr Beaton's history can be seen at the Ancestry Research Society in Edinburgh. The name Beaton has varied in spelling from ancient times. 'Beath' was one of its earliest forms, and from this derives MacBeath or MacBeth, Son of Beath—or Son of Life as it is aptly translated. The name Beaton probably came into common use in the seventeenth century when this spelling, and a large number of variants, are documented.

There is a story told about John Beaton, who was said to be the greatest doctor of his time, whose simple advice to the people

163

in his care was 'To be cheerful, temperate, and early risers'. He was summoned to appear before the King of Scotland, along with twenty-four other leading physicians, to undergo a test which would decide who was the most skilled among them. This took place probably at the Court of King James VI in Edinburgh, at the end of the sixteenth century, before that monarch took up permanent residence in London after the Union of the Crowns in 1603.

The test set by the King was to feign an illness which had to be diagnosed by the medical men without seeing the Royal patient. A specimen of urine was provided for examination, which, however, was not that of the King. Beaton was the only one to call his bluff, and for his discernment he was admitted to the Royal favour. In fact, it is recorded that in 1609 James VI granted a charter to 'Fergus McBeath, of Ballinaby', possibly the son of this same John, confirming in him the office of 'Chief Physician of the Isles' as well as in his hereditary title to lands, which presumably were connected with John's successful consultation in Edinburgh.

There is a sad sequel to the triumph of John Beaton. Soon afterwards poison was administered to him secretly by his jealous rivals, who with a healthy respect for his skill first of all took the precaution of hiding all the antidotes for which the expiring doctor called in his last agonies.

The medical branch of the family appears to have died out in Mull in the early eighteenth century. Rev Dugald Campbell, writing in the Statistical Report of 1795, mentions 'a large folio MS in gaelic, treating of physic, which was left with a woman, the heiress of the Beatons, seen by some now living; but what became of it the incumbent [Campbell], after all his inquiries, could not find. It is perhaps lost, as the heirs of this woman are quite illiterate.'

The memory of the Beatons is preserved in a cairn erected above the shore of Loch Scridain near Pennyghael. It is surmounted by a cross whose shaft bore the initials of two of the Beaton family and the date—GMB 1582 DMB—although the lettering can now hardly be traced.

A colourful sixteenth-century islander was Ailean nan Sop, Allan of the Straws, so called because his first act after being born

164

out in the barn was to grasp a handful of straw. He was brother of Eachann Mor, twelfth chief of Duart. As a youth he took to the sea, and throwing in his lot with the Danes, who still occasionally raided the islands, he rose to be admiral of their raiding fleet and the fiercest pirate who ever roamed the Hebrides. Later he gave up his roving life and retired to his native Loch Tuath, where he is (wrongly) said to have founded the family of the Macleans of Torloisk. His tomb is in Iona, where his body lies under one of the carved slabs in Relig Oran.

One of the most famous natives of Mull was Major-General Lachlan Macquarie of Jarvisfield (an estate which included Salen and Gruline) who was born in 1761, son of a small farmer in Ulva. Later the family moved to Oskamull, near Ulva Ferry, where his mother lived until her death. Lachlan MacQuarie rose to be Governor-General of New South Wales in 1809, in which office he continued for the next eleven years, retiring honoured and respected as the 'Father of Australia' to his native Mull, where he died in 1824. He is buried with members of his family in the mausoleum at Gruline which was maintained in his memory by the National Trust for Australia, now by the National Trust for Scotland. In 1808 he established the village of Salen, with sixteen crofts, a blacksmith, a tailor, carpenter, and weaver, also a shoemaker, with an inn and a shop. Salen is one of the few places in Mull to have expanded naturally during the last century.

A famous member of the Clan Maclean was Colonel Sir Fitzroy Donald Maclean, Chief of the clan and twenty-fifth of his line, who after a lapse of ownership for 220 years purchased back the ancestral home, Duart Castle, which was restored and formally opened in 1912. Sir Fitzroy, who had fought in the Crimean War, died in 1936 after reaching his 101st year. The present Chief, Sir Charles H. F. Maclean, brought the name of Mull into almost every corner of the world during his extensive travelling as Chief Scout.

The late Neil Cameron, who belonged to Tobermory, rose to be the head of a large fashion and textile business in Sunderland. He donated £50,000 to expedite the building of Craignure pier.

Carrying on the traditions of their warlike ancestors, Mull families have made the Regular Army their profession and sent

165

high-ranking officers to every war of the last 250 years. In the Napoleonic wars up to 1815 there served in the British Army five generals, one lieutenant-general, three major-generals, seventeen colonels, three lieutenant-colonels, eight majors and seventy-eight officers of lower rank. During the same period one admiral and a number of officers served in the Navy, mainly in the Marines. Many of those men were Macleans. The rank and file of Mull men would themselves have made a formidable army, many of the tenants following the laird to the wars. Conditions were different when it came to the Crimean War and the Indian Mutiny. Only a handful of Mull men served at the Crimea, including Colonel Sir Fitzroy D. Maclean of Duart, who has been mentioned earlier. The people of Mull could well have repeated the words of an old Ross-shire man uttered at a recruiting rally at the time of the Crimean War. The Duchess of Sutherland (whose lands had been subjected to wholesale clearances) had expressed her disappointment at the lack of response by her tenants: 'The people are all gone,' cried the old man, 'you can send your sheep.'

The old Volunteers of the last century, and the later Territorials, attracted numbers of Mull men. Like so many of the islands, Mull sent a higher than average proportion of its male population to the two world wars, especially into the Navy and Merchant Navy. The Argyll and Sutherland Highlanders was naturally the regiment most favoured, together with the Argyll Mountain Battery and the Scottish Horse.

Typical of the inshore fishermen-crofters were the MacDougall family, who fished entirely for their own requirements until the export of lobsters became profitable. There were two families, who lived at Haunn, Treshnish, where their dwellings existed from the beginning of the nineteenth century and may still be seen, some in ruins, some converted to holiday cottages. In past times the men-folk were not above running the still below Crakaig which is described on pages 188-9.

One of the last surviving members of the families was Alick MacDougall or Alick Ban (fair); he was also called the Rubber Man because of his great strength and endurance, in spite of having a leg crippled by an accident when serving in the Royal Navy during the first world war. Well-loved in the community, he spoke gaelic in preference to English, and had a store of old gaelic songs, most of which—regrettably—died with him unrecorded in 1961. He also had a wide knowledge of local lore and history, for he had spent his whole life on and beside the seas and islands off Mull. Alick's first words on going out of doors were never 'What's the weather like?' but 'How's the tide?'

One of his stories reflects the experience and supreme confidence of the hardy fishermen in handling a boat. One morning during the second world war, he rose early to prepare his gear for setting lobster creels. In his latter years he was no longer staying at Haunn, but at Quinish, two miles north of Dervaig, where his tiny cottage and store stood beside a natural jetty formed by a geological dyke in the sheltered inlet. Then (in his own words), 'Ass I wass going to the chetty I saw a great big mine, with its horns sticking out, floating in with the tide chust fifty yards from the shore. I knew if this went off in here it would blow the house and the poat, and maybe maself, to bits. So I got a length of pig-iron I used for ballast and lashed the end of a rope round it, and put it in the stern of my wee dinghy that wass tied up pesite the chetty. I pushed her off with the oars and backed up to the mine. Well, I got a grip on it by the bottom of the horns and turned it over 'til I came to a ring bolt; so I tied the end of the rope to that, put the pig-iron overboard for an anchor, and pushed the mine away. I rowed to the shore, had my breakfast, then walked in to Dervaig to telephone the Mine Disposal to come. Man, I wouldn't care for their chob! When they wass making the mine safe I wass half a mile up the hill behind a rock with my hands over my ears!'

Romantic and historical references to men of the past may be found scattered about the island. For instance, in the old graveyard which lies almost forgotten within a pine wood near the sea at Gruline, there are two interesting tombstones; one bears the inscribed story of an ensign who fought at Waterloo. The other reads: 'James Stewart, died 1828, aged 22. A relative of Prince Charles Edward Stewart'—though so far it has not been possible to find the connection between this young Mull shepherd and the Prince.

AROUND the coast of Mull, on the small patches of *machair* and in a few favoured spots, such as the lower fertile hill slopes with natural drainage, the level raised beaches and flatter areas on some of the smaller islands, the people used to win a bare living from the land in past centuries. The clan territory was worked by families jointly, several cultivating their plots on the inbye land, with crops of bere, oats and, later on, potatoes, while their cattle and sheep—which were then roughly equal in numbers—grazed on the common pasture land on the hill. Some upland grazing could be got in the summer, the women-folk taking the stock up to summer shielings. The wealth of the islanders lay in their cattle for, in time, these became an 'export product', driven on the hoof and shipped to the mainland markets. At that time the lands were not enclosed and the drove roads passed through areas that yielded grazing to passing herds, including those in transit from more distant islands.

Cultivation was a laborious task, carried on in an often inclement climate. The arable land, cultivated in rotation in lazybeds, narrow raised strips, was fertilised by the application of seaweed and shell sand carried up in creels from the shores, of manure accumulated during the wintering of the stock in byres, and by the old and sooty thatches when they were replaced on the houses. Implements were primitive; the cumbersome *caschrom* or foot plough was used. The art of tile drainage was as yet unknown and waterlogged but fertile land remained unreclaimed. Crop yields were often low; some barley and oats yielded only three-fold, potatoes (introduced during the second half of the eighteenth century) only four-fold.

There was no incentive for the individual to set about improving his plot or his crops, because in winter his land was open to pasturing beasts, along with his neighbour's. Nevertheless the people drew a subsistence from their lands and used what nature provided in the way of fertilising agents and timber in a way of life tied to the land until the social and economic eruptions that started in the eighteenth century.

In more recent times some of the fertile waterlogged land has been reclaimed by field drainage, though the potential extension of the arable area is restricted by the nature of the relief and the elevation of much of the land—rather less than half of the total area of the island lies below the 500ft contour. The introduction of improved seeds, modern fertilisers, implements and motor-driven vehicles has both improved the output of the land and eased the lot of those who still farm these marginal lands. Nevertheless present-day farming on Mull is a very different proposition from farming on the lowlands of the mainland. The amount of land level enough to cultivate occurs only in small patches, and while the climate is comparatively mild it is also cloudy and rainy. The small crofter-farmer has increasingly had to contend with the problems that beset small farmers on marginal land throughout the country in times of rapidly increasing industrialisation and changing economic relationships overseas.

However, the resources and opportunities for alternative work on the island are limited; tourism, much talked of as a panacea for island ills, can occupy only a part of the whole year. Some 31 per cent of the effective labour force of Mull were occupied in farming and forestry in 1969, a total of 259 persons. Of these, 95 were farm employees, mostly full-time and mostly men. The number of people employed on farms is steadily declining—there were 147 in 1962.

Many farm owners and tenants themselves undertake the whole operation of the holdings, where the size of the farm or lack of capital cannot justify employing labour. In terms of the area of crop and grass land on holdings (ie excluding the rough grazing land), well over half the farms are under 20 acres. The Ross of Mull had far more of these small holdings than either of the other two agricultural regions in 1969 (the regions coincide roughly with the parishes).

Crop, fallow and improved pasture land actually occupies only 3 per cent (6,723 acres in 1969) of the total area of Mull, but the farm holdings have a much larger area in rough grazing land, notably in central Mull where the larger farms and estates lie.

Area of crops and grass	Number of holdings		
	North Mull (Kilninian and Kilmore)	Ross of Mull (Kilfinichen)	Central Mull (Torosay)
Under 5 acres	29	23	23
Between 5 and 20 acres	23	45	14
Between 20 and 50 acres	18	33	5
Between 50 and 150 acres	12	8	5
Over 150 acres	3	–	–

The following data derived from the agricultural returns of June 1969 illustrate the regional differences.

Region	Number of holdings	Area of crops, fallow and grass (acres)	Area of rough grazing (acres)	Dairy cattle	Livestock Beef cattle	Sheep
North Mull	85	3,418	61,357	38	2,292	28,977
Ross of Mull	109	2,394	44,277	12	1,550	23,768
Central Mull	47	911	82,736	36	1,030	25,580
Mull	241	6,723	188,370	86	4,872	78,325

The numbers of farms in the north and centre have declined markedly since the 1920s, but in the Ross of Mull, where crofting has had a stabilising influence and where forestry plantation is less intensive, changes have been less evident. This is the region where common grazing land is most extensive. There were 10 common grazings in the Ross in 1969, totalling 10,262 acres, in contrast to 3 in the north (2,350 acres) and 2 in the centre (391 acres). These rough hill grazings are shared by a number of farming units whose stock may become intermixed on the open hill. There is a legal entitlement to the continuing use of the grazings which has ensured their preservation; for instance, the common grazings on the hills above Tobermory were granted to the settlers when the town was established as a fishery station, and the right to graze livestock was embodied in their charters in the same manner as the perpetual grant of land for building.

CROFTING

In the agricultural economy of Mull crofting plays only a small part, compared with the thriving crofting communities in Lewis and Harris, and in Skye. There are in fact only 31 crofting holdings, one in north, one in central, and twenty-nine in the Ross of Mull. Here, at the extreme south-west of the island, the crofts lie between Bunessan and Fionnphort, at Ardtun, Kintra and Uisken, and in Iona. There are tiny crofting villages at Kintra and Uisken, but the old thatched cottages are gone, being replaced now by modernised, but still substandard houses. Lacking the wide *machair* lands of the real crofting areas, with a cattle and sheep rather than a purely agricultural economy, Mull never developed as a crofting island.

Agricultural methods have been brought up to date, but only within the limited capacity of the under-capitalised crofters. Subsidies on livestock figure largely in their incomes. Common grazings within the area are still shared by the neighbouring crofters, whose cattle may be wintered there, or brought within the owner's enclosed fields, or confined within the byre (with the extra problem of providing winter fodder) when the winter is unduly severe.

Few of the crofts—even the largest—can provide a living, and the holder himself must work long arduous hours when it is financially impossible to engage helpers. In most cases income is below subsistence level and crofters are obliged to engage in part-time work; in fact, they can turn their hands to a surprising number of sidelines, as varied as forestry work and house-building. Some inshore fishing is carried on, but in order to augment the food supply rather than to bring in cash.

Rights of tenancy for crofters were secured by the Crofters' Acts of the late nineteenth century but, by other provisions, these measures also fixed the holdings in an unchangeable pattern which prevents progressive development of the farm land to keep up with modern technical and economic agricultural changes.

Crofting, like agriculture generally, is steadily declining in Mull, and is carried on mainly by an older generation. Unless some effective form of encouragement is introduced at official level its future prospects are poor. Crofts, as agricultural units,

171

may cease to exist if a proposed enactment converts the crofter-occupier into crofter-owner-occupier, with powers of disposal. If Mull develops as a holiday island, land of this type may become a new and valuable capital asset for the crofters.

Highland cattle, as we know them today, were originally the small black hardy breed known as kyloes, which were particularly adapted to the highlands and islands through their ability to thrive on the natural coarse grasses of that environment where other breeds could hardly find a living. They became the mainstay of the economy of Mull, the main source of cash for crofters and small farmers. By the end of the eighteenth century Mull was exporting 2,000 head of cattle a year, excluding the transit herds from outlying islands, to markets in the Scottish lowlands and the English lake district, for they stood up well to the rigours of droving. On some of the grassy islets even a certain kind of seaweed was added to their diet. Their shaggy coats protected them in the damp changeable weather, and with their sturdy frames and restless disposition they fared better on the open range than in confinement.

The enclosing of lands, begun on the mainland early in the eighteenth century (although not until the last quarter of that century in Mull), began to speed up after the rebellion of 1745. Access to wayside grazings along the traditional drove roads of the mainland became so restricted that herds were forced on to the longer, harder military roads, where animals were sometimes shod. Gradually competition came into the cattle trade from growing herds in Aberdeenshire and later from imported foreign beef, while the intensification of sheep grazings through the nineteenth century ousted the cattle from their pastures. Despite advances in scientific breeding and feeding since 1800 the cattle-carrying potential of Mull has failed to expand. Old records of the Agricultural Society state that in 1814 there were between 80 and 100 breeding cows in the two small offshore islands of Staffa and Gometra. The owner of those vanished herds was MacDonald of Staffa, a famous cattle breeder and progressive landowner. In 1815 he sold a herd of three-year-olds at an average price of fourteen guineas per animal. In the same year he sold for 130 guineas a bull for which he had refused an offer of 200 guineas two years earlier. Another bull realised 100 guineas. Even allowing for the depreciation of the value of money these prices reflect the quality of his stock.

Early in the nineteenth century, driven to take action perhaps by the increasing profits being made through the rearing of sheep, cattle owners began to cross-breed the kyloe with certain mainland strains in an effort to produce a larger-boned animal carrying more beef which still retained the hardy nature and economical grazing habits of the original kyloe. The resultant breed is the picturesque shaggy Highland animal, with colourations shading from cream and light brown to dark reddish brown, with the rare appearance of the original black. Experiments in cross-breeding Highland with Beef Shorthorn cattle in the island of Luing, south of Oban, have produced the new and highly successful Luing breed which was registered in 1965. Hardy, docile, wintering well in the open, as well as quicker maturing than the Highland breed, and able to graze freely at and above 1,000ft, it is ideally suited to Mull, where it has been successfully introduced into four of the main herds.

Mull now supports just over 5,000 head. The rising cost of maintenance has meant withdrawing them from such rich outlying grazings as the Treshnish Islands and centring them in more accessible places like Torloisk, Ulva, Glen Aros and Glen Forsa. Although potential expansion is still very great, it is inhibited by the island's unbalanced economy; the cattle have to compete with sheep and afforestation for both land and capital.

SHEEP

The indigenous Mull sheep were akin to Soay sheep, often four-horned, a small animal yielding only a quarter the products of the heavier mainland breeds. As cash-earning exports they were valueless to the eighteenth-century crofters. After 1745 flockmasters from the southern uplands of Scotland gradually extended their sheepwalks northwards, bringing larger hardy stock to the highlands. By the end of the century Cheviot flocks were widespread in Mull, superseding the indigenous stock by about 1810 as the landlords turned their lands over to the more profitable leasing to the flockmasters. For a time there was a rich harvest in rents and produce; in 1843 the parish of Torosay alone realised £17,500 from the wool crop.

The intensification of sheep grazing during the nineteenth century not only exacerbated the rate of emigration amongst evicted and unemployed crofters and their families, but also destroyed the cattle grazing lands, which became seriously over-cropped and fouled. Grazing sheep also damaged tree seedlings and checked woodland regeneration. In the end deserted sheep lands became infested with bracken and rabbits and in places reverted to peat and sour bogland.

Although sheep rearing in Mull has suffered a setback through imports of foreign wool and mutton to Britain, the island continues to support a considerable number of sheep: about 80,000 Blackfaces, of which 20,000 are exported annually. This trade, along with the wool crop, is important to the island's economy, though a better balance between sheep and cattle would, it is believed, be more profitable.

PONIES

Hill ponies, a small type of garron, used to be bred in Mull in association with cattle and sheep rearing. They were used for carrying loads—creels of seaweed for instance—and for deer stalking. These ponies were famed for their endurance, believed by some to have been derived from the strain introduced from a few horses of Andalusian breed landed from an Armada ship in Tobermory Bay. Few ponies have been raised since the 1920s. Recent interest in riding and in pony-trekking holidays may cause a revival in pony breeding on Mull.

FORESTRY

Afforestation is frequently a cause for controversy, for there is a conflict of interests between the farmer, the sporting-estate owner and the forester. In Mull the Forestry Commission is now the largest land-owning body and the plantations are extending steadily.

The first land was taken over by the Commission in 1924 on the Aros estate, followed between 1928 and 1930 by areas at Lettermore (Loch Frisa) and Fishnish (near Craignure), a total of 1,700 acres that now produces about 5,000 tons of thinnings annually. Post-war expansion of the forests started in 1952, on ground that came on to the market through the abandonment of sheep and cattle farming and the termination of leases. By the autumn of 1967 the Commission had increased its holdings to 38,000 acres, of which the Department of Agriculture managed 16,000 acres on behalf of the Commission. Of the remaining area, nearly 10,000 acres are now under trees, plantings amounting to 1,000 acres a year. A proportion of the total holdings—under rocks, gulleys and bog for example—is unusable.

The plantations are chiefly of Sitka spruce (57.6 per cent), which has proved to be the most adaptable, and Japanese larch (12.3 per cent). Larch is often planted for aesthetic purposes and as windbreaks. The plantations are healthy, with few traces of disease which cannot readily be eliminated. During severe gales there is some loss through wind-throw, but on a surprisingly small scale. Red deer—and sheep—will nibble the tender growing points of young trees, and the cost of fencing young plantations for protection against them is £15 per acre. Wire netting of $1\frac{1}{4}$in mesh was formerly required to exclude the hordes of rabbits that infested the island, but their extermination by myxomatosis in the early 1950s eliminated this need. One enemy of very young trees, which it damages by gnawing and ring-barking, is a species of the humble vole peculiar to Mull, which is so far confined to the Ardmore plantations. The Mull Forest will mature and come into full production after 1980.

The steady employment that the Forestry Commission provides is greatly welcomed in Mull. Permanent work is ensured for a labour force of about seventy foresters and twenty casual road-makers. A basic wage, augmented by 40–50 per cent piece-work, provides a reasonable standard of living. The Commission has also brought new amenities to the island, in the form of houses and new roads. Housing is provided for the forestry workers, as well as agricultural holdings (now nine in number). In addition to houses built by the Commission, Argyll County Council has an expanding programme of house building centred on Aros (Salen) and Bunessan. There is one chief forestry officer based on Aros, with deputies at Dervaig, Kinloch and Craignure. Little increase in the labour force is likely until the plantations reach maturity; even then, with mechanised techniques, little expansion may be required.

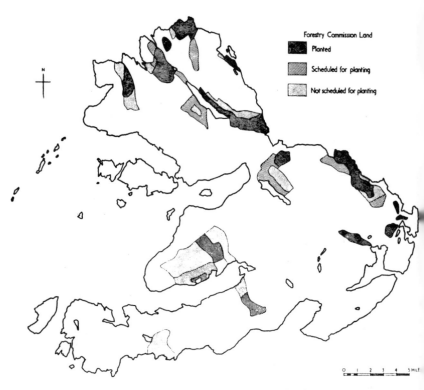

The distribution of Forestry Commission land

The output of the Mull Forest will be taken up by the Wiggins Teape pulp mill at Fort William and it is unlikely that any local timber-processing industry beyond a chipping plant and sawmill will be set up in Mull itself. At present timber is shipped by a small timber-carrier boat from Craignure to Fort William, but there is some doubt as to the ultimate adequacy of Craignure pier, which is designed to store no more than 100 tons of timber. Moreover, the existing roads in Mull are unsuitable for economic load-weights for timber haulage; there is already an 8 ton limit on loads.

Unless there is an early halt in the decline of hill farming more land is likely to go under trees. The Commission and the Department of Agriculture work jointly to preserve a balance of land use and the Highland Development Board has conducted a complete land-use survey of the island which it hopes to publish late in 1970.

Local interests are closely watched by the Mull and Iona Council of Social Service and there is collaboration with the Red Deer Commission and the Nature Conservancy. The Forestry Commission therefore is endeavouring to compromise with the interests of all these agencies. Nevertheless some over-hasty plantations have been made on valuable agricultural lands, at Aintuim, Aros, Lettermore, Gruline, Tiroran, Kilfinichen, Fishnish and Ardtun, which have aroused some bitter criticism in Mull farming circles.

FARMING VERSUS FORESTRY

Land acquired by the Forestry Commission loses is productivity so far as stock raising is concerned, for it quickly reverts to sour bogland or is invaded by bracken, and it may be several years before it is planted to trees. Moreover the normal periodic burning of heather is restricted on moorland grazings adjacent to young plantations, thus inhibiting the regeneration of the grazing. After the trees are tall enough to escape the attentions of browsing animals, the fences are allowed to deteriorate. Grazing stock can then wander into the woodlands—for shelter or to escape the flies in the heat of summer—and it is difficult to observe and control them. More serious than these causes for concern, however, is the spread of Forestry Commission acreage at the expense of both arable land and marginal grazings (as opposed to upland grazings).

The Forestry Commission is not unsympathetic to farming land use though many farmers may not agree, and some agricultural areas are incorporated within its boundaries. Good-quality land, at low altitudes, is to be set aside as holdings for forestry workers or as large-scale tenanted farms run by the Department

L   177 of Agriculture. In Glen Forsa the cattle herd run by this department is a successful venture and confirms the fact that cattle raising on progressive lines can be quite profitable, despite the heavy overheads.

THE FUTURE OF FARMING

Because farming is of paramount importance in Mull's economy if it is to continue as a living island, the satisfactory solution of several problems is essential. The search for the right road to prosperity is shared by all Hebridean islands. Some of the factors in the problems are external, such as the vagaries of the beef trade or the consequences of the attempts of a distant government to ameliorate the islands' ills by legislation. Others are internal—the inherited attitudes of island farmers and crofters, their lack of accumulated capital, and the sheer physical fact of insularity. Yet others are the result of the historical combination of internal and external factors that has led to the emigration of young folk from the island and to the misuse of the land.

The solution is believed to lie in the expansion of cattle breeding—to quote Fraser Darling, Mull is cattle country equal to the best in the land. The best use of that land would be the rearing of large numbers of stock of reliably high quality for sale to mainland farmers for fattening on richer lands in the south. In many respects Mull is more favoured than other islands: it is in a more sheltered southerly location and nearer to the mainland markets; and over much of the island, because of the underlying basalt rock, less acid grassland conditions could be achieved through improvement. Whether this solution can be achieved in the face of existing conditions would involve considerable changes in the attitudes of the islanders and of the government as well as in practical land use and economy.

Under existing conditions sheep farming is a vicious circle for the small farmer or crofter tenant of a small or medium sized holding. He has little or no capital to invest and the balance of his economy depends on the Hill Sheep Subsidy; he cannot afford to improve his stock which gradually deteriorate in quality. Direct, unconditional subsidies per head of stock are not to the advantage

178

of the quality of the sheep, and it is considered that subsidies should be related to land improvement or reclamation, fertilising and fencing of pastures and selective breeding. Annual subsidies are at present 23s per head for hill sheep plus 1s 6d for winter keep. Hill cows, on the other hand carry a subsidy of £16 5s, calves over eight months £11 for a steer, £9 for a heifer.

The balance of grazing between cattle and sheep, that has come about since sheep grazing ousted the cattle, now represents a gross misuse of the land and, frequently, the under-use of the uplands. The best cattle grazing land lies below the 500ft contour, on the wet moorlands carrying molinia grass. Above that generally lie the high acid grazings of fescue-agrostis grassland which are excellent for sheep. But sheep take first place in the farm economy now and they graze unrestricted on the lower grounds. This practice has led to the deterioration of potentially very good cattle grazings, since sheep by their feeding habits destroy or retard fresh growth. They do not, as cattle do, trample down young bracken which invades poor pastureland and their droppings do not enrich the soil, rather do they sour it.

Fundamental to the improvement of farming conditions on Mull are the reclamation of former cattle grazings and marginal land and the extension of the arable area. If more ground could be put under the plough and grassland could be improved to yield an annual hay harvest for silage, the age-old problem of winter fodder for the cattle could largely be overcome, thus reducing the island's imports, though an initial and recurrent investment in the materials for improvement would be necessary. Intensively used arable ground could also yield vegetables to meet the demand created by tourists. Private experiments in reclaiming land have been successful, using deep ploughing to eradicate bracken, reseeding, fertilising, and treating the boglands with basic slag and lime. Minimum requirements for this treatment are three tons of lime and one ton of slag per acre. Towards the end of the 1960s and allowing for subsidies, the cost of spreading lime in Mull was 66s 2d per acre, compared with 43s in Dalmally, central Argyll, 22s in the Cotswolds, and 16s in Eire, an indication of the island's large handicap.

Livestock producers are in conflict with MacBrayne and the British Transport Commission over high freight charges and the

lack of convenient, co-ordinated transport, especially for imported fertilisers. No facilities exist to import and stockpile com-
modities in bulk at more competitive rates, such as might be done
by the car ferry at off-peak periods. While farmers are allowed
as a concession to transport empty vehicles on the car ferry at a
cost of 30s, the minimum loaded charge is £7 10s (30s per ton
load). The following freight rates for feedingstuffs and fertilisers
taken at random in the late 1960s indicate some of the overheads
the small Mull farmer has to find.

Glasgow to Mull (by sea, per ton)
½ ton or less   71s 2d
over ½ ton   60s 3d
10 tons   52s 5d
Oban to Mull (by car ferry, per ton)
1 ton or more   57s 8d

It costs 78s per ton to transport hay from Oban to the island by
car ferry. Outgoing charges are equally crippling. To transport a
calf from Mull to Oban costs 10s for conveyance to the pier, plus
11s 6d freight for the sea journey; for a lamb the respective
charges are 3s and 1s 7d. On land MacBrayne run stock floats
in the Tobermory, Salen and Ross areas. All these freight rates
are by no means stable, but periodic increases are not offset by
higher prices got for the livestock exported. The most recent
threat to the livestock trade is the reluctance of stockbuyers
to continue their agencies in Oban; the withdrawal of these
would involve yet another overhead expense to be borne by
the island farmer, on transport between Oban and southern
markets.

To expand cattle breeding in Mull would require a balanced
plan for sheep and cattle stocks and good management of the
grazings. Cattle numbers could be increased to some 22,000 and
sheep reduced to a similar total, reverting to the 1 : 1 ratio of the
early eighteenth century, and the two kinds of stock could be
allocated to the appropriate grazing areas. Such a scheme, however, could be successfully carried through only if the under-
capitalised small farmers would adopt a sufficiently forward-
looking approach, given the necessary government aid, *and* if
the size of individual units were rationalised—in general, that is

to say, increased. There are at present far too many flocks of uneconomic size struggling for a bare living. The larger farmers can market uniform lots of selected stock in worthwhile numbers which attract the buyers, whereas the small lots of the smaller farmers are passed over and obtain a poorer price.

The reorganisation of farming and the consolidation of hold-ings are not uncommon in current agricultural reforms every-where in the world and in many agricultural communities the days of the smallholder are numbered. Seen at close quarters and in the perspective of the history of the past 150 years in Mull, as in the other western islands, such a rationalisation of land use is hard for the small tenant farmers, once the backbone of the island's farming economy, to face. Their attitudes are largely con-ditioned by the struggles and the fears of their forebears and they may be very loath to relinquish the security of tenure achieved through the Crofters' Act of 1886. Subsequent Crofters' Acts (1955 and 1961) and the efforts of the Crofters' Commission since 1955, while attempting to preserve and reinvigorate crofting in the western highlands and islands, have not succeeded notably in changing the conservative attitude of the crofters and small farmers themselves. Young persons have continued to emigrate from the islands, leaving an ageing farming population, and incen-tive as well as capital have to be found to put through land re-forms of the kind described here.

The ideal size for a cattle-sheep holding is considered to be 1,000 acres. At present there are only some twenty units of this optimum size on the island. If the land is to be reorganised into units of this more economic area, for the sake of Mull's future prosperity, some small tenant farmers will be forced out of busi-ness. Economic rationalisation will inevitably cause temporary hardships.

The findings of an investigation of Mull's stock-raising possi-bilities, made in the mid-1960s, and quoted in the Mull Survey, 1965, are impressive. They even suggest that principles success-fully applied between 1960 and 1964 could be adopted as a long-term government policy in the island. On the basis of an area of 21,000 acres (assessed as the amount of land which could be improved with government aid), the outlay on improvement costs was estimated in 1965 to be :

181

5,000 acres ploughed, rotavated, reseeded, fertilised and slagged, at £35 per acre	£175,000
16,000 acres limed, slagged and surface seeded, at £15 per acre	£240,000
100 miles of fencing at £5,000 per mile	£50,000
	£465,000

It was estimated that this improved area would support 5,500 cattle (140 per cent increase on the number of cattle grazed there before the experiment) or 30 per cent more lambs, in each case with better breeding quality. A rise of productivity on this scale for a single grant of half a million pounds could barely be found by the government in the industrial world.

Livestock production has already been increased by as much as 50 per cent (and even more), through private initiative in the twenty-five years prior to the mid-1960s, on the very small number of estates or large farms which could afford to organise their businesses on modern lines. The authorities concerned with the future well-being of Mull—and of other islands, too—and the government should seriously consider a state-assisted scheme based on the principles of the improvements already shown to be successful, to benefit the ambitious but under-capitalised stock raiser, to help the general economy of the island and, with it, that of the country as a whole. At the same time the farmers of Mull would have to be willing to collaborate in the necessary reorganisation of some of the holdings, and the interests of those unable, for whatever reasons, to maintain larger holdings would have to be protected.

Afforestation and farming could be co-ordinated in a well-balanced policy—though this must be done soon, before a fifty-foot high carpet of green timber spreads too far over the island. Much new planting could be fitted in as shelter belts for existing arable land, giving the benefit of lusher growth and better cropping within the shelter.

11 INDUSTRIES PAST AND PRESENT

THE island's natural resources for economic development, other than pastoral farming and forestry, are very limited indeed. Of the industries developed in the past the burning of seaweed (kelp) probably had the greatest social impact, coinciding as it did with a large increase in population. Tourism may yet play an important part in changing some aspects of the island's economy—and its landscape. But the development of new light industry, with necessary financial investment in the island, is probably an essential accompaniment to a more rational policy for modern pastoral farming and forestry, aiming towards the stabilisation of Mull's population trend and economy.

THE KELP INDUSTRY

The kelp of the western isles is the *laminaria* seaweed, the 'tangle of the isles', which grows in vast beds, with long thick stems and large glossy leaves, especially on the western coasts of the islands. The beds are half exposed at low tide and there occurs a natural thinning of the weed, especially in the late autumn, when immense quantities of the tangle are torn from the sea floor by wave action and tossed up on the beaches. Originally the name 'kelp' was applied not to the weed itself, but to the alkaline ash produced after burning. In the early farming economy, the kelp, which is relatively rich in potash, was of great importance, for it was used as manure on the light shelly *machair* land, and with even more beneficial effects on soft mossy ground. In addition to kelp, every variety of seaweed was used for this purpose. The crofting family depended on providing sufficient labour to harvest this natural resource and to convey it to their fields. This was all part of a carefully balanced natural economy.

183

The exploitation of both the kelp and the people came when a new industry was developed which was profitable to the lairds but which led many of the crofters, who were by the nature of the island confined to live around its shores, into the harsh life of kelp burning. The industry originated in France at the end of the seventeenth century, when it was discovered that the alkaline ash, known then as *Soude de Varich*, obtained from calcined seaweeds, was an effective substitute for barilla. Although it was introduced into Scotland about the middle of the eighteenth century, and had a small measure of prosperity at the time of the American War of Independence, the rise and decline of kelp is more associated with the Napoleonic wars, at a time when the addition of the potato to the islanders' diet in fact led to an increase of population and a ready supply of labour within the island. The harvesting of what amounted to an export crop that had no part in the food economy contributed little to their welfare, for tenancy rights were commonly involved in the remuneration for their work. However, additional wages were usually paid to the workers, which although low according to modern standards were a new and valuable source of income in a community where hard cash was scarce. The crofters were sometimes accused of neglecting their lands by diverting too much kelp to the new industry instead of spreading it on the food-producing ground. Much profit went to factors and lairds, who were able to let out their shores for kelp collection and burning.

Kelp when burnt produces an impure alkali, which can be used in the manufacture of glass, soap and bleaching agents, and in the processing of linen. Twenty tons of tangle would be needed to produce one ton of kelp ash. This processing agent was originally imported largely from Spain, for the barilla is a maritime plant which grows around the shores of Spain, the Canary Islands and Sicily, and which is burnt for the soda ash thus produced. This source was cut off by the outbreak of the Napoleonic wars, and the kelp provided a substitute. When the Napoleonic blockade was broken, and barilla could again be imported, the kelp industry of the western isles collapsed, with far-reaching social consequences.

The collecting and burning of kelp was very hard, distasteful work and, being exploitive of the crofters' labour, was a degrading one. The work involved much hardship and required great physical endurance and in fact, the incidence of rheumatism in the Hebrides is described in the Statistical Account of 1845 to have been at its highest during the intensive period of the kelp industry. The plants were collected at low water by wading far in, and with the assistance of boats under suitable conditions, cutting the stems with a special long-handled hook, and dragging the tangle ashore. The load then had to be carried up to the drying and burning area in creels on the backs of every member of the family old enough to help, or on ponies, or in carts, according to the nature of the shore. After drying, the kelp was burned in kilns or trenches, or between carefully arranged layers of peat, where it melted down into a kind of slag. Burning was a skilled task, requiring that a close watch be kept on the temperature of the burning mass. A close watch was also kept by the buyers on the finished product, into which unscrupulous workers sometimes inserted stones or sand which affected both the quality and the price. In Mull certain of the lairds intimated that any tenant found guilty of this practice would be instantly evicted from his holding and prosecuted.

Mull produced about 600 tons of kelp ash annually, 8.5 per cent of the total production of the west highland region. At peak prosperity this brought in £12,000 to £15,000 in hard cash to the island. The alkaline content of the Mull seaweed was high, but its distribution was so affected by the nature of the rocky shores that the potential output was comparatively low. 'Kelp' included other forms of seaweed in addition to the tangle, which, although bulky, did not yield such high-quality ash as 'button wrack' and 'lady wrack', described in the Statistical Account of 1795 as being the best to use for burning 'unless the price is very high'. The chief centre was Loch na Keal (that is, Gribun, Ulva and Inch Kenneth), with other corners of the island adding their quota.

The profits belonged to the landlords. In order to attract workers they set aside land and divided it into what became known as 'crofts', with common grazings. Whole families who engaged in this seasonal work could earn as much as £8 in the year, a wonderful cash addition to the produce of their crofts. Rents in kelp-producing areas soared; in the twenty years ending

1791 the rents paid to the proprietors of the parish of Kilfinichen and Kilviceon alone rose from £961 to £2,711.

Thirty years later the kelp burning industry declined suddenly and rapidly. It was later restarted on a very small scale when it was discovered that iodine could be extracted instead of the unwanted alkali. As long as barilla could be freely imported there was no stimulus for a kelp-burning industry. But during the American War of Independence and the Napoleonic wars, not only were imports of barilla drastically reduced, but they also had to bear a heavy import duty. The price of kelp consequently soared—from as little as £1 per ton to a peak of £20. By 1825, however, the imports of barilla had been restored, and the import duty was repealed. By 1834 the price of kelp was down to £3 per ton. Workers suffered through loss of earnings; but some landlords, who had come to depend on this new and easy source of income to finance a wider and more luxurious way of living, were faced with ruin. This was one of the factors leading to the development of the sheep grazings and to the land clearances, account of which is given in chapter 5.

The Statistical Account of 1845 summarises the contemporary situation :

'The manufacture has entirely disappeared, with the exception of a very little made at Innis Kenneth and Gribun. Before barilla was allowed to enter our market duty free, and thereby exclude the kelp, there were no less than 150 tons annually manufactured in this parish [Kilfinichen and Kilviceon], and of course it, in common with the Highlands in general, has felt the loss . . . In previous years this manufacture employed and gave bread to many thousands in the Highlands and Islands, and the price it drew, . . . being circulated through the Kingdom at large, kept that money at home, which now goes to enrich the foreigner at the poor Highlander's expense; a measure of policy which cannot be too strongly condemned—for whether it arose from ignorance on the part of the Government, or from any other cause, the Highlands have since the admission duty free of barilla and other substances, presented scenes of much distress, bankruptcy, and poverty.'

Mull has not yet shared in the new industry producing sodium alginates from seaweeds, which started up in two places in the

Hebrides in the 1960s, the product being processed at two factories on the mainland. Kelp, bladder wrack and brown ware are collected, dried, crushed, bagged and sent in this compact form to the factories where it is chemically processed to yield alginate, a general name given to purified chemicals obtained from brown seaweeds. There are many uses for alginates: controlling the viscosity of food products, gel formations for various desserts, in pharmaceutical products, the formation of surface films, even the control of the rate of flow of welding materials.

Although Mull is reported to have too low a concentration of seaweeds to justify setting up a collecting and drying plant, yet thorough research and local pressure might attract such a unit, and thus diversify the island's industrial capacity.

DISTILLING

In 1823 a distillery was set up in Tobermory at Ledaig, at the foot of the Eas (Cataract) Brae, where the Tobermory Burn, flowing steeply down from the upland moors and peat bogs, enters the sea. The owners were John Hopkins & Company, of Glasgow. A conduit was built under the main road to carry the water of the burn straight into the distillery. The quality of the water was good —one of the vital factors in producing a good whisky.

Malt whisky of excellent blending quality was the type distilled here. The specialised process for making malt whisky with malted barley differs from the making of grain whisky, which uses a wider variety of grain, though including barley; distillation from mixed grain is a more continuous process, giving a correspondingly larger output. The average annual output from the Tobermory distillery between 1900 and 1920 approached 250,000 gallons of malt whisky. The registered brand was 'Old Mull', and to this day there is a popular whisky bottled under that name but, sadly enough, it contains none distilled in Mull. John Hopkins & Company Limited were taken over by the Distillers Company Limited in 1917, and production stopped in Tobermory in 1924. The distillery was dismantled and sold, and the site is now taken up by the generators of the Electricity Board. The former owners still carry on business under their original name in Glasgow, though as a subsidiary of the Distillers Company Limited.

This is a case of the eclipse of a valuable Mull industry through rationalisation. The more compact grouping and lower transport costs of the mainland distilleries at Glenlivet, just south of the Moray Firth, made the Tobermory subsidiary too expensive to run in comparison. In the island of Islay, on the contrary, the distilleries have remained under local ownership, and now provide an established industry for the island as well as a high excise revenue for the Exchequer.

In Mull, as well as in so many other remote districts, there was a large undercover industry at one time, right up to the early nineteenth century. This was one industry which flourished on remoteness and bad communications.

Whisky as a drink is a comparative newcomer. The art of distilling was known in the Middle Ages, but whisky did not become a popular drink until the mid-eighteenth century. Up to then ale was the drink of the people : in gaelic the term for a public house is *tigh leann*, which means an ale house.

In 1660 excise duty was imposed on *aqua vitae*, as it was called, but no records were kept until 1684. An Act was passed in 1736 to prohibit the manufacture of the drink, for certain varieties were being distilled as much as four times, making them so strong that a small glassful endangered life. This Act was bitterly resented; so the law was evaded, and smuggling and distilling became rife. In Mull distilling was carried on with impunity in such wild and remote corners as Carsaig, Burg, Lochbuie, Loch Ba, and Treshnish.

The foundations of a large still can be examined at the entrance to a deep dry cave below the old township of Crakaig, west of Torloisk. It lies at the base of the cliff, just above the reach of the highest tides, the only approach from inland being down a steep cleft or gully in the cliff. A zig-zag bridle path had been built down this, starting cunningly at the outer edge of the cliff above, which was passable for ponies carrying loads of peats and grain one way, and kegs of spirits the other. The staves of old kegs still lie at the inner end of the cave. A tiny stream had been diverted to drop across the front of the cave just a few feet from the still, conveniently close for cooling the 'worm' from the distillation pot—or *poit dhubh* (the black pot), as it was called. This sat over a furnace, a hemispherical hollow 8ft in diameter by 3ft deep, with an air duct led in from below, the whole enclosed in a circular platform of rocks 15ft in diameter. Outside the cave are the remnants of a turf wall which would have been built high enough to hide the reflection of the furnace from passing boats. The writer once lit a huge fire of driftwood in the furnace and watched how the dense smoke pouring out of the cave seemed to cling to the face of the cliff and dissipate. On the raised beach 120ft above the cave there are many bright green patches of former cultivation, where much of the barley was grown to supply the still. These plots of ground were worked right to the dangerous edge of the cliff; now they are covered with thick tangles of bracken.

The cove in front of the cave had a channel which had been cleared of boulders to allow boats to be run in. From here early last century the still was being operated by the forefathers of a local family who rowed and sailed all the way across to Ireland in their open fishing boat to sell some of their produce. Mull people must certainly have had the art of producing high-quality whisky, when they could compete profitably in the land of the poteen.

Another still of the same type, but much smaller, takes up one room in a tiny two-roomed cot-house, one of half a dozen or so lost and forgotten in a wood not fifty yards from the present main road in the north of Mull. A burn had been diverted to supply the cooling water.

Illicit distilling ended as an undercover industry in the 1830s, when it was enacted that the owner of the ground on which a still was found would be heavily punished along with the operators. Up to then the landowners, benefiting indirectly from the extra cash raised from spirits, were on the side of the producers.

It is a sad fact that Scotland is the only country in the world which has to bear the most penal excise duty on its own traditional drink, its *vin du pays*!

FISHING

With a maritime background such as that of the Mull people, one may well ask why there is no worthwhile local fishing industry. In 1789, as a result of several factors—industrial expansion on the west coast of the mainland of Scotland, the urgency of finding work for the expanding population, and the difficulties of obtaining salt privately under new tax laws—a fish marketing agency was set up at Tobermory. This was founded by the British Society for Encouraging Fisheries through the efforts of the then Duke of Argyll. The plan was to establish sixty settlers, including a few experienced men from the east coast, each with twelve acres of land, a common outrun on the hill, and rights of peat-cutting.

However, although the well-sheltered bay seems to be an ideal site for such a project, it came to nothing. Tobermory offered a good enough haven for the fishing fleets, but it was too near the commercial facilities of Oban to compete in the fish market. A good deal of reclamation of the foreshore was carried out, which allowed an extension of the main street across the burn, and the erection of a number of new buildings. Those improvements were of lasting benefit to the town, some local trading developed, and for some time a small boat-building business was carried on.

Fishermen from Tobermory and the whole of Mull had to face strong competition from larger and better equipped boats from the east coast, manned by professional fishermen whose livelihood depended entirely on fishing. The west coast fishing was for subsistence rather than for commerce, and the crofter fished for his family, using out-dated methods and equipment. There was further competition from foreign boats, which were exploiting the west coast from as far back as 1632, and which continue to do so to the present day.

About the time of this Tobermory venture the Duke of Argyll tried to establish a similar scheme in his own lands at Crieth, near Fionnphort. He granted individual loans of £25, repayable in annual instalments of £5, to help crofters to purchase boats, nets, and gear. He divided up a large farm to provide holdings for crofter-fishermen. This project failed after struggling along for a few years; but the agricultural side of it expanded and developed with the improving methods of cultivation. Today this is the only true crofting district in Mull.

There is no lack of variety in the fish to be caught around Mull: herring, cod, ling, mackerel, saithe, lythe, rockfish, flounders, plaice, sole, turbot, skate, and others. Along some of

190

the bays clams and oysters are found—in fact, experiments in growing oysters in Loch na Keal, at Kilfinichen (Loch Scridain) and a few other places might be rewarding, for natural conditions are good, and oysters are already established at the first two. Cockles, whelks and mussels are found all along the coasts.

One thriving industry is lobster fishing, and Mull contributes a substantial proportion of the west coast production. The lobsters are of excellent quality. Alick (Ban) MacDougall was one of the last surviving members of the old crofter-fisher family who lived at Haunn, Treshnish. He fished for lobsters round the coasts of Caliach and Treshnish, and the quality of his catches was so high that up to the time of his death in 1961, he had a firm order from the Cunard line to supply them with as many lobsters as possible for use on the *Queens* on the North Atlantic run. Careful packing and express delivery ensured that the lobsters carried well to the London market, and the inevitably high freightage was offset by the uniformly good prices obtained. The air-lift is now sometimes used for urgent consignments of this nature.

The lobster pot, or creel, is home-made; a flat board on which a heavy stone is lashed as a sinker, with semi-circular hazel withies fixed to support a net of stout cord or nylon, with a small built-in section for access to the bait, and to remove captive lobsters. The shellfish can enter by two opposed funnel-shaped openings, one of which is always exposed invitingly no matter how the creel is lying. The creels are dropped in water between five and twenty fathoms deep, near rocks, in lots of half-a-dozen upwards, and connected by one rope which is marked by a buoy.

Loss of tackle can be serious when a storm blows up with a heavy ground swell; worse still is the wholesale scooping up of 'everything that crawls' (as one exasperated lobster fisher described it) by large modern boats, often from the Brittany coast of France, which can smother a bay with modern gear and clean it out in a night, seldom observing the regulations governing minimum size under which our fishers must operate. Add to this the illegal inshore trawling by large craft which goes on, and some picture can be formed of what the crofter-fisherman is up against.

One of the largest lobsters to be caught around the British Isles was taken in Calgary Bay, below Craig-a'Chaisteal in the 1920s

191

by Alick MacDougall, who is mentioned above, and his cousin. Three feet one inch from tail to tip of feelers, the span of its claws was 2ft 10in. The circumference of a claw was 13in. Weighing over 12lb, it sold for £5 and it was on show for months in the window of a leading Glasgow fishmonger. Too large to enter and too greedy to let go, this monster clung to the top of the creel as it was drawn to the surface, where a rope was quickly passed round it.

Another profitable small-scale business is salmon fishing. Certain stretches of coastal waters are let to salmon fishers, whose nets are set across the tidal paths that the salmon follow round the coasts, especially off promontories and river mouths. The floating nets consist of two long leaders 12ft deep kept taut by a number of stakes which are held upright by the action of the tide against the floats on the surface and anchors below. Salmon follow the leaders (which are set at right angles to the paths taken by the fish) until they reach a central 'bag' in the nets through a narrow vertical slit, and through which they cannot easily escape.

The boat is drawn up against the upper edge of the bag, which is then manhandled to the surface, a detachable section opened, and the salmon taken out, killed, and stored in the boat. On shore the fish are weighed and packed in boxes holding a dozen or so salmon each of 10 to 25lb in weight. The boxes are taken by van to Craignure, where they are conveyed to Oban by the last car ferry of the day. The night journey to Glasgow lands them early next morning in fine condition for the fish market there. Total freight to Glasgow is £1 per box, of which 8s 6d is charged for the crossing from Craignure to Oban. Prices of salmon are good and reasonably steady, which serves to offset the high freight charge. Damage to nets can be severe and costly at times when seals pursue the fish into the meshes, or when basking sharks become entangled, and when they become dislodged in stormy weather.

The Herring Industry Board has suggested that a fish-drying plant could be set up in Mull to handle surplus fish from the Oban-Mallaig area, but no progress has yet been made with this idea. The White Fish Authority has been conducting experiments in fish farming at one or two centres elsewhere, that is, the rearing of fish from selected eggs or hatched fish, particularly flatfish, such as Dover sole, and feeding them to marketable size. This has proved to be successful in the experimental stages, so much so that fish farming might well become a crofter-fisher industry of the future, using submerged cages conveniently sited in sea-lochs and other sheltered coastal inlets. Mull would be an excellent area for such a venture.

At present there are four boats based on Tobermory, each operating independently with a crew of four, fishing for prawns and lobsters; this is a nucleus which may expand as time goes on. There are smaller centres in the island, often with only a single boat. A new and profitable line in sprat netting was introduced by one observant local fisherman. Observing fine scales on the wide meshes of some of his nets, and suspecting the passage of shoals of sprats, he tried out a few experimental 'shots' with sprat equipment, with very satisfactory results.

Tough endurable nylon has replaced the old cordage for nets, eliminating much of the constant examination and repairs formerly required. High freight charges are a deterrent to development. From Ulva Ferry it costs four guineas for one collection per week by motor lorry, and on the car ferry each box of fish costs 5s 3d, of prawns 7s 2d. Nevertheless transportation of this kind saves a ten-hour sail by the fisherman to Oban and back for direct disposal of his catch.

MILLING

In Mull's self-supporting community there were many small industries which developed to meet local wants, of which milling was one. Up to the middle of the nineteenth century there were at least six sizeable water mills actively working, each producing about 300 bolls of meal in the year (a boll was approximately 168lb). In 1892 there were still two oatmeal mills working, one in the Ross of Mull and one in the north. Water mills in Mull were used also by the grain-growers in the island of Tiree to grind the abundant harvests grown in this 'land of corn', as the name is said to mean. Mills were owned and run by landowners as profitable sidelines. Long ago the people were forbidden in some parts to use the small hand quern, as this would have deprived the mills of custom.

M   193

There were two types, the 'clack' mill, built directly over the stream which turned the wheel and delivered power through a vertical shaft and gearing; and the more conventional type where water led along a mill lade poured on to the flanges of a large revolving wheel which transmitted power along a horizontal shaft. The introduction of cheap foreign grain to Britain during the nineteenth century and of commercial milling have led to the availability of flour and oatmeal for import to the island and, as elsewhere, to a decline in the local grain trade and milling. Where formerly there were many small mills throughout the island, not a trace now remains except a place name such as Tom-a'Mhuillin and the faint line of the mill lade.

A small industry connected with milling was the cutting and shaping of millstones, some of which measured up to 5 feet in diameter. This was carried out at Gribun, where there is an outcrop, just above high-water mark, of a pebbly siliceous gritstone of Triassic age, which is of high quality for this purpose. It lies 150 yards west of the shed and garage of the Inch Kenneth ferry; one defective millstone can still be seen lying in the bed from which it was cut. Twenty or thirty millstones were made annually, and most were exported to the islands, from which boats or smacks came right inshore for loading.

THE TOURIST INDUSTRY

In recent years this has become a valuable source of revenue for Mull, as the statistics of the car ferry service indicate. The overall income is worth close on a million pounds annually when every angle is taken into account; but there is plenty of scope for expansion. If not properly controlled and correctly catered for and fitted into the economy of Mull it could lead to a false prosperity, and yet another exploitation of the land and the people in an industry that would flourish for a time and then decline.

Mull is not yet ready for tourism; the demand is far ahead of the organisation. Accommodation, for instance, is sadly lacking. It is estimated (1969) that hotels, boarding houses, holiday houses and caravans provide a total of 550 beds for visitors. During the peak holiday months the car ferry can bring a maximum of sixty

194

motor cars and their occupants to Mull on each of its three or four daily trips; the consequent shortage of overnight accommodation can be imagined. Most of the hotels and boarding houses are fully booked six months in advance; some holiday houses a year ahead. The problem is alleviated somewhat by the bed and breakfast service. Craignure, not Tobermory, is now the main dispersal centre of the island, and considerable expansion must take place there.

At Craignure a sixty-bedroom hotel, to cost £300,000, is projected for opening in the early 1970s, sponsored by the Highland Development Board, and to be run by the Scottish Highland Hotels group. This project has received only qualified approval from Mull people, who consider such a sum might have been more effectively spread over the whole island.

Mull, though still comparatively unspoilt, is becoming much better known. For instance, the island was chosen as the venue, in October 1969, for a major motor rally held under strict club rules, on a double circuit of ninety miles covered after dark. This was the first event of this kind to be held there, and with few objectors it met with the general approval of the local people; in fact it may become an annual event and a profitable off-season one for the island.

The Mull and Iona Council of Social Service encourages local projects and makes recommendations to the Highlands and Islands Development Board for the granting of loans, which by 1969 amounted to a cumulative investment of £100,000 in the island. Most of this is devoted to extending services for visitors.

Although there is a Tourist Association and an Information Centre in Tobermory, there is still a large gap to be filled to give full coverage on the island, including wider information on its many attractions. Mull has much to offer : places of historical as well as geological and archaeological interest; yachting; golfing; pony-trekking; hill-walking; fresh- and salt-water fishing; skin-diving; bathing beaches—all set in typical Hebridean scenery; but many of these amenities are still underdeveloped and have insufficient financial backing.

The establishment of a tourist industry in Mull to convert the island's natural assets into capital would demand the ploughing back of substantial profits in order to consolidate and expand local tourist services. One answer would be the formation of a Mull Tourist Board as a development company, invested in jointly by the Highland Development Board and the Mull people themselves, and covered by government guarantee. This would give scope for controlled expansion.

Reference is made in other chapters to quarrying and peat cutting, as well as to iron working. Most settlements had their local blacksmith or iron-worker, descendants of the craftsmen who forged and shaped the tools of war when those were in greater demand than agricultural implements. The word *gobhainn* (anglicised to Gowan) is the gaelic name for a black-smith; it appears in many place-names, marking the site of a former smithy, but the smithies themselves have, like the water mills, disappeared, except for a few workshops run as a sideline to cater for odd repairs. There is an excellent repair garage and service station at Tobermory, and smaller ones exist at Salen, Craignure and Pennyghael.

The arts of weaving and dyeing were naturally known in the old self-supporting communities. Heather, crotal (lichen), iris root, bog myrtle and the bark of certain trees were the chief sources of dyes—whose secret is now lost. Flax was grown for making linen. In 1789 the Duke of Argyll hoped to develop from this a small industry in yarn and net making, but this came to nought. Tweed weaving was started up in the 1950s in a disused church in Tobermory, but the business ran into financial difficulties and had to be closed down.

DRYSTONE WALLING

This began first in the district of Kirkcudbright, about 1710, after the passing of the early Enclosures Act. In Mull it was intro-duced in the late eighteenth and early nineteenth centuries to fix the marches between farms and the new estate boundaries, arable lands and grazings, and to contain livestock which had hitherto to be watched or tethered to protect the crops. Some of these dykes were massive, measuring as much as 6ft in height and 3ft in width at the base. Some of the heavy rocks used in the building had to be sledged or carried long distances over rough and hilly ground. The craftsmen who built the 'black houses' (whose walls were formed virtually of two high drystone dykes built close together, with an in-filling of dry peat) easily adapted their skill to the building of drystone dykes. In 1820 they worked from 7am until 6pm, walking time extra, for a weekly wage of 4s 6d plus an allowance of oatmeal. Now-a-days, when old boundary walls become ruinous, they are replaced by the stob and wire fence.

ELECTRICITY

Electricity for public use was first generated in Tobermory in the middle 1920s. A small hydro-electric generating plant was erected below the waterfall halfway down the Eas Brae, and driven by water supplied by a small storage dam built on the Tobermory river at Tom-a'Mhuillin Bridge. This supply was later augmented by a diesel generating plant, which was housed in the disused distillery buildings. A supply of power was extended from Tobermory to the adjacent district of Mull.

In 1947 the undertakings at Tobermory were acquired by the North of Scotland Hydro-Electric Board. In that year the diesel units had a capacity of 92kW, and the hydro generator 25kW. Together they gave a total output of about 96,000kWh. Between 1950 and 1953 the Board expanded the service by installing additional generators, until by 1964 the total capacity had been increased to 1,575kW; in 1965 the Tobermory plant (which also supplied Iona) had an output of 4,254,000kWh.

Then in 1966 Mull was connected to the mainland grid of the Board by two submarine cables, one crossing the mile-wide Sound of Mull from Ardtornish (near Lochaline) to Fishnish Bay, north of Craignure, the other running from Oban across to the Island of Kerrera, then crossing for four miles under the Firth of Lorne to Grass Point. Since 1966 the Tobermory plant has been on stand-by duties.

The Electricity Board offered favourable terms to the first consumers when power was brought into their district; later consumers had to pay a very high connection charge unless the power lines passed close to their house. Installation costs can be estimated roughly at £70 per pole. One owner was charged about £800 to bring a domestic supply by overhead poles from the mains line about three-quarters-of-a-mile distant. Torloisk is the only district of importance still lacking electricity, but a survey was made in 1969 with a view to extending the supply there within two years.

SPORTING ESTATES

In Victorian and Edwardian times sporting estates provided steady employment for gamekeepers, stalkers, boatmen, and domestic staffs. An extract from the records of a large Mull estate illustrates the employment conditions of the time (30 September 1865):

Servants who are worth keeping and necessary for the place :–

Gamekeeper W. Curie	£45 a year, pint of milk per day or a cow's grass, and seven tons of coal per annum.
Forester J. McGregor	15s a week or £40 a year, pint of milk and his bothie [his bed, bedding, and fuel]. Unmarried. A good servant.
Ploughman J. Campbell	£24 a year, milk, house, 6/7 tons coal. £6 10s in lieu of $6\frac{1}{2}$ bolls of meal and 12 barrels of potatoes per annum. A first-rate man.
Gardener G. Cruikshank	14s a week; wants 17s. Milk and bothie. Fuel, say 6 tons coal.
Two Apprentices	£5 a year each. £6 10s in lieu of meal. Milk, and their bothie.
Fisherman J. MacKinnon	10s a week and house. 3 tons coals. (He pays for his milk). A first-rate boatman and desirable in other ways.
Sawman Sandie Lamont	11s a week and a house. 3 tons coals. No milk. Attends to gasometer. Boatman on the place.
Dairy or Cow Woman	5s a week and a room over the bothie.

In those days there was a fair income from the letting of shootings and fishings, but such times have gone. Unless financially independent of their estates, the landowners can barely afford to maintain their houses and policies, let alone grouse moors, shootings and fishings. Many sporting estates have already been made over to the Forestry Commission.

MARKET GARDENING

In the gardens of Glengorm Castle, in the extreme north of Mull, a newcomer to the island has set up market gardens which have proved so successful, especially with the seasonal demands of summer visitors, that he has had to extend the original three acres. His most remunerative crop is celery, for thanks to the mildness of the climate he can export high-quality celery to the post-October and Christmas markets of the mainland. These are just as profitable as the early markets, for bulk supplies of celery end in October in England. One large multiple store has contracted to take up his whole stock for years ahead. The chief practical difficulty is the shortage of local manpower to work the gardens.

The growing of daffodil bulbs for export was carried on for a time at Dervaig, and is still continued on a small scale at a few other places in the island.

BANKING

The first bank in the vicinity of Mull was a branch of the Paisley Bank, opened in Oban on 8 September 1790. It received rents on account of the Duke of Argyll in exchange for 'receipts payable in Edinburgh at twenty days' currency'.

Although a good deal of Mull's financial affairs are still handled at Oban, Tobermory has for over a century catered adequately for the banking requirements of the island. Just before the middle of the nineteenth century a branch of the Western Bank was opened in Tobermory, but the office was closed down in a few years through the disastrous failure of its esteemed but short-lived parent institution in Glasgow. Its business was taken over in Tobermory in the same year (1857) by the Clydesdale Bank. Then early in the twentieth century the North of Scotland & Town & County Bank Limited opened a branch in Tobermory, and the two offices operated in friendly competition

199

until just after the 1939–45 war, when the two Scottish banks amalgamated under the name of Clydesdale Bank Limited. The businesses of the two Tobermory offices were combined shortly afterwards into the office of the former North of Scotland Bank Limited, and the old Clydesdale Bank building was sold.

A branch of the Royal Bank of Scotland was opened in the 1920s but closed down in 1969. For a year or so about 1878 the Clydesdale ran a sub-office at Salen under the control of the Tobermory branch. The Clydesdale Bank Limited now serves the whole island through the medium of the 'Bank on Wheels' which goes the rounds on several days a week.

EMPLOYMENT AND THE FUTURE

Because the island's population is an ageing one and its economy is weak, unemployment benefit, social security and retirement pensions play all too large a part in maintaining standards of living in Mull. Many people are glad to retire to the island in financial comfort but others, for lack of opportunity during a lifetime spent there, have been able to make little provision for their later years.

In 1969 the Highlands and Islands Development Board estimated that the effective labour force in Mull was 840 persons (40 per cent of the whole population) while retired people and housewives numbered 819 and children under 15 years 441. The greatest part of the labour force is engaged in agriculture, forestry and fishing, but a large percentage is also concerned with secondary employment—in general and personal services—as the following statistics show.

Percentage of labour force engaged in :

Agriculture and forestry	30·8
Fishing	2·8
General services	27·9
Personal services	4·2
Hotels and accommodation	13·6
Transport	7·3
Labouring and manufacturing and artisans	13·4

In the early summer in 1968 and 1969 the numbers of unemployed in Mull were 37 (including 15 men and 18 women) and

29 (18 men and 9 women) respectively (the others were adolescents). Total unemployment varies between 25 and 40 persons, averaging 1·5 per cent of the population, which suggests that Mull has no surplus of labour with which to staff new industries that might be introduced. Of course, lacking the inducement of new industry to keep them on the island, many unemployed persons leave to seek work elsewhere, and the figures are artificially low.

Mull's difficulties are a compound of the lack of manpower, high overhead costs, lack of co-operation locally and lack of official interest and constructive support at government level. The objective seems to be to provide solutions to the social problems through the provisions of the social security and welfare services rather than by solid, if slow, commercial development, suitably financed, to establish an economy which will expand to support a correctly balanced population level. At the same time, there seems little initiative among the islanders to start up local businesses, such as laundering, shoe repairing, barbering or such traditional industries as weaving, handicrafts, even the carving of crooks and walking sticks, which could be collectively important in a tourist economy. It is astonishing that in Mull fish, meat, vegetables, even some milk, have to come to the island from Oban. Hotels even send hampers of soiled linen to Oban, where the nearest laundry is situated; with freight added this is a costly procedure.

Sixty years ago, in a good season, an apiary of six beehives produced several hundredweights of the finest heather honey—which no one would buy, even at 6d a pound section. Now, although it is eagerly sought in mainland markets, Mull produces very little honey.

MYTHS, FOLK-LORE AND CUSTOMS

THERE is a story on the island of an estimable lady, a regular church-goer, who was one day challenged by her minister. 'Tell me,' he remarked reprovingly, 'Why do you, a good Christian, always bow when the name of Satan is mentioned?' 'Ach, weel, minister,' she replied thoughtfully, 'Ye never know, dae ye? Ye never know!'

It may seem strange that superstition and folk-lore should figure so strongly in the lives of a religious people like the inhabitants of Mull, whose religion would seem to have been kept in a watertight compartment, isolated from the beliefs and practices of their pagan background. Perhaps the Mull people have sought to have a foot in both camps—to have the best of both worlds, as it were.

The real reason, of course, is that the Celtic character is highly imaginative and perceptive. The early island-dwellers lived very close to nature, and explained away unaccountable happenings as the work of supernatural beings, fairies, or the 'little folks' (both benevolent and malevolent), giants, dragons, water-horses, witches —an unseen horde.

In the great days of clan culture the *seanachies*, or wise men, the successors of the druid-priests, were the recorders and counsellors of the chiefs. They kept no written records, memorising their knowledge and imparting it to their successors by word of mouth. They could relate the genealogies of the leading families for hundreds of years back. But while word-perfect in this type of memory work, they were doubtless only human in the correct recording of more intricate subjects over a long period; ritual and ceremonial as well as romantic stories might differ considerably from the original. The *seanachies* are gone long since, but something of their art has been preserved in story-telling, and tales of old ways of life and incidents of the past are still related by raconteurs beside the winter firesides.

Story-telling may concern three types of subject : traditions and folk-lore, witchcraft and superstitions, and second sight and the supernatural.

TRADITIONS AND FOLK-LORE

Broadly, these concern ancient myths, heroes of old, ways of life, clan battles, local place-names and so on. There are few references to the Fingalian giants in Mull beyond the name Fingal's Cave and Clach Sguabain (Sguabain's stone). This is a great pointed boulder projecting from the bank of a lay-by in the old Glen More road above Loch Sguabain. It is said that two of the Fingalian giants, Nicol and Sguabain, became involved one day in a playful argument which became rather heated. Nicol was standing just about this point above the loch, while Sguabain was over on the shore of Loch Spelve, from which he could doubtless see his colleague across the intervening hills. Picking up this boulder, Sguabain hurled it petulantly over the hills at Nicol, who in return playfully lobbed back another huge rock which landed beside Sguabain and which can still be seen lying beside Loch Spelve.

Many myths and stories are associated with this lonely glen in the neighbourhood of Loch Sguabain. South of the loch stands Beinn Fhada (the long hill), where once a dragon is reputed to have had its lair—one can still see the hollow supposedly worn on the top of the hill by this terrifying monster as it crouched there on the look-out for wayfarers and livestock which it devoured until the glen was empty of cattle and shunned by way-farers. In despair the local king offered a substantial reward and the hand of his daughter to anyone who would rid him of this importunate beast; many adventurers were tempted, but all fell victims to the dragon, until one day a young man came forward with a new scheme. He anchored a ship close to the shore in Loch Scridain, laying down a floating causeway of barrels, with long projecting spikes, between ship and shore. Then he began to drive a herd of cattle up the glen towards the dragon's lair.

The beast came bounding down to devour this herd and its herdsman; but quickly turning about, the young man slaughtered one of the herd, and began to urge the others back to the ship. Again and again the dragon approached, but each time it was delayed by the sacrifice of another animal, which it stopped to devour. The herd lasted out as far as the shore of Loch Scridain and the young man was able to escape to the ship along the floating causeway. But when the dragon began crawling after him to seize the ship and her crew, it became impaled on the spikes and finally expired. Its body was towed to the seaport of the local king, where the young man claimed his just reward.

Another myth is connected with the spectacular surroundings of Loch Ba. It concerns the Cailleach Bheur, a giantess so tall that when she waded the Sound of Mull the waters barely reached her knees. She lived for countless ages in the square of large granite rocks near the shore in south-west Mull, from which her herds of deer used to graze on lands now reclaimed by the sea—so long was the span of her life.

Every time her hundredth year came round she renewed her youth by going down to Loch Ba in the early morning and immersing herself in its waters, whereupon her years fell away and she became a young girl once again; but it was imperative that the immersion took place before any creature had awakened and given its first call of the day. Her end came as she tottered down to the loch on the early morning of her last centenary, long before daybreak. Unfortunately for her, there came the faint bark of a shepherd's restless dog from the far distance. The spell was broken, and the Cailleach Bheur expired before she could reach the life-giving waters of the loch.

A more authentic story has come down from the sixteenth century, which describes the death of Eoghann a'Chinn Bhig (Ewen of the Little Head), only son of a chief of the MacLaines of Lochbuie, whose island-home lies in Loch Sguabain, centre of the myths described above. It is related that, on the flat green bogland beside the loch a fight took place (to settle Eoghann's claim to a larger share of the Lochbuie lands) between Eoghann and his old father, who on this occasion was supported by the Macleans of Duart. In the course of the fight young MacLaine

204

was decapitated, and his headless body, still mounted on his black charger, was carried for two miles from the field. The spot where he fell off, above the Falls of Lussa at Torness, is marked by a small dilapidated cairn.

Eoghann a'Chinn Bhig had been warned the day before the battle that it might be his last; this he heard from a fairy woman he came across washing clothes of green cloth by a riverside. She warned him that if butter were placed on the table on the morning of the fight he would win; but if he were obliged to ask for butter, he would lose the fight and his life. Unfortunately for him, the serving maid forgot to place butter on the table, and forgetting the fairy's warning, he asked for it to be brought. Although downcast when he recalled this symbol of calamity, Eoghann went boldly into the fight—and indeed it was his last. He is the ghostly headless horseman who is said to frequent the roads of Mull mounted on his black charger, and who gallops furiously round the ancient MacLaine keep of Moy, at Lochbuie, when death or some tragedy is about to strike the family. Sir Walter Scott referred to him in the *Lady of the Lake* :

'Sounds, too, had come in midnight blast
Of charging steed, careering fast
Along Ben Talla's shingly side,
Where mortal horseman ne'er might ride.'

Thomas Campbell, also impressed by the number of traditional stories connected with Mull, wrote two poems describing events of the past. *Lord Ullin's Daughter* was a poem popular in the schooldays of the early 1900s. In it Campbell describes the elopement of the daughter of Sir Allan Maclean of Knock with a young MacQuarrie chief. Fleeing to the security of Ulva, with the irate parent and his men hot on their heels, the young couple were overwhelmed by a sudden squall and drowned as they attempted to cross the ferry to Ulva at the height of a storm. The Ulva Ferry of those days was more probably the longer crossing of stormy Loch na Keal from Gribun to Ulva than the short sheltered stretch of water from the Torloisk shore which is the modern ferry. The body of Lord Ullin's daughter was washed up on the rocky shore after the tragedy, and is said to lie under a rough stone slab, surrounded by a ring of large stones, twenty

205

yards above the shore of the Sound of Ulva below Oskamull farm.

Glenara is a less well-known poem. It tells the story of the Lady Rock, a tidal reef surmounted by a warning beacon, which lies off Duart Point on the eastern end of Mull and just south of Lismore lighthouse. Seeking to rid himself of an unwanted wife, a Duart chief had her marooned on this reef, and to explain away her death he prepared a story of accidental drowning. Unknown to him she was rescued by a passing fishing boat and restored to her parents and family on the mainland. Later, her brother met the guilty Duart chief and stabbed him to death. The rock has been known as Lady Rock ever since.

Away in the northwest of Mull, in a little boggy hollow in a loop of the Dervaig road just beyond the watershed at Achnadrish, there is a triangle of three small cairns, deeply embedded in the soft ground. They are reputed to mark the three leaps of the Gille Reoch—that is, the sandy or reddish young fellow— who was of the clan MacKinnon who occupied the lands of Mishnish around Tobermory about the sixteenth century. He was an expert swordsman, and possessed of great agility. One day he was surprised at this spot and hemmed in by a raiding party over from the island of Coll, all set to pay off old scores. Although defending himself stoutly he was so hard pressed that he was obliged to give the first of his three great jumps—thirty feet if it was an inch! However, he could not elude his numerous attackers except by taking a second leap, to find himself still so hemmed in that in desperation he executed his final leap, which was one of forty-five feet, and backwards at that! This landed him back at the spot from which he had originally started.

Exasperated by the agility of this nimble opponent the chief of the Coll men hurled his battle axe at the Gille Reoch—who, deftly avoiding it, darted in and despatched the now defenceless chief with a cunning sword thrust. The discomfited Coll men gave up, and picking up the body of their dead leader they retired down Glen Gorm, to their galley at Loch Mingary, leaving the Gille Reoch master of the field. To judge by probing the depth to which the stones have sunk, this triangle of cairns has been preserved for centuries, and has been constantly added to; however fanciful the legend appears to be, it is doubtless based on some real incident.

A story of a different type comes from Ulva, from the old days when it was a prosperous and populous island, when the people used to drive their flocks and herds up to the sheilings, the rough shelters set up at the rich summer grazings in the hills, where they lived until the crops had been harvested and the livestock could return again to their winter quarters. Up there the women-folk used to prepare butter and cheese for the winter, and carry out their weaving and dyeing, while the men attended to the crops and fishings at the lowland settlement.

One such sheiling, Ari-Chreag-nan-'Ighinn (the Sheiling of the Maiden's Rock) lies quite near the large cave on the raised beach above The Castles on the south shore of Ulva. One industrious woman, inspecting her store of food one day, discovered that a *cabag* (kebbuck, a round of cheese) was missing, and at once accused a certain young girl of having stolen it. The girl denied this indignantly; but the angry woman, to extort a confession or to prevent a repetition of the theft, dragged the girl to a high rock nearby, wrapped a plaid round her neck, and lowered her over the edge.

To the horror of the woman the plaid slipped and tightened, and the poor girl was strangled. Although the woman was inconsolable (for the girl had been a relative) the rest of the people would accept no excuses or expressions of repentance from one they regarded as a murderess. After a hasty trial the guilty woman was bound in a sack, carried to the Ormaig shore below, placed on a rock which was covered at high tide, and thus executed. This tidal rock is still known as Sgeir Charistiona, after the unfortunate woman, and the whole incident gave the sheiling its name.

WITCHCRAFT AND SUPERSTITIONS

It is said that when Columba began to build on Iona, even he could not overcome the powers of evil spirits who caused walls to fall down as fast as they were set up. Supernatural word came to him that no building would stand unless a human victim were first buried alive under the foundations. Oran, a companion of Columba, was chosen by lot to be the victim.

After three days Columba felt an urge to have one last look at his friend, and ordered the earth to be removed. When Oran's face was uncovered, he immediately uttered the words: 'There is no wonder in death, and Hell is not as it is reported.' Shocked by this impiety Columba instantly ordered the workers to fling back the earth, saying, 'Earth, earth, in the mouth of Oran that he may blab no more'—a gaelic saying that has become proverbial in Mull. This was said to be a fictitious story spread around by his druidical opponents to discredit the Saint.

The fairies, wee green people not three feet tall, still live in Mull. They are there in the woodlands; you are aware of them, but they 'flit e'er you can point the place' when your eye is about to alight on them. They were prepared to work industriously for human beings, but their wages were extortionate, unless the person for whom they were working could utter the magic words which would unloose their spell. They lived, too, in the depths of old duns (forts) and hillocks. A story about the fairies comes from Dun Bhuirg, an ancient fort on an eminence beyond Burg farmhouse, on the south-west corner of Ardmeanach.

In one of the many old households that once stood there a woman was planning her domestic duties, in particular how to deal with a heap of wool she had collected to be woven into cloth. Now, it was customary for neighbours to rally round and lend a hand when such a large job was to be undertaken and the woman remarked aloud to herself, 'It is about time the people of the hill were coming along to give me a hand.' This was overheard by the little people who lived in the dun, and who thought she was inviting them in to help—so in poured a host of fairy people until the whole house was packed. They sang a fairy song, each line of which referred to a certain process in the operation of spinning, weaving and dyeing: and even as they sang it, so also was the process magically completed, step by step, until, by the time the song was over, the whole store of wool had been beautifully processed into cloth (the gaelic words of the song are still preserved in the island).

Then the fairies immediately crowded round the woman demanding the customary payment of food. She was in despair, for even if her stores had been ample—which they were not—she could never have catered for the voracious appetites of her self-invited guests. Seeing a wise old man passing by, she managed to attract his attention and quickly whispered her predicament. 'Just you go back in,' he advised, 'and call out to them "Dun Bhuirg is on fire! Dun Bhuirg is on fire!"'' This she did and at once there was panic—'My house—my children,' they cried; 'My hammers and anvils!'—and out poured the panic-stricken *sluagh* (fairy host) which vanished into the dun, never to be seen again.

Certain rites used to be performed to avert or cure such troubles as cattle disease. One of these, which dates from the time of the Norsemen and continued to the middle of the eighteenth century, was *Tein Eiken*, or oaken fire. When disease appeared among the black cattle, an oaken wheel was set up over nine spindles made of oak on top of a nearby hill. Then every single fire in every house within sight of the hill had to be extinguished, and the wheel was rapidly rotated widdershins, or anti-clockwise, to the accompaniment of repeated incantations known only to a privileged few. At last, if all the conditions had been carefully observed, the friction against the spindles produced fire, which was fanned into a blaze and fed with fuel to make a bonfire. A heifer suffering from the disease was then sacrificed, the diseased parts being cut from the animal when it was still alive, and burned over the fire. Thereafter the household fires were relit with flame carried from the bonfire, and the ceremony ended with feasting on the remains of the sacrificed animal.

The Armada ship sunk in Tobermory Bay was, according to one story, destroyed by an army of fairy cats conjured up by witchcraft at the instance of the then Lady Maclean of Duart. Suspecting her husband of being infatuated by a Spanish princess on board, she determined to get rid of the whole ship. First of all she contacted the Doiteag Muileach, the most gifted witch in Mull, but without success; nor could the Laodhrag Thiristeach (the Tiree witch), nor the Glaistig Illeach (the witch of Islay) achieve any better success with their spells. They complained it had something to do with the number of holy silver crosses on board. However, an appeal to the Gormshuil Mhor (big blue-eyed one) of Lochaber was successful at last. She worked her spells, calling together an army of fairy cats, which swam out, climbed on to the decks, and destroyed the ship and her crew. The final explosion was set off by the sparks given off by the fur

N

of one cat which had pursued a member of the crew into the magazine. It is obvious in this story, from the catalogue of names of those illustrious practitioners, that there was no lack of efficient spell-binders in the land.

It may be the same Lady Maclean, together with her husband, who are said to lie under the two recumbent stones outside the south-east corner of Pennygown chapel, which stands in the old cemetery beside the Salen–Craignure road just three miles from Salen. Suspected of necromancy, they were denied interment in the holy ground of the chapel itself, but were allowed to lie as near its influence as possible. This same Maclean may have been the chief who is supposed to have called up Satan himself by roasting a live cat, this unseemly rite having the effect of obliging Satan to carry out the wishes of the spell-raiser. Pennygown chapel itself, now a ruin, of which only the four walls stand, is reputed never to have carried a roof; as in the building of Columba's church on Iona, the building work was undone overnight by the forces of evil.

SECOND SIGHT AND THE SUPERNATURAL

The 'second sight' is something which even in modern times is still possessed by a few people—often to their embarrassment. This is the prerecognition of coming events, usually of a tragic nature, such as the sudden deaths of local people. St Columba is the first person to whom the faculty was attributed in Mull. It is typically a manifestation of the mysticism inherent in the Celtic people. The possessor falls into a kind of trance when the power falls on him, and he describes in vivid detail what he is seeing in the vision. The difficulty is to record first-hand examples. Two which can hardly be disputed are as follows.

The first was told to the writer by his father (a Mull man) who was quite upset by the experience. Walking with a local man up the road one day, his companion suddenly halted, drew him to the side of the seemingly empty road, and doffed his hat. 'Do you no' see them?' the man whispered 'There's —— and —— [mentioning the names of a number of local people]. It is the funeral of old John —— and they are taking him over to Kilmore.' Kilmore is the old cemetery above Dervaig. The man's eyes followed the funeral procession which only he could see, and when it had passed he donned his hat and resumed his walk. Now, John —— was in excellent health at the time; but a fortnight later he died very suddenly, and sure enough, the cortège passed along the road at the exact time of day of the vision, and was indeed attended by the people named.

The second incident concerned a strange but happier experience of a friend of the writer, a man so well known to him that the facts related are quite undoubted. This man had a friend who in his later days became very religious. He had a limp and walked with the aid of a stick. They used to spend many evenings together talking by the fireside. One evening this man remarked in a manner that was strangely convincing, 'You know, I have the knowledge on me that I am going to die soon. We have talked plenty about this. Now, after I pass over, and if everything on the other side is as fine and happy as they are telling us, I will come back to see you. I don't know how that will be—but you will know that I am there beside you, and that all is well and I am happy.'

Sure enough, the man died soon afterwards. The sequel came a few weeks later when the relator of the experience was sitting smoking in his easy chair by the fire and reading the paper. Suddenly he heard the handle of the front door turn; the door clicked open, and shut again. There came a halting step and the sound of a stick tapping across the hall; the sitting-room door opened, and the steps crossed the floor to the fireside—just as the deceased used to do all unannounced in the past. But strangest of all, the cushion of the chair on which he used to sit sagged under an invisible weight. Newspaper in hand the man sat watching, until after a short space the cushion eased up, the sound of steps and the tapping stick faded away, the outer door opened and finally shut. 'No', he said; 'I was not frightened at all. I knew he had kept his promise to come back and tell me all was well with him on the other side.'

Yet another expression of the supernatural was the sight of a winding sheet, high in front of a perfectly cheerful and normal person. This vision was a warning of their death : the higher the sheet appeared to be, the sooner the demise. A belief once held was that the spirit of the last person to be interred in the cemetery was obliged to keep watch, and could not be at peace until the duty was passed on to the next comer. While one may discount many such reports of the second sight, of sympathetic reactions, and of the supernatural, enough still remains to establish that there is still something in the make-up of the island people which cannot be explained in scientific terms.

FUNERALS

Up to the earliest years of the twentieth century funerals, especially to remote cemeteries, were not always the decorous ceremonies we know today. They were occasionally anything but depressing. Extravagant sums of money were raised even by the poorest families in order to provide a funeral with all the traditional hospitality, even to parting with their last horse or cow. This generally included the provision of a quota of spirits; when this became too generous trouble sometimes started. In fact, back in the days when illicit distilling was prevalent the generosity of the family was measured by the number of kegs provided.

Long distances had often to be covered by the cortège, the coffin being carried on wooden bearers by relays of mourners, or on a horse-drawn cart. Every wayfarer met on the road was invited to accept a drink 'to the health of the corpse', and to refuse was something of an insult. Old people will still tell you tales of days when the mourners arrived at the place of interment with so much drink taken that they found the coffin had been left behind at some halting place along the road, or had even fallen unnoticed off the open back of the cart on some extra steep hill. It is not so long since one funeral took place where, at the last wish of the deceased, hospitality was lavish. For days afterwards forgotten bicycles lay unclaimed against the walls of the cemetery. One douce citizen awoke the day after the ceremony and in something of a daze began to shave, having first looked out his Sunday suit. He only came to when his wife assured him the funeral had taken place the day before. However, the ceremony of interment itself had been reverent and seemly, for the deceased was a prominent and well-loved member of the community.

Along many of the Mull roads there are little cairns of stones at the summits of steep hills, or beside water. These mark the spots where the cortèges generally halted for a rest. On departing, every mourner left a stone until a little cairn was built up. This custom may have connections with a very ancient custom by which small stones or pebbles were placed beside the bodies of the dead.

At remote cemeteries relatives often had to dig the grave themselves, there being no official grave-digger. A macabre story related to this custom concerns a young man who was busy with a spade deep in the old family grave. Presently he stooped down and picked up a skull he had just uncovered, and held it up for inspection by the folk above. 'This will be my grandfather', he announced proudly 'Man, man, had he no' a grand set of teeth!'

It may surprise readers to know that Resurrection Men, or body-snatchers, operated in Mull, certainly up to 1870. It was quite common for local men and relatives of the deceased to take it in turn to watch over a new grave for the first ten nights or so after an interment. About 1870 the writer's father remembered, as a boy, seeing the watchers sitting against a wall of Pennygown churchyard under a sheltering tarpaulin, with a loaded gun beside them and a cheerful fire of driftwood for company. In the old cemetery at Tobermory a tombstone can be pointed out which is badly chipped on one corner by a stray bullet fired by the watchers at grave-robbers who were interrupted at their gruesome trade.

This trade (if it be so called) existed between the island and the anatomists in the Glasgow medical college. The retail price paid by the agent to the local operators for a reasonably fresh corpse was £5. The agent (a man not unfamiliar with the medical profession, and who lived all alone) prepared the goods for transport in casks of brine, which were shipped direct from Tobermory to the city quayside for collection, by the regular Glasgow steamer which served the islands. Suspected of the practice, the agent was never identified until a fearsome prank was played on him by a party of the young sparks of the village.

One day, just after an interment had taken place in the local cemetery, a big ship called in at Tobermory, with a mixed crew

213

on board. That evening, in one of the hotel bars, the young plotters met one of the crew, a huge, cheerful and accommodating negro. Over a few drinks they hatched a plot into which the negro gleefully entered. Later in the evening, when the agent answered a gentle knock on his back door, he saw two dim figures in the darkness with a long canvas-wrapped bundle at their feet. The agent, not unprepared for a deal, silently passed out a £5 note and dragged the bundle into his kitchen. Presently, in the light of a flickering candle, he bent down to inspect and prepare the goods in the sack. With excellent timing a glittering knife blade slashed through the canvas under his very eyes, a huge grinning black face rose up, and a large black hand flourished the knife. The agent is said to have carried the front door of his house with him on the way out, and he finished up cowering under the bed of an astonished, alarmed, and very respectable citizen and his wife in their house a quarter of a mile away, to the vast amusement of the small audience watching from the slope above the houses, where they had been joined by the conspiring negro sailor.

13   THE SMALLER ISLANDS

PROPERLY speaking Mull is an island group consisting of the one large island and a number of much smaller ones on the western side. Chief among these are Staffa, Inch Kenneth, Ulva and Gometra, Erraid, Erisgeir, the Treshnish Isles, Eorsa, Little Colonsay and, of course, the sacred island of Iona. The economy, history and social problems of these islands are so closely interrelated with Mull itself that with it they form a comprehensive whole. The surface geology of all the islands, except Inch Kenneth, Iona and the southern islets, is similar to the volcanic basalts of western Mull.

ULVA AND GOMETRA

These are the largest of the islands, divided from the north-western promontory of Mull by the waters of Loch Tuath. Both are formed of basalt like the neighbouring part of the main island. Ulva (Wolf Island) is roughly four and a half miles from west to east and two miles from north to south; its basalt terraces rise to 1,025ft in its higher western portion. The coastline is very indented and has several striking basalt formations, numerous off-shore rocks and islets. A raised beach, possibly pre-glacial in age, may be observed at about 150ft above sea level on its southern shore between Tor Mor and A' Chrannag and, at the back of this level, there is a huge sea cave, about a quarter of a mile inland from the present sea shore.

A 'glen' that is deepened into a narrow sea channel completely separates Gometra from the western end of Ulva. A bridge traverses the channel and carries the rough road from Ulva Ferry to Gometra House. Gometra, also with a very indented coastline and numerous offshore rocks, is only two miles long and one mile

215

wide. Although most of the surface is under 500ft in altitude, the island is rugged, with steep coasts. There is a private anchorage and quayside at the sheltered eastern end.

Ulva Ferry is a crossing of only 150 yards from the Torloisk shore of Mull. Although Argyll County Council maintains the piers and some of the roads in Ulva, permission to visit the island should be sought from the proprietor—this is to discourage casual sightseers who might disturb stock and spoil the amenities of this quiet island.

These islands have fertile, porous soils and a mild humid climate that combine to give a natural grassiness very well suited to cattle grazing. However, the disturbance of the natural balance through the introduction of sheep has led to the spread of a rampant bracken growth and the islands' potential resources are no longer fully utilized.

Ulva and Gometra were formerly densely populated. In 1843 some 800 people lived there but five years later, hit first by the potato crop failure and immediately afterwards by the clearances and evictions, the population had fallen to 150 persons and was still falling. Now only a handful of estate workers live on the islands. The sheltered eastern side formerly produced splendid crops; some of the best potatoes in the Hebrides were grown in the rich basalt soil, with a surplus for export. Ruins of old houses and settlements are a sad memorial today to past prosperity.

Ulva was the clan territory of the MacQuarries; the chief of the clan who entertained Dr Johnson and Boswell on the island in 1773 was a man who lived to be 102. The father of Lieutenant-General Macquarie, Governor-General of New South Wales at the beginning of the nineteenth century, was a small farmer on the island. The father of Dr Livingstone, the explorer, also originated in Ulva. Ulva House, a modern mansion about half a mile from the ferry, replaces the building where MacDonald of Staffa entertained Sir Walter Scott and other famous visitors.

INCH KENNETH

This fertile island has a level surface, rising only to about 160ft at its highest, but it is fringed by low broken cliffs. It measures about one mile by half a mile and lies just south of the entrance to Loch na Keal. The grim cliffs of Gribun a mile away dominate it. The proprietor runs a private ferry boat and there are convenient landing places on both sides of the ferry. There is a fine nineteenth-century mansion house on the island and an attractive bungalow-style farmhouse for the farmer who leases the ground for crops and grazing.

Like Iona, the island differs in character from Mull, for the overlying lavas have been worn away to reveal sedimentary rocks that break down into a sandy soil capable of producing good crops. In early times the island was a veritable granary for the monks of Iona, like the more distant island of Tiree.

The island is named after Kenneth, a contemporary of St Columba, who is said to have saved him, through the power of prayer, from drowning. Kenneth died abbot of Achabo, in Ireland, in AD 600. In 1549 Inch Kenneth, with other concessions, belonged to the Prioress of Iona. In ecclesiastic importance it was second only to that island, and although no trace now remains of the monastery, there is a ruined chapel, measuring 40ft by 30ft, the remains of a cross, and many tombstones marking the graves of prominent persons of the past.

In 1773 Dr Johnson and Boswell were impressed by the ' . . .pretty little island . . . all good land', where they were entertained, 'not by a gross herdsman or amphibious fisherman, but by a gentleman and two ladies of high birth, polished manners, and elegant conversation, who in a habitation raised not far from the ground but furnished with unexpected neatness . . . practised all the kindness of hospitality and refinement of courtesy'. Their hosts were Sir Alan Maclean, chief of the clan, and his two daughters. The low-roofed stone building where they met is still in good order though no longer used as a dwelling house.

EORSA

This rugged island lies in the centre of Loch na Keal. Once frequented by wild goats along its western cliffs it is at present uninhabited but supports a fair stock of sheep. At one time, like Inch Kenneth, it belonged to the Prioress of Iona.

LITTLE COLONSAY

Lying a mile south of Ulva this fertile island is smaller than
Eorsa. Up to the time of the clearances it provided a living for
several families.

STAFFA

Staffa lies off the mouth of Loch na Keal, roughly half way
between the northern and southern promontories of western
Mull. Its Norse name means Pillar Island and graphically describes its striking formations of columnar basalt. A mile long
by a quarter wide it slopes gently upwards from the low northern
shore to the bold cliffs along the south side which rise at one
point to 135ft and are penetrated by a number of sea caves,
some of which can be explored only by boat.

Best known of these is Fingal's Cave, 227ft deep 66ft high and
42ft wide at the entrance. A path can be followed far into the
cave along the tops of the wave-cut basalt columns which form
a natural landing stage in front. Its former gaelic name was the
'melodious cave' and the echoing surge of the waves and the cry
of the sea birds inspired the composition of Mendelssohn's over-
ture that takes its name from the spot.

In the Clamshell Cave, which is 130ft deep, 30ft high and
18ft wide, the basalt columns, instead of being vertical, are angled
or fantastically curved. The peculiar rock *Buchaille* (the herdsman) is a conical pile of 30ft columns on a foundation of curved
and horizontal pillars visible offshore from the Clamshell Cave.
The Cormorants' (or Mackinnon's) Cave is 224ft deep, and the
Boat Cave, 150ft deep.

All these caves are at their most impressive under conditions
of morning light. In stormy weather, all over the island the noise
of breaking waves can be deafening. Mackinnon, Abbot of Iona
(whose tomb lies beside the altar in the cathedral there) was so
disturbed by the roar of the waves that he moved his cell from
Staffa over to the vast dark quiet cave below Balmeanach farm,
Gribun, which now also bears his name.

Staffa was unknown to the outside world until 1772 when Sir
Joseph Banks, on board *St Lawrence* on his way to Iceland, put
in to Mull for shelter on 12 July. He learned of the existence of

Staffa and its wonders from an enthusiastic Irish gentleman. Queen Victoria and Prince Albert landed on Staffa in 1847 and the Queen's impressions are recorded in her diary of the tour. For over a century now the island has been a centre of attraction for tourists and, together with Iona, it is visited every summer by tens of thousands.

The landing of sightseers from the daily cruise ship from Oban was discontinued in 1968, partly because of the rising costs of this operation, partly because of the increasing danger from rockfalls in Fingal's Cave. The ship now lies close in to the island when weather permits, giving the opportunity to view and photograph the coastal formations. From Mull, however, a fast motor cruise launch based on Ulva Ferry now provides sightseeing trips off the west of Mull which include, by arrangement, a landing on Staffa.

ERISGEIR

This rocky islet is isolated in the seas west of the Ardmeanach promontory. It is no more than a wide grassy rock on which a few sheep can graze. Probably because of its central position in the Mull group, Erisgeir figures prominently in a traditional story handed down from the fourteenth century. It is said that a chief of the clan Maclean, who up to then had had few connections with Mull, married a daughter of the Lord of the Isles, whose large possessions in the Hebrides included the island of Mull. In due course when a child was born of the union, and when the Lord of the Isles promised a gift of land to his grandchild, the shrewd family nurse suggested that he be asked to convey a grant of 'Little Erisgeir and her Isles'. To this the great chief thoughtlessly agreed and although he found to his chagrin that this included among the 'Isles' Mull itself, he held to his word. This, it is said, was the foundation of the subsequent power and possessions of the clan Maclean.

TRESHNISH ISLES

This island group, strung out in a line from north-east to south-west, lies to seaward some four to five miles west of Gometra. They are the marine-eroded remnants of a lava sheet. From north

219

to south, the main islands are Cairnburg Beag, Cairnburg Mor, Fladda, Lunga, Bac Mor and Bac Beag; between and around Fladda and Lunga there lie numbers of small islets and reefs. Seen from Loch na Keal and the north-west of Mull, the Treshnish Isles present arresting profiles, especially when standing out boldly against the unforgettable colours of a Hebridean sunset.

Although difficult of access because of the steepness of their rocky shores, these islands were formerly a convenient base for local fishermen who built rough huts or lodged in the caves. They are now uninhabited. Even the largest of them lacks surface water. On Fladda cattle and sheep depended on the dew-covered grass for moisture and although the grass is indeed lush and green on all the islands neither cattle nor horses (they were sometimes grazed here) are now found on them; only sheep are now grazed there, and they too may soon be withdrawn because of the difficulties of collecting and handling the stock. The islands form a natural sanctuary for sea birds and for a breeding colony of grey seals.

Cairnburg Mor and Beag are divided by a narrow chasm between steep cliffs, for the islands are no more than precipitous rocks with just enough space on top to house a small garrison and, on Cairnburg Mor, a few head of livestock. Access to this island is by a steep narrow path running up between massive man-made walls from a difficult landing place. The Cairnburgs were strongholds in the distant history, even prehistory, of these western waters.

The Dutchman's Cap—Bac Mor (the great hump)—is aptly named from its resemblance to a wide-brimmed flat-crowned hat. The 'brim' is an eroded lava platform, the 'crown' is capped (and thus protected) by the remnant of an overlying lava flow.

IONA

A great deal has already been written about various aspects of the history of Iona. Indeed its significance is such that it warrants full treatment in a separate book and what follows is no more than a brief, general summary. It is now a quiet sunny holiday island with bays of dazzling white sand and green translucent water in the mile-wide Sound of Iona that separates it from Mull on its eastern side. There are fine views from Iona towards the massive mountains of central Mull which not only protect it from the worst of the east winds but also attract the westerly rain clouds upwards before they have had time to precipitate their heaviest rains on the little island.

Three miles from north to south and one and a half miles from east to west, Iona is about 2,000 acres in extent, rising at its highest point to 332ft at Dun-i. Its shores are washed by the relatively warm waters of the North Atlantic Drift and its climate is even more equable than that of Mull. It is composed mainly of ancient Lewisian gneiss, in contrast to its large neighbour. What were once bands of limestone in this rock have been recrystallised by heat and pressure and altered into the marble for which Iona is famous. The island is sandy and fertile. One-third of its area is cultivated and the rest is grazing and rocky bogland.

The present permanent population is about sixty, mostly centred in the little village connected by ferry with Fionnphort, the Mull terminus, across the Sound. The population stood at 500 in 1842 but, as in the surrounding districts, fell rapidly thereafter. In summer accommodation is strained to the limit to meet the holiday requirements of hundreds of visitors. Fresh water used to be in limited supply but the shortage has been overcome by the construction of a small reservoir on the south-west side of the island. In early days a small burn, large enough to turn a little corn mill, flowed near the village, with a shallow dam (or fish-pond) beside the abbey garden. Few traces of this remain. With under three miles of passable roads all but a few essential vehicles are absent from Iona, and any proposal to introduce a small car ferry and to bring cars to the island should be firmly rejected.

Iona, the island of St Columba, is steeped in history and tradition. Here we can 'See the moon on royal tombstones gleam' and read in carved coats of arms the story of men who lived, preached, fought and died, back to the dawn of Christianity in this part of the world. The atmosphere is well conveyed by Dr Johnson's words: 'We are now treading that illustrious Island, which was once the luminary of the Caledonian regions, whence savage clans and roving barbarians derived the benefits of know-

221

ledge and the blessings of religion . . . That man is little to be envied whose . . . piety would not grow warmer among the ruins of Iona.'

The magnificence of Iona began in AD 563 when Columba with his twelve disciples landed on the southern tip of the island at Port na Churaich—the Harbour of the Coracle. The coracles of those days were sometimes quite large craft, built of wickerwork over a frame of wooden strengtheners, covered with hides and well caulked. The Woodrow MS, dated 1701, which is kept in the Advocates' Library, Edinburgh, records that the coracle of St Columba measured 60ft in length, being the distance between two stone pillars set up on the shore as markers (and still visible there). On the shore too are to be seen piles of stones said to have been raised as penances by the monks; as Pennant wrote rather pawkily, 'To judge by some of these heaps it is no breach of charity to think there were among them enormous sinners'.

Columba was a descendant of Niall of the Nine Hostages, High King of Ireland, and in religion a follower of St Patrick. The monastery which he established was built about a quarter of a mile north of the present-day cathedral. This 'morning-star of Scotland's faith' brought with him from Ireland the traditions of the Celtic Christian church and thus to the seclusion of Iona there came a school of learning, that attracted scholars and pilgrims, and the practice of writing, that during the next century through monkish evangelism was to influence not only the Dalriadic Scots the neighbouring mainland areas but also the Picts and the Northumbrians and, beyond their lands, far into the European continent.

In the seventh century the monks built an abbey church which was subsequently pillaged by invading Norsemen, in search of the gold and other treasures that could usually be found in Irish churches. Between 794 and 986 the island was pillaged six times. After 1069 the abbey church was restored and about 1200 a Benedictine monastery and convent were established there, as well as a nunnery, which is now a picturesque ruin from every chink of whose stones flowers grow in profusion. In spite of this resurgence the great days of the island as a source of Christian teaching were long past, and three centuries later Iona was turned into a sacred desert more systematically and finally than had been achieved by any earlier ravages. In 1561 an Act was passed at the desire of the Reformed Church in Scotland 'for demolishing all the abbeys of monks and friars, and for suppressing whatsoever monuments of idolatrie were remaining in the realm'. Armed with this authority the fanatical reformers ruthlessly destroyed the learning of ages, records of Scots and Irish nations, beautiful archives of remote antiquity, and revered and lovely buildings. Of the 360 crosses said to have been standing in Iona only three can now be seen. Many of the books and records were carried away by the fleeing monks. Some still lie at the Vatican, others in Switzerland and elsewhere. A few—very few—remain in our own museums. Hearsay has it that many such relics were hidden away in the fortress-island of Cairnburg Mor but were retrieved and destroyed by Cromwell and the Covenanters.

Iona belonged to the Macleans of Duart until it passed into the hands of the Dukes of Argyll. Restoration began in a small way in 1899, when the eighth Duke made over the abbey buildings to the Church of Scotland for the use of all Christian denominations, in the hope that it might be rebuilt. This has now been done by the dedicated work of the Iona Community, a body of voluntary workers founded in 1938 under the inspiration of Rev George MacLeod, now Lord MacLeod of Fiunary.

In the reconstruction by the Iona Community, one can trace much of the original structure, for which most of the red granite must have been rafted across by the eleventh-century builders from the Tormore quarries across the Sound of Iona. The monkish architects and masons painstakingly hammered and chipped the walls to a plain surface. They were not without an impish sense of humour, to judge by some of the original whimsical and symbolic carvings around the tops of arches and pillars. A permanent light, marked on Admiralty charts, is in the St Columba Shrine, adjacent to the west door of the Abbey.

An old Mull tradition has it that St Columba would allow neither woman nor cattle to live on Iona during his lifetime, and there is a gaelic saying attributed to the saint that is still current in the islands:

> *'Far am bi bò bithidh bean;*
> *Is far am be bean bithidh molluchadh!'*

> 'Where there's a cow there's a woman;
> And where there's a woman there's mischief.'

The women were banished to Eilean nam Ban (Women's Island), the rocky islet which lies below the Tormore quarries and shelters the ruined jetty and the anchorage in the bay, known to yachtsmen as the Bullhole; ancient ruins are still visible on the island. The ban was relaxed after the death of Columba and by 1203 the convent of the Black Nuns had been founded on Iona.

Iona became a place of interment for great men from far places. Forty-eight Scottish kings lie there, from Fergus II to Macbeth, as well as kings from Norway and France, clan chiefs and dignitaries, and holy men associated with the monastery. According to tradition (for there is no record of this) an Archbishop of Canterbury is buried there, and a Norwegian princess, interred with a treasure of gold around her.

There were two reasons for the desirability of Iona as a last resting place. One was the comforting thought of lying for all time in such holy ground. The other was more subtle and secular —to lie for all time in an island of lasting permanence. It is remarkable how the unscientific peoples of those early days were aware of the geological antiquity and endurance of Iona as an island. A very old gaelic prophecy translated and paraphrased long ago by Dr Smith of Campbeltown illustrates this :

> 'Seven years before that awful day
> When time shall be no more,
> A watery deluge will o'ersweep
> Hibernia's mossy shore.
>
> The green-clad Isla, too, shall sink
> While with the great and good
> Columba's happy isle will rear
> Her towers above the flood.'

The sanctity that Columba brought to Iona seems to be preserved there and it is striking how easily the gap of 1,400 years seems to be bridged. St Columba might have lived there no more than a century ago. His sayings are common in Mull and Iona, as are stories of his life, traditions and accounts of the miracles

attributed to him. Places where he preached are still pointed out;
indeed at Salen, his congregation is reputed to have been rather
scanty!

ERRAID

This island, roughly a mile square, lies close to the south-west
tip of the Ross of Mull. It is accessible dry-shod at low tide.
Until recent years it was the shore station for keepers of the lighthouses of Skerryvore and Dhuheartach which stand 24 and 15
miles away respectively, on their dangerous submerged reefs in
the open sea. The station was abandoned in 1967 and the houses
sold by the Commissioners of Northern Lights.

This is the inhospitable island that Robert Louis Stevenson
described so vividly in *Kidnapped*, on which David Balfour,
after being confined on the brig *Covenant*, was cast away and
began his adventurous flight through the heather. It is little
wonder that Stevenson described the background so well, for
he had lived there and explored the district during the time his
father was engineering the construction of the two lighthouses.
His lesser known story *The Merry Men* also relates to this coast.

Three miles south of Erraid lie the Torran (Thunder) rocks,
so called on account of the roar of the Atlantic rollers breaking
over them in stormy weather. This is a wild and dangerous coast
that is given a wide berth by shipping.

14   A VIEW OF THE FUTURE

FOR one born of Mull parentage and brought up on the island, it is sad to realise that over a lifetime one has unconsciously watched it slowly dying as an economic unit. With its dwindling population, an increasing proportion of older people and a falling birth rate, the island is in a critical social and economic position. The 1970s may be one of the most decisive periods in its history.

Subsidies alone are not enough—they lead to social security rather than to solid commercial development; their benefits are largely offset by the heavy freight charges of monopolistic communications services, which affect the whole cost of living on Mull, from groceries to agricultural production. The island needs support and encouragement for small industries to be added to pastoral farming, forestry and tourism; it needs immediate substantial financial aid; and it would benefit by a population growth to about 5,000 people.

Over the last 200 years successive governments have failed to appreciate or been indifferent to the domestic problems of the Scottish highlands and islands. Now it is essential to have the fullest support from an understanding central authority. The administration of other marginal areas—Norway, Iceland, the Faeroes—might be examined for lessons that might be applied in the northwestern islands, for the protection of their fishing industries. And every country from Eire to Morocco has something to teach us in running a flourishing tourist industry.

However, the people of Mull—with a few notable exceptions—have not themselves been blameless with respect to the decline of their island. Granted that memories are long and two centuries of commercial failures and disappointments have left uncertainty and distrust in the islanders' minds, nevertheless the evolution of

226

the national society of which Mull is a part has to be accepted. The traditional way of farming in crofting communities in Mull as elsewhere in the north-west did not breed individual initiative or accumulate working capital and the tempo of life, tied to the seasons, was slow. Amongst many of those who do not emigrate there is little inclination towards radical change, even resistance to the adoption of improved techniques.

But while the tides ebb and flow along the coasts of Mull, and the seals and sea birds return in their season to their island sanctuaries, there must be change in the human scene. In official circles there is a slowly increasing awareness of the problems that beset Mull, for which a comprehensive survey is in preparation (1970) by the Highlands and Islands Development Board. Recent interest in Mull both as a place in which to work and as a place to live in, on the part of people tired of the exacting standards of modern life in urban and industrial areas, may have been stimulated by press reports on local depopulation. One would hope that small factory projects already under consideration will come to fruition.

There is a heartening stir as construction work proceeds on the new road from Iona to Craignure. A large modern hotel is projected in Craignure itself. Tourism, though, is likely always to be seasonal; and forestry alienates land that could be used for farming and food production. Neglected fields and hill grazings have already been hidden under the deep carpet of green plantations. Unless the right path is taken now towards prosperity and repopulation, the trees may lean to each other in the sea winds and whisper 'Eisd! Eisd!' but few will be there to listen to them.

PLACE-NAME ELEMENTS

THE descriptive and imaginative nature of the gaelic tongue is revealed in many of the topographical names in Mull. Some place-names perpetuate the personal names of people who once lived on the island, the actual memory of whose deeds or fame has long since been lost. Examples of this kind are: Loch Sguabain (Loch of Sguabain, a Fingalian giant); Sgeir Charistiona (a rock off Ulva on which a woman was tied and drowned by the rising tide as a punishment); Kilninian, Kilbrennan, Kilpatrick, etc (the cells or chapels of the various missionaries and saints).

Other place-names are either entirely Norse in origin (especially on the western side of the island) or have Norse elements in them, for example: Rossal (hross volr, horsefield); Scridain (skrida, a landslip); Burg (a fort); Forss (cataract or waterfall); Loch Frisa (the chill loch).

Some place-names are now known only by an Anglicised version of their original form, such as: Ballygown (baile, homestead, and gobhainn, blacksmith); Ben (beann, a mountain); Knock, (cnoc, a ridge).

A few names have no exact English equivalent. The original word form has been lost, and remains as hearsay by the older people, through gradual changes in local dialects which have taken place over the long period of time when such records were preserved by the spoken, and not the written word. Examples are Mishnish, Urgabul.

abhainn	river
allt	stream or burn
ach, achadh	field (cultivated)
Acharoinich	field of bracken
Achnadrish	field of brambles

229

-aig, -uig, -vik (*Norse*)	suffix meaning bay or inlet
-airidh, -ary	suffix meaning summer sheiling
aluinn (aline)	beautiful
aoineadh, aoinidh	steep rocky brae-face
ard, aird	high headland
-ay, -a (Norse)	suffix meaning island
bad	thicket
bàgh	bay
bal, baile	township, homestead
ban	woman; female
beag	small
bealach	pass between the hills
beann, beinn	mountain
blar	small marshy plain, often battlefield
bo	cow
bodach	old man
bogha	sunken rock or curving reef
breac	speckled
Buie	yellow
bun	river mouth
Bunessan	river mouth at the falls or cataract
Burg (Norse)	fort
cabar	log, rafter
cadha	steep path
cailleach	old woman, nun
caisteal	castle, castle-like rock
cam	crooked
camas	small sandy bay or beach
Calve (calbh)	calf (island)
caol, caolas (kyle)	narrow strait
caorach	sheep
carra, carragh	standing stones
ceann	head (see kin)
cille	see kil
clach	stone or boulder (on dry land)
clachan	stones, stepping stones, helmet
cnoc (knock)	ridge
coille	wood
coire	corrie, or hollow in the high hills

230

craig, creag	a high rock or bluff (on dry land)
crasg	crossing
dal (Norse)	valley
damh	stag
Dervaig	little grove (doire, a wood, bheag, small)
dhu, dubh	black
doire (derry)	wood
dris	bramble, brier
druim	ridge
dun	old fort or fortified hill
each	horse
eas	waterfall, cataract
eilean	island
fan	gently sloping
fang (fank)	sheep fold
fad, fada	long
fiadh	deer
fionn	white
forss (Norse)	waterfall, cataract
fraoch	heather
Frisa (Norse)	cold, chill
gall	stranger
gaoth	wind
Dun na Ghaoithe	hill of the two winds
garbh	rough
geal	white
geard	garrison
gille, ghillie	young fellow, servant
glac	hollow
glas	green, greyish
gobhainn (gown)	blacksmith
gobhar	goat
goirtean	enclosed field
gorm	blue
Gribun	origin doubtful, but said to be 'high rocky shore'. Might be from sgrioban, furrowed, from the regular lines of eroded escarpments which run for miles along the cliffs and slopes.

231

gualann	shoulder of a hill
iolair	eagle
kil-, keal-, cille	cell of early missionary, old chapel, burying ground
Killiechronan	murmuring grove, from coile, wood, cronan, humming or murmuring
Kilviceon	chapel of the son of Ewen
kin (ceann)	at the head of
knock	see *cnoc*
laggan	fertile little hollow
laogh	calf
Lathaich	(loch) bottomed with clay
leac	flat stone or slab
leitir (letter)	fan-shaped grassy slope, especially at burn mouth on steep lochside
leum	leap
liath	grey or blue
linn	long deep pool
lios	enclosed garden
Lismore	great garden
machair	level grassy sward above sandy beach
magh (moy)	plain
mam	bald rounded hill; sometimes a pass between such hills
maol, mel	smaller bald rounded hilltop
marbh	dead
meadhonach (meanach)	middle
min	smooth
mor, more	large, great
muileann	mill
muir	sea
Mull	high flat land
nathair	snake
nighean	young woman
-nish	suffix indicating a high flat peninsula

232

penny	old unit of land division ('Pennyland', 'Farthing land', based on rent paid); lowland Scottish origin.
poll	pit or hollow
rhu, rudha	point, cape
righ	king
roid	bog myrtle
ron	seal
ros (ross)	promontory
ruadh	red
sagart	preacher
Salen (Sailean)	deep bay
Scridain (Norse)	(Loch) surrounded by landslides, from skrida (Norse) a landslip, sgriodan in gaelic
sean	old
seilisdeir	iris
sgarbh	cormorant
sgeir, skerry (Norse)	isolated sea-girt rock or reef, from Old Norse sker, skerry
sgurr, sgor	jutting conical peak
Siaba	'six-cow land' an old form of Hebridean land measurement related to amount of grazing land available per animal
sith	fairy
slochd	deep hollow
sron, stron	nose, point
stac	very steep pointed hill
Staffa (Norse)	pillar island
stuc	sharp peak
suidhe	seat
Teanga	tongue
tigh	house
tir	land
tobar	well, spring
Tobermory	Tobar Mhoire, well of Mary
tom	knoll, or rounded eminence
torr, torran	small flat-topped hill
Torrunn	thunder

P

233

THE ISLE OF MULL

traigh	wide sandy bay
Tuath	north
uaine	green
uamh	cave
uan	lamb
-uig	see *-aig*
uisge	water
Ulva (Norse)	wolf island
-vik (Norse)	see *-aig*

BIBLIOGRAPHY

Most of the literature about Mull is descriptive and was published before the first world war. Little was conveyed in it of the great and permanent changes in the ways of life of the islanders or in the island landscape over the last two centuries. More recent material than this is most frequently in the socio-economic and historical fields and occurs in books and articles that in general cover a much wider region than the island or even Argyll—usually the highlands and islands of Scotland.

The earliest to write about the island were without exception travellers—explorers might be a more apt description—from the Lowlands of Scotland and from England. Not all accounts were flattering; hardly surprising in view of the tedium and austerity of contemporary travel.

Sir Donald Monro, High Dean of the Isles, travelled extensively throughout the western isles. In 1549 he produced his *Genealogies of the Chieff Clans of the Isles*, in which Mull and its inhabitants are described. This and other descriptive writings of his were published in 1773–4 as *Description of the Western Isles of Scotland called Hybrides* and were included in a second volume *Miscellanea Scotia*. Copies of the manuscripts are preserved in the Advocates' Library in Edinburgh.

In 1702 Sacheverell, Governor of the Isle of Man, published a report of his excursion through Mull in 1688, when salvage operations were being attempted on the sunken Armada galleon in Tobermory Harbour. It has not been possible to trace the title or whereabouts of this report, but a quotation from it by MacCormick in 1923 describes the dress, armour and general appearance of the people of Mull with a certain admiration and respect.

Martin Martin, after extensive travelling among the western

235

isles, published a short paper in 1697, which was more formally presented in London in 1703 under the title *A Description of the Western Islands of Scotland.*

Thomas Pennant's *A Tour in Scotland and Voyage to the Hebrides,* published in 1772, is well known. It describes his journey of 1769 when he had 'the hardihood to venture on a journey to the remotest part of North Britain', of which he brought home an account so favourable that 'it has ever since been *mondée* with Southern visitors'. His research into local history and traditions makes fascinating reading.

Among the tourists of the eighteenth century who visited Mull were Dr Samuel Johnson and Boswell, both of whom described their island journey of 1773, respectively in *Journey to the Western Islands* and *Journal of a Tour to the Hebrides with Samuel Johnson.*

In 1772 Sir Joseph Banks first described the marvels of Staffa and Fingal's Cave; his description was inserted in Pennant's *Tour.* John MacCulloch, geologist and scientist, published among other papers *A Description of the Western Islands of Scotland* (1819) and *Highlands and Western Isles of Scotland* (1824). His was the discovery and interpretation, in 1819, of the famous fossil tree in the headland of Ardmeanach that bears his name (see pages 29-30).

Descriptions of Mull or references to it have come into the writings of Thomas Campbell, Robert Louis Stevenson and Sir Walter Scott, all of whom drew on their experiences there. Even Queen Victoria's diary has a reference to the island (*Leaves from her Journal*), describing her visit to Staffa in 1847.

ARGYLL, DUKE OF. 'On Tertiary leaf-beds in the Isle of Mull', *Quart Journal Geol Soc,* vii (1851), 89–103

BAILEY, E. B. *Tertiary and post-Tertiary Geology of Mull, Loch Aline and Oban* (1924)

CREGEEN, ERIC R. (ed.) *Argyll Estate Instructions (Mull Morvern and Tiree) 1771–1805* (Edinburgh 1964)

DARLING, F. FRASER. *A Herd of Red Deer* (Oxford 1937)

DARLING, F. FRASER (ed). *West Highland Survey. An Essay in Human Ecology* (Oxford 1955)

DARLING, F. FRASER AND BOYD, J. MORTON. *The Highlands and Islands* (1964). (A revised and rewritten version of F.

Fraser Darling, *Natural History in the Highlands and Islands* 1947)

DUCKWORTH, C. L. D. AND LANGMUIR, G. E. *West Highland Steamers* (Prescot 1967)

ELLIS, M. H. *Lachlan Macquarie, His Life, Adventures and Times* (1958)

EWING, P. 'Contribution to the topographical botany of the West of Scotland', *Proceedings and Transactions* of the Natural History Society of Glasgow, New Series III (1892)

GERRANS, M. B. 'Notes on the flora of the Isle of Mull', *Proceedings* of the Botanical Society of the British Isles, 3 (1960), 369–74

GLOVER, JANET R. *The Story of Scotland* (1960)

GORDON, SETON. *Highways and Byways in the West Highlands* (1935)

GORDON, SETON. *The Land of the Hills and the Glens* (1920)

GRAHAM, H. D. *The Birds of Iona and Mull* (Edinburgh 1890)

GRAHAM, H. G. *The Social Life of Scotland in the Eighteenth Century* (1906, 1937)

GRANT, I. F. *Economic History of Great Britain* (1934)

GRANT, I. F. *Highland Folk Ways* (1961)

GUNN, NEIL. *Off in a Boat* (1938)

HANNAN, THOMAS. *The Beautiful Isle of Mull* (Edinburgh 1926)

HARKER, ALFRED. *The West Highlands and the Hebrides* (Cambridge 1941)

JOHNSTON, W. J. *History of the Celtic Place Names of Scotland* (Edinburgh 1926)

MacCLURE, V. *Scotland's Inner Man* (1935)

MacCORMICK, JOHN. *The Island of Mull; its History, Scenes and Legends* (Glasgow 1923)

MacDONALD, JAMES. *General View of the Agriculture of the Hebrides* (Edinburgh 1811)

MacKENZIE, OSGOOD. *A Hundred Years in the Highlands* (1949)

MacLEOD, R. C. *The MacLeods of Dunvegan* (Clan MacLeod Society Publication for members of the Society, Edinburgh 1927)

MENZIES, LUCY. *St Columba of Iona* (Edinburgh 1935)

MUNRO, NEIL. *The Lost Pibroch and other Sheiling Stories* (Edinburgh and London 1923)

MUNRO, NEIL. *Para Handy and other Tales* (Edinburgh and London 1923)

O'DELL, A. C. AND WALTON, K. *The Highlands and Islands of Scotland* (1962)

PIGGOTT, STUART (ed). *The Prehistoric. Peoples of Scotland* (1962)

PLANT, MARJORIE. *Domestic Life of Scotland in the Eighteenth Century* (Edinburgh 1952)

PRYDE, G. S. *Scotland from 1603 to the Present Day* (1962)

RAINSFORD-HANNAY, F. *Drystone Walling* (1957)

RICHEY, J. F. *British Regional Geology, Scotland, the Tertiary Volcanic Districts* (1964)

RITCHIE, T. *Iona Past and Present* (Highland Home Industries Ltd, Edinburgh 1945)

Ross, G. 'On the flora of Mull', *Transactions*, Botanical Society Edinburgh, XIII (1878)

SKENE, W. F. *Celtic Scotland*, vol III (Edinburgh 1880)

SMALL, A. 'Historical Geography of the Norse and Viking Colonisation of the Scottish Highlands', *Norsk Geografisk Tidsskrift*, 22 (1968)

THOM, A. *Megalithic Sites in Britain* (Oxford 1968)

THOMPSON, D. C. AND GRIMBLE, I. *The Future of the Highlands* (1968)

WILMOTT, A. J. 'Report on an excursion to the Isle of Mull July–August 1939', *Report* for 1939–40, The Botanical Society and Exchange Club, 12 (1942), 236–50

Mull, 1965. A Study in Rural Planning (Argyll County Council, Lochgilphead 1965)

Official Report of Court Proceedings of Royal Commission (Highlands and Islands), 1892

Proceedings of the Society of Antiquarians of Scotland, 1914–15 to 1946–47

The Statistical Account of Scotland, vols II and III (Edinburgh 1791–9)

The New Statistical Account of Scotland, vol VII (Edinburgh 1845)

Third Statistical Account of Scotland, vol IX, County of Argyll (Edinburgh 1961)

MAPS

The current one-inch Ordnance Survey maps covering Mull are the Seventh Series Sheets 45 and 51; the Treshnish Islands lie on sheet 44 (with Tiree and Coll). Bartholomew's half-inch Contoured Map Great Britain No 47 (Mull and Oban) includes Mull and all its islands. Sheets 43 and 44 of the Geological Survey one-inch maps cover western Mull and central and eastern Mull respectively.

ACKNOWLEDGEMENTS

It would be wearisome for readers and embarrassing for individuals to give the names of the many people whose valuable help and interest contributed to the preparation of this book. However, I must single out the name of Mr Donald MacKechnie of Dervaig, on whose knowledge of Mull and its people I have drawn extensively, and on his collection of old books and records. I also thank the following for their patience in answering my queries and the useful technical information they supplied: Director-General, Meteorological Office; Forestry Commission, Scotland; Public Relations Officer, GPO and Telephones, West of Scotland; John Hopkins & Co Limited, Glasgow; David MacBrayne Limited, Glasgow; Campbell K. Finlay, Mull and Iona Council of Social Service; County Clerk, Argyll; Town Clerk, Tobermory; County Librarian, Ayr; North of Scotland Hydro-Electric Board; Department of Agriculture and Fisheries for Scotland (Economics and Statistics Unit).

INDEX

Page numbers in italic indicate illustrations

INDEX

INDEX

244

245

INDEX